Andrew McDona

The Pattern of Time

Andrew McDonald is a professional astrologer specialising in traditional Natal, Electional and Horary consultations. He is also a musician and an artist. Andrew lives with his wife and family in London. He has astrology clients in many countries across the world and his paintings are in private collections in the UK, Europe and the USA.

www.andymcdonaldartist.com

Cover painting, *The Pilgrimage,* Andy McDonald

The Pattern of Time

Essays on Traditional Astrology

Andrew McDonald

© 2014 Andrew McDonald

Copyright © 2014 Andrew McDonald

Published 2014 by Caeli Enarrant
London

All rights reserved. No part of this work may be used or reproduced in any manner without written permission, except in critical articles and reviews.

ISBN 978-0-9928711-0-9

Cover painting *The Pilgrimage* copyright © Andy McDonald

Foreword

What is it to be a human being? What is our relationship to That which is beyond ourselves? How can our own free will be compatible with God's omniscience? These are questions which any thinking person must ask, yet the asking of these questions and the refining of their answers is the work of a life-time. If at some point in our life we begin to see through that glass slightly less darkly, such insight is to be treasured.

Three of the tools we have been given with which to address these questions are philosophy, art, and astrology. Each in its own way enables a standing back from our daily existence, in order that we may observe this with some degree of objectivity so that we might better understand.

As Andrew explains, the astrology that allows us to do this is something far from the common idea of astrology as wish-fulfilment: that a few words from the seer in rapture can somehow empower us to renegotiate our life so we can have whatever it is that we think we want. Astrology as Fairy Godmother granting us our wishes. It is something far more interesting than that: a tool for understanding what is going on, a way of looking at the underlying structure of both our life and the Creation within which we dwell. Particularly in trying to grasp some better understanding of the intangible, elusive, but all-pervading medium that surrounds us and within the constraints of which our every thought is shaped: time.

It is our everyday experience that time does not conform to the strict and regular discipline we seek to impose upon it by the movement of a clock. It slows down, it races ahead – and every now and again it seems to double back upon itself, giving those intriguing moments which we feel we have seen before, or know we shall see again. So with astrology, we see the same events in a person's life shown with clarity, and often in the same way, from the placement of the planets at moments that have, apparently, no connection to each other. Why should the positions of the planets so many days after the birth display the same events as their positions so many years after the birth? No reason at all, according to much of contemporary thought. Yet as the Bible's 'I give you a day for a year' shows, taking a less superficial view gives insight to the structure that underlies what we perceive as reality.

This structure underlying life remains stable. This is why the creator of the *Odyssey* speaks to us of things that are not foreign to us, despite the millennia and huge cultural shifts that have passed since it was made; or why Michelangelo - the subject of one of Andrew's studies – resident in an age

Foreword

very different from our own, can speak to us so clearly across the centuries, helping us perceive something of this deep structure.

Astrologers can be a parochial bunch, innocents lost abroad when straying beyond the safe confines of 'this planet aspects that'. Informed by his knowledge of painting and music, Andrew's essays take us beyond the narrow boundaries of the astrological parish to explore the countryside beyond. In the meadows through which he leads us, astrology deepens our perceptions of art, art deepens our perceptions of astrology. Such perception is a fine thing, so I am happy to commend this work.

John Frawley

Preface

When I was a child sometimes I dreamed things before they happened. I don't know how or why, I just did. Call it sensitivity, call it psychic ability call it what you like, I had no control over it and it seemed to happen at random. As I grew older many times I'd see events happen in my head and then see them play out in life. These visionary experiences were often of simple, every-day passages of time …

I pass through hilly Victorian streets. Sunshine sparkles upon the roads and pavements. Birds wheel above me and I taste sharp cold sea air. To my right, patterns of light flash against white weather boarding. And further up, upon the hill, houses stand like elegant ladies and gentleman. I turn right, and I wind my way down to the sea.

I felt I was there. Yet physically I was not.

Years after this I moved to Los Angeles and on a weekend trip to San Francisco with my girlfriend we drove through the very streets I had seen so many years before. I'd seen those trees I'd seen those houses and felt the breeze. I'd even reached the crest of that particular hill and looked at the harbour and sea below. Part of that weekend I had experienced before - part of it, somehow, I had already lived.

Many years later I became a clinical and analytic hypnotherapist. I worked with people in various trance states and when appropriate, I used regression therapy to go back in time with them. On odd occasions we found memories that puzzled us both. Sometimes, by my client's admission, these memories could not even have been their own. If we were able to date the original memory my client often looked at me with surprise and assured me that at that date they'd physically been elsewhere; it was as if they had inadvertently tapped into someone else's memory or experience. At other times the puzzling memory was clearly their own, but in the memory they were older, suggesting that the event contained within the memory had not yet happened and it was something that they'd have to later catch up with in their life. This was very similar to my own experiences that somehow life caught up with the vision.

Time is a very strange thing. Astrology deals with time. The planets may be its language but time - past, present and future is the page that it is written upon. Yes, it is possible to see into the future, but is this really the goal of astrology? Is this what it exists for - is this its raison d'être? I don't think so.

Astrology, at its metaphysical roots, is essentially two things. It is a tool and it is a sign.

Preface

As a tool it can be used for all kinds of dubious goals and in the hands of a skilled astrologer it can even appear to give the person wielding it some kind of power. This power is of course an illusion. It is an illusion born of the age old battle to control one's destiny tragically misplaced into the muddy realm of conflicting desires. As all the great faiths attest, it is indeed possible to have control over one's destiny, but not in the way that most modern people think.

Astrology is also a sign. A sign by its nature points beyond itself, therefore as a sign astrology points towards something greater. It should dawn on anyone who seriously practices traditional astrology that there is a greater will at work in the world than ours. This was obvious for most people before us who still believed the human mind could come to know the truth of things. The contradictory ideas that all truth is relative or that now we've advanced so far that we can hold an impartial or neutral view are commonly taken for granted. These too are illusions, born of the desire to control life - to make it obey our whims, to make it conform to the patterns that we wish to impose upon it. Traditional astrology will show us that these things are not possible.

There is an underlying pattern within our lives that is objective and not superimposed by subjectivism; a Truth which, despite our best efforts, we are unable to make up as we go along. It is our recognition of this and our attempts to understand it that can bring us to not only ask the important questions in life but to realise that there may even be answers to such questions after all.

The essays in this book are about how we can use astrology as a tool to see that it points beyond itself. If we do this much, we are better placed to see what it points toward. This is not about projections, wish fulfilment or fantasy. Instead, it is about *what is*.

Again I saw that under the sun the race is not to the swift, nor the battle to the strong, nor bread to the wise, nor riches to the intelligent, nor favour to the men of skill; but time and chance happen to them all.

Ecclesiastes 9:11

Acknowledgements

Some of the chapters in this book previously appeared as articles in various magazines.

Chapter 1, *The Divine Michelangelo* appeared in 2008 issues of Aspects magazine, Anima Astrologiae, and Saptarishis Astrology. Chapters 2, 4 and 5, *When Will I Find My Next Job*, *Starry, Starry Night* and *The Nativity of a Lady* all appeared in Saptarishis Astrology. They appear here with minor changes.

My thanks go to Sunil John and his team at Saptarishis Astrology. Saptarishis are predominantly Vedic astrologers but they have shown great interest in the background and techniques of traditional western astrology and have supported and championed my work.

Special thanks to John Frawley for his Foreword and for the generosity of spirit with which he has encouraged the development of my work and supported and promoted my endeavours.

Thank you to my clients. Without them calling upon me to help unravel the thorny problems that life throws at us all, my work would not have developed in the manner that it has.

And lastly my thanks go to my wife and family; without their love, support and understanding none of this would have been possible.

'But, you will reply, if it lies in my power to change a proposed course of action, I will be able to evade Providence, for I will perhaps have altered things which Providence foreknows. My answer will be that you can alter your plan, but that since this is possible, and since whether you do so or in what way you change it is visible to Providence the ever present and true, you cannot escape divine foreknowledge, just as you cannot escape the sight of an eye that is present to watch, though of your own free will you may turn to a variety of actions.'

Philosophia to Boethius, Book V, Consolation of Philosophy

'And in His will is our peace: that will is the sea to which all things flow – all that it creates and nature makes.'

Dante Alighieri, Paradiso III, 85–86

'Lift up then, reader, with me your eyes to the great wheels, directing them on that point where one motion strikes on the other, and there begin to delight in the art of the Master who so loves it in Himself that His eye never leaves it.'

Dante Alighieri, Paradiso X, 1–12

Contents

Foreword by John Frawley	v
Preface	vii
Acknowledgements	xi
Introduction	xvii
The Divine Michelangelo	1
When Will I Find My Next Job?	22
The Colour of the Spheres	31
Starry, Starry Night	37
The Nativity of a Lady	46
Fate, Freewill, Fortuna and the Soul	59
The Forge of Vulcan	110
Act and Potency – The Nature of Change	114
Impressionism, Saturn and Ivory Black	124
Epiphany	141
Appendix: The Table of Essential Dignities	143
Bibliography	145
Index	147

Introduction

If we stand still and watch the horizon we can count the time when the sun rises in the morning and sets in the evening. At night we can look to the sky and measure the courses of stars and planets. On paper we can divide day and night into segments and assign a planetary ruler to each segment. Every hour will have its ruler and every ruler will have its associations with the things of this world.

Astrology is built upon simple foundations.

In the traditional view of the cosmos the earth is surrounded by spheres. From wherever we stand upon the earth, up to the sphere of the Moon all is change, the elements of Air, Fire, Water and Earth ceaselessly combining in a dance of generation and corruption. Above this mêlée is the sphere of Mercury. Then we come to the sphere of Venus, then the Sun and then the sphere of Mars. Above this is the great benific Jupiter and then Saturn. After Saturn we reach the sphere of the Fixed Stars. Above this is the Primum Mobile, the first movable heaven and beyond that is the *Unmoved Mover*...

Aristotle said time is, 'number of motion[1] in respect of before and after'[2]. He describes time as the counting of a succession of moments of before and after. To do this counting we use *now* as a marker, as a boundary. Yet as he says in his *Physics*: 'now is no part of time nor the section any part of the movement, any more than the points are parts of the line...'[3] *Now* is not in time – it is a boundary between before and after that we use to count the passing of time. Aristotle insisted on the need for there to be a soul to witness each *now* in order to count each moment. Without a soul to witness and count there could be no time. To count each *now* there has to be a soul there doing the counting. This is us being present to perceive something real in a world outside of us.

We are here now – we exist. It is this existence that is the most mysterious thing of all.

If we use a clock to isolate a moment in life, Aristotle's *now*, we can make the calculations necessary to erect an astrological chart. From this specific point, this mathematical moment, we can watch time appear and symbolically expand to give us a qualitative spatial picture. It is a picture constructed out of time and place; it is partly of the mind and partly of the world. We can

---

[1] Motion refers to change in general not merely movement from place to place which is known as 'locomotion'.
[2] Aristotle *Physics Book IV 219b1*
[3] Aristotle *Physics Book IV 220a18*

Introduction

extrapolate from these simple beginnings to a complete birth chart with 4 angles, 12 houses, and 7 traditional planets. From this, a visual pattern of time is woven for the soul that is doing the counting, for the person that is *there*. At first glance this pattern can appear abstract, as if we must impress meaning upon it. But, if we still our gaze, if we look to see what is before us, the abstract will coalesce into something else: unfurled like a medieval work of art will be a narrative tapestry in glorious colour. Complete with its own intrinsic meaning, its own story to tell.

Traditional astrology can help us read this tapestry, this work of art, this Pattern of Time.

'I copy what I think fate says I am ...'
Michelangelo Buonarroti, Sonnet 104

1
The Divine Michelangelo

There is an old story, told in different forms throughout history, that when mankind reaches a low point in our activities down here on Earth, a messenger from God will be sent from the Heavens to show us the way, to show us how to do things properly. And so it was in the world of art, when, in the year 1474, 'the benign ruler of heaven,' saw fit to send us, 'an artist who would be skilled in each and every craft.' An artist, 'whose work alone would teach us how to obtain perfection in design.'

The sending of such a genius, we imagine, would be trumpeted in the stars, and it was, as Giorgio Vasari (16th century artist/biographer) in the second edition of his book, *Lives of the Most Excellent Sculptors, Painters and Architects*, goes on to tell us: 'under a fateful and lucky star, the virtuous and noble wife of Lodovico Buonarroti gave birth to a baby son,' his father saw in him something, 'supernatural and beyond human experience.' 'This was evident in the child's horoscope,' and that, 'his mind and hands were destined to fashion sublime works of art.' That genius was known as The Divine Michelangelo. Michelangelo Buonarroti.

His birth data has been disputed as to whether it was 1474 or 1475 by the old style or new style calendar. Almost all recent art historians now favour 1475 new style. But Benedetto Varchi, the Florentine historian, who gave the eulogy at Michelangelo's funeral, Vasari and Ascanio Condivi, another biographer, all give 1474 new style. So does Michelangelo's father's record, which survives in a 17th century copy. This has an added note in brackets essentially saying, 'old style not new', but the record is a copy, and of course nobody knows when the note was added. Besides all this, if we let the astrology speak and set the chart for the time suggested by Vasari, Varchi, Condivi and Michelangelo's father, it fits his contemporaries' astrological description which the 1475 chart does not. And if we delve further, it speaks eloquently. In short, the astrology stacks up.

The earliest astrological description we have is in Condivi's biography, *Life of Michelangelo Buonarroti*. This was published in Rome in 1553 and written with Michelangelo's guidance. In fact, in a letter dated 14 April 1548, Michelangelo had written from Rome to his nephew Leonardo asking for a copy of his 'nativita'.

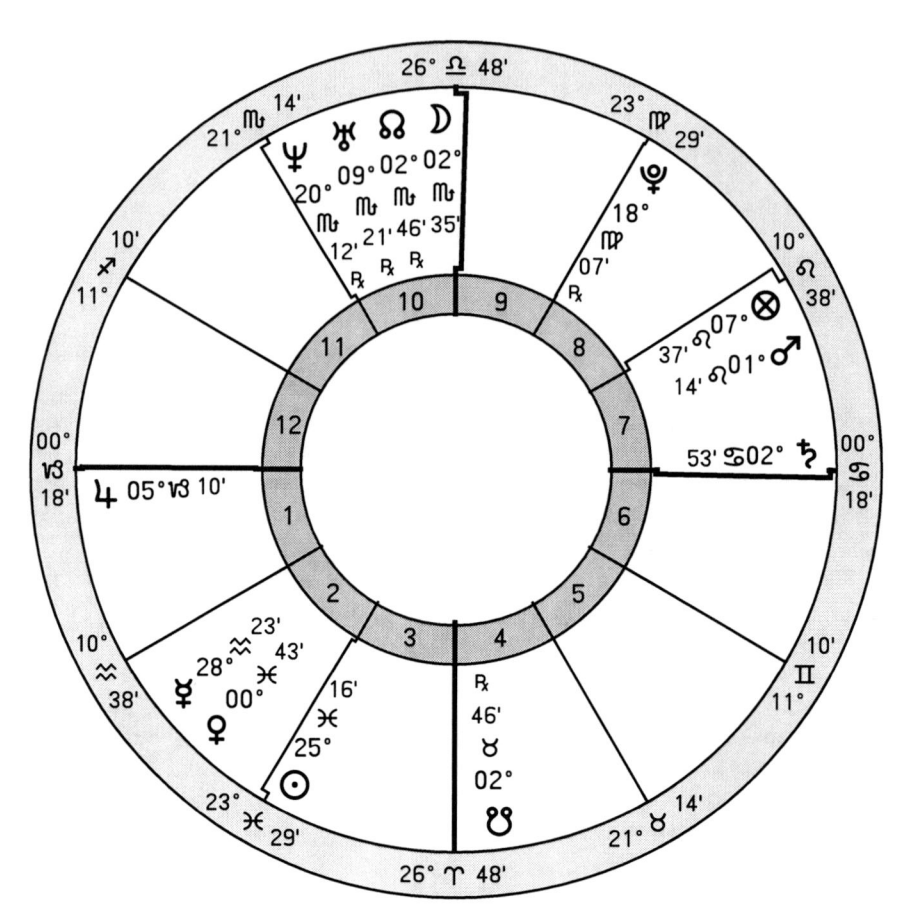

(Fig 1) Michelangelo, 7 March 1474 AD JC, 2.06 LMT, Caprese Michelangelo, Italy

Condivi states: (Michelangelo was born) 'in the year of our Salvation 1474 on the sixth day of March, four hours before daylight on a Monday. A fine nativity truly, which showed how great the child would be and of how noble a genius; for the planet Mercury and Venus in seconda being received into the house of Jupiter with benign aspect, promised what afterward followed.'

'Four hours before daylight' is approx 2 am which we would now call the 7th March but it is still the 'sixth day of March' until sunrise, the sixth day lasting from 6 March sunrise to 7 March sunrise. It is also a Monday following the Paschal calendar as Condivi and Michelangelo's father both noted.

But however we count it, the point is, it fits his contemporaries' description of his nativity.

Around this time we have a choice of Jupiter or Saturn as Lord Ascendant. The Lord Ascendant is the planet that rules the sign on the Ascendant, from this, and the Ascendant itself, we can judge the physical appearance of the native. I have set it for 2:06am with Capricorn rising, as Saturn in Cancer as Lord Ascendant, fits the description that Condivi gives us in his biography, far more than Jupiter in Capricorn: He was, 'of middle height,' with a 'round skull, (prominent) square forehead,' 'little eyes,' 'flattened (broken) nose,' 'few eyebrow hairs,' and 'hair black and not very thick.' Condivi also mentions, 'He suffered for many years with difficulty in passing urine'. This, for our purposes, points to restrictive Saturn in watery Cancer in the seventh house of his pelvis and genitals, trine by the Moon in its fall in a fixed water sign.

Traditionally planets are said to be in certain 'dignities' depending on their location in the chart. These dignities are known as 'essential' and 'accidental'. Essential dignities are derived from the sign in which the planet falls, in some places they are 'good' strong or 'happy' shown by a planet falling in its own sign, exaltation or triplicity, and to lesser extent term and face. In others they are problematic, weak or unhappy shown by a planet in its detriment or fall.[1] These distinctions are also qualitative and so we can also see a planets attitude toward other planets by essential dignities. For example, if a planet falls in the exaltation of another then it exalts whatever that particular planet signifies. If it is in another's sign then it is ruled by or 'loves' that planet. In another's detriment it dislikes that planet, in its fall; it hates it. This technique is called 'reception'. Planets that are simultaneously in each other's dignities are in 'mutual reception' signifying understanding between them. This can be positive or negative depending on the state of the planets and the dignities involved.

Accidental dignities basically show how much ability a planet has to act in the world, this is shown by various factors such as its position in the houses, aspects by other planets, speed and direction, placement on fixed stars etc.

Using this time of 2:06am for Michelangelo's birth, the planet Jupiter is inside the first house,[2] this could be seen literally as the 'fateful and lucky star' that Vasari mentions, Jupiter traditionally being known as the great benific and thus, lucky. Though, of course, Vasari may have been speaking generally about the auspicious astrological moment Michelangelo was born. Any planet in the first house close to the Ascendant will have some affect on the native's appearance, the native being 'born under' it. But this will only qualify, it will not change the primary testimonies, these are drawn from the Ascendant and Lord Ascendant, so as a first choice between Saturn and Jupiter as Ascendant ruler, one must go with Saturn in Cancer.

A quick look at the chart reveals the thoughtful, contemplative melancholic nature Michelangelo was known for. His Ascendant, Lord Ascendant

---

[1] See Appendix for the table of Essential Dignities. Following traditional practice I omit mention of Uranus, Neptune and Pluto.
[2] All natal and related charts are set using Placidus cusps.

and Moon are all judged as cold and dry by traditional method, thus giving him a melancholic temperament.

He was generous by nature, benific Jupiter is in his first house and so is significator of his manner, of his motivations. This generosity was very important to him as shown by his Lord Ascendant exalting this Jupiter and can be seen by the work he sometimes just gave away. For example, Michelangelo's statues, *The Dying Slave* and *The Rebellious Captive* that are now in the Louvre in Paris, he simply gave to his friend Roberto Strozzi. Also Condivi quotes him: 'rich man as I have made myself I have always lived as a poor one.' Michelangelo's Lord Ascendant Saturn is in its detriment in Cancer, sign of the 'poor and common people.' He was a devout Christian: his significator of manner, Jupiter is on the fixed star Pelagus. Vivian Robson in his book: *The Fixed Stars and Constellations* tells us that Pelagus gives the native, 'a religious mind and ecclesiastical preferment.' And as Condivi tells us, Michelangelo had a great affection for the famous Florentine preacher Girolamo Savonarola, 'keeping always in mind the sound of his voice.' With the ruler of his 9th house of religion being in a fixed, 'voiced' sign, this should not surprise us.

The Moon and Mercury are traditionally seen as the rulers of a natives mind and their condition and relationship with each other describe the particular qualities that mind has. Michelangelo's show his ingeniousness: his Mercury is conjunct fixed star Deneb Adige, which, according to Robson, whose book is the standard traditional text on the fixed stars, 'gives an ingenious nature and clever intellect.' His Moon is conjunct the North Node. William Lilly, the great 17th century astrologer, in his indispensable book *Christian Astrology* points out, this position of the Moon 'shows active spirits, prompt to any science'. The Moon and Mercury behold each other by a square aspect giving ruggedness to his mind, and Mercury is below the horizon, a position that particularly frames his mind for the Arts. Michelangelo's Moon and Mercury are also conjunct by the traditional method of 'antiscion'. This is whereby a planet is reflected through the solstice points of 0 degrees Cancer and 0 degrees Capricorn, thus giving the planet an alternate or second placement. This is traditionally read in much the same way as a bodily position and according to William Lilly this conjunction of Mercury and Moon 'in any sign, declares ingenious persons'.

His art is powerful and passionate: more planets are in Mars dignities than the dignities of any other planet. Mars rules the Moon, which as it is a night time birth, is known as the 'Light of Time'. Venus is his 'Lord of the Geniture', the strongest planet by essential and accidental dignities in his chart. Venus is the natural ruler of art and is powerful, having just entered her exaltation in Pisces. It is in the second house with Mercury, in mutual reception and sextile ('benign') aspect with Jupiter; exactly as Condivi had noted. Venus is also conjunct his Midheaven, his place of work, by antiscion and is ruler of his 10th house of action.

The Divine Michelangleo

Traditionally the eclipse before birth will show the 'life and times' in the mundane world, the big wide world that the native is born into. It is set for the latitude and longitude of birth thus linking it to that particular place. It can be seen as a set of potentials, if a native sets himself out from the crowd, somehow he will plug into these potentials shown by the eclipse before birth, attempting to bring to fruition the seeds that are planted there. This will be shown by significant points or planets in the natal chart falling on significant places in the eclipse chart. After the eclipse and before birth there may also be a pre birth lunation; a New or Full Moon. This seems to act as a narrowing of focus as if the manifestation of the potentials of the eclipse are now restricted to less possibilities and these possibilities are then further restricted by the birth chart. Connections are seen or not seen between the charts and this is all read back into the potential that is shown in the 'bigger picture' of the eclipse. Only what is shown there can be achieved.

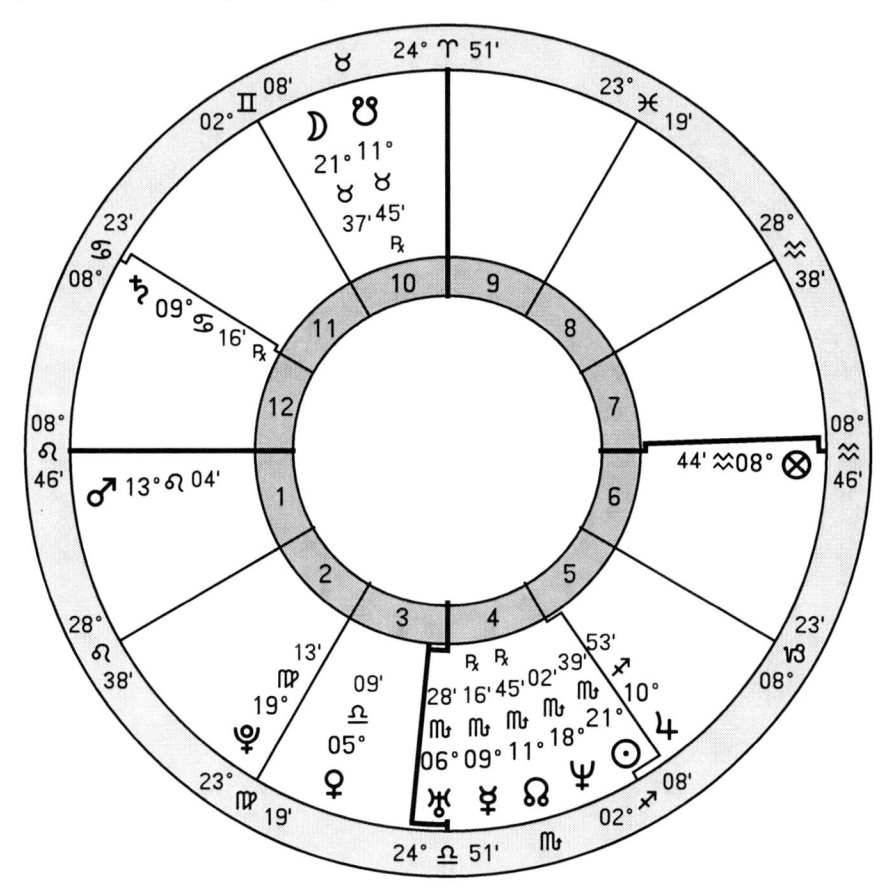

(Fig 2) Michelangelo's pre-birth eclipse, 4 Nov 1473 AD JC, 22.00.20 LMT, Caprese Michelangelo, Italy

The Pattern of Time

With our eyes open to these connections we can see Michelangelo's Light of Time, the Moon, powerfully applying to conjunction with the benefic North Node in the 10th house of his career and, by antiscion, this falls on the Mercury and Venus conjunction of the pre birth lunation. His Mercury also picks this up, plugging him in to the life and times of his era and fuelling his powerful artistic imagination. Mercury is ruler of his 9th house of visions and dreams and is on fixed star Deneb Adige so favourable for artists. Venus gives him the eloquence and Mercury provides the facility to portray the cosmic vision, to bring it to earth. The pre birth conjunction of Mercury and Venus occurs in Aquarius, traditionally seen as the most 'humane' of signs and ruled by Saturn, who in turn is traditional ruler of matter, marble and stone. Poetry was another of Michelangelo's artistic gifts, Venus providing Mercury with the poeticism to speak beyond the mundane; Aquarius is fixed air and is a voiced sign.

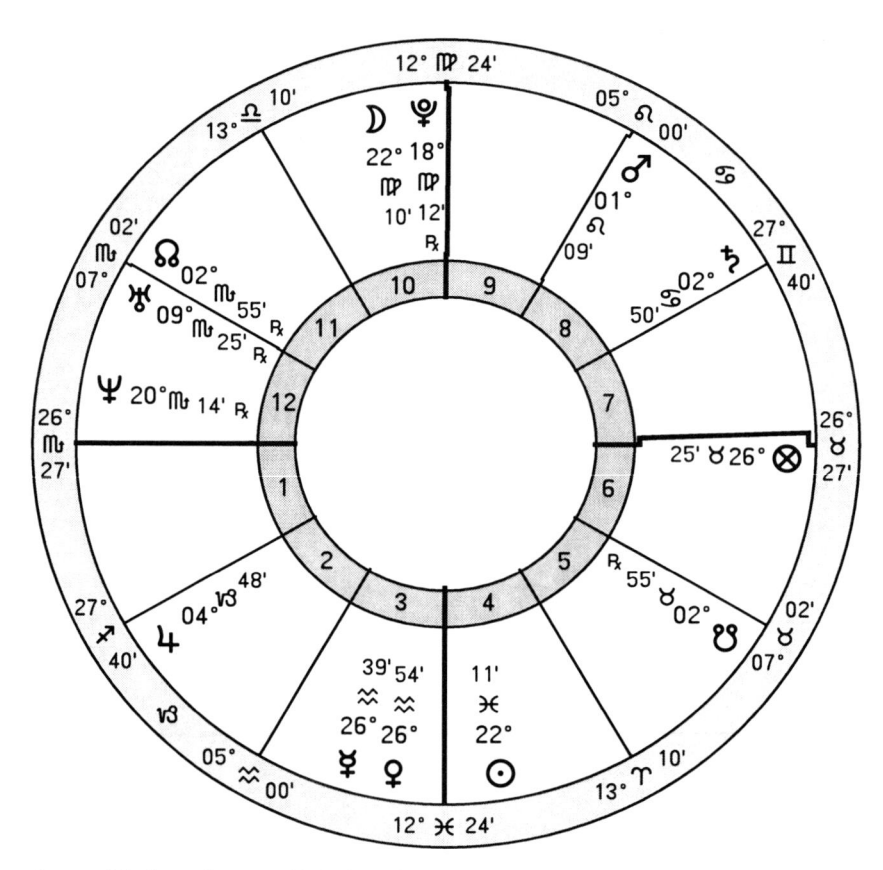

(Fig 3) Michelangelo's pre-birth lunation, 3 March 1474, AD JC, 23.33.58 LMT, Caprese Michelangelo, Italy

His work will make its mark on the world: Michelangelo's 10th house/4th house axis, known as the MC/IC, reverses the MC/IC of the pre birth eclipse. As the MC is the Heavens, the IC can be seen as the lowest point, the ground, or the world down here. It will be through art, and the portrayal of the divine and the human that he will make his mark: his Sun, by antiscion, is conjunct the ruler of the eclipse, a dignified, and again humane, Venus. His creations, shown by Venus as ruler of his 5th house, are of an exalted religious nature as Venus is exalted in Pisces, a Jupiter sign and Jupiter being the traditional ruler of religion. They are in mutual reception, showing understanding between them and in sextile aspect, again showing influence and access to one another. His Midheaven is on the fixed star Princeps, which is located on the spear shaft of Bootes, said to give a profound mind. As this star is on his MC, this profundity will come out in his career. That it is on the spear shaft shows again it is aspiration, in the best sense of the word that is driving the career, as the spear shaft is thrust up towards the Heavens. Princeps can also show him working for 'Princes,' which of course, he did.

He has a great love and understanding of religion, shown by his Lord Ascendant Saturn, exalting, and in mutual reception, understanding, with Jupiter, natural ruler of religion. Jupiter as mentioned above is on Pelagus. Pelagus is situated on the vane of the arrow at the Archer's hand, and so shows him aiming for the Heavens, aspiring. Yet even someone as great as Michelangelo can only 'see' so far: fixed star Facies conjunct his Ascendant will obscure his view.

Saturn is conjunct Alhena a Venus/Mercury fixed star, favourable for artists and artistic expression, in the seventh house of other people, thus, portraying visions directly to them in the 'plastic' materials, (Saturn in Cancer) of art.

Exalting Jupiter, this artist will favour a large, grand vision, Jupiter being ruler of large and grand things, attempting to contain, as Saturn is the ruler of boundaries, the uncontainable; Saturn being in Cancer is in uncontainable cardinal water.

There are problems and injuries to his eyes, as indeed he had while painting the Sistine Chapel ceiling with paint dripping into them. Saturn as Lord 2 is seen as his tools, his brushes and paints, and as Saturn is in its detriment they afflict the Moon, 'his eyes' by trine. He tells us himself in this extract, from 'Sonnet 5', written while he painted the ceiling:

> … the brush keeps dripping till my face looks gaudy more like mosaic than anything you'd tread on …

And there were problems after completing the ceiling, as Condivi tells us, when he could no longer lower his eyes, so long had he stared upwards: 'When he had finished this work Michelangelo, because he had painted so long a time with his eyes turned upward towards the vault, could hardly see any thing when looking down, so that when he had to read a letter or look at a minute object it was necessary for him to hold it above his head.'

Unfortunate fixed star Facies, on his Ascendant, also brings injuries to his eyes, Facies being the nebula on the Archers face; as the Archer aims upwards to Heaven, so his eyes suffer.

The Sun and Moon, 'the Lights' are the traditional rulers of the eyes and his Moon is in its fall afflicted by that trine from Saturn which is also Michelangelo himself. His Sun is exactly conjunct the fixed star Difda, a yellow star on the Whale's tail. This Whale is Cetus the sea monster sent by Poseidon to ravage the land and devour the beautiful Andromeda, to avenge the claim by Cassiopeia, Andromeda's mother that Andromeda was more beautiful than the sea nymphs the Nereids. And so this Whale, this sea monster, is born from the endless ocean of desires and from envy too, it is driven to ravage the epitome of beauty that is Andromeda who is more beautiful than even desire itself. The hero Perseus intervenes changing the sea monster into stone by showing it the head of Medusa, originally a beautiful young woman, but whose beauty turns all who look at her to stone. She is born from desire for the material world, being daughter of Pontus, the ocean and Ge, earth or matter. Her gaze shows Cetus the sea monster that his origin is in avarice and his nature is the desire to devour material beauty. Michelangelo's eye is on the tail of this thrashing beast. This is not a fish whose tail is vertical and shares in its steering like a rudder on a boat, this is a mammal and its tail is horizontal, acting as the 'motor', the powerhouse or engine room that propels the beast; this is where Michelangelo's eye is located. With realization of its true nature via the gaze of Medusa, the Whale is transformed into stone. Which on the one hand because of his mighty artistic gifts Michelangelo can turn to his advantage as a sculptor and creator of static images, taking this driving desire for material beauty and capturing and containing it in stone, and on the other hand, later in life, realizing that this can only take him so far, this quest for material beauty, before he realizes one can make an idol of it instead of seeing it for its true nature which is always to lift one's eyes beyond itself, beyond the material. Michelangelo, near the end of his life, wrote 'Sonnet 285', in it he tells us:

> Through stormy seas and in a fragile bark
> my life has reached at last the common port
> where all must come to render their report,
> accounting for each good and evil work.
>
> So the fond fantasy that used to make
> an idol and a tyrant out of art,
> I now see as it is, with error fraught,
> like what men love despite the harm they take.
>
> What of these vain and wanton thoughts of love
> now I approach two deaths? I know that one
> is certain, and the other threatens me.

The Divine Michelangleo

> Painting and sculpture will no longer serve
> to calm my soul, turned to that love divine
>
> whose arms were opened for us on the cross.

Perseus was riding through the air on Pegasus. That Pegasus was born from the head of Medusa shows that he too is representative of desire. But this desire has wings, lifting him upwards towards the Heavens, aspiring and enabling the hero to slay the beast and free Andromeda. She is now seen, because of the elevation of his desire, as she truly is: a reflection of divine beauty. The hero then marries her. It is clear that Michelangelo managed this feat many times in his long artistic career, both in paint and stone. From the stamp of Pegasus' hoof comes the fountain Hippocrene sacred to the Muses where poets are said to draw their inspiration. Michelangelo clearly was no stranger to this place either.

Fixed star Bungula sits on his 11th cusp; a Venus/Jupiter star traditionally seen as bringing 'beneficence, friends, refinement and honour.' On his 11th cusp these qualities will manifest through his friends; after all, this was the man who spoke familiarly with popes and as a youth wandered sketching and studying in the gardens of the Medici princes under the wing of Lorenzo the Magnificent. Yes indeed, he had powerful friends. The Pope, after Michelangelo's death, even expressing he wanted 'a personal memorial and sepulchre for him in St Peter's itself.'

Michelangelo clearly had empathy for others with his Lord Ascendant on the 7th cusp in trine with Lord 7, 'other people' and his Moon so high in the chart, making his empathy visible. He portrayed humanity as exalting the religious quest back to God, shown by Saturn in the 7th house, exalting Jupiter on Pelagus. These planets are in opposition, showing the tension of separation, they are also in mutual reception showing the possibility of resolution, but they are both essentially debilitated, (as is Lord 7), showing the inability to do it by one's self, hence the need for Grace; God reaching down to humanity. This constant theme in his visual work is also shown, especially later in life, in his poetry. In 'Sonnet 292' he cries out:

> ... The prayers I offer would be sweet indeed
> If only you would lend me power to pray ...

And in 'Sonnet 289'

> ... Stretch down to me, dear Lord, the chain that with
> itself brings linked each heavenly gift: I mean
> faith that I catch and course at, while I rue
> my sin that checks full grace that comes from faith ...

The Arabian Part of Vocation falls at 4 degrees Gemini, within 2 degrees of the royal fixed star Aldebaran. It is ruled by Mercury in Aquarius the most humane of signs, and as mentioned, this Mercury (also conjunct his Moon by antiscion) falls conjunct the Mercury/Venus conjunction in the pre birth lunation, giving him the job of articulating the artistic vision of his time. Occurring in a fixed sign shows this is a vision that will last.

That this is for his generation and more is also confirmed by his natal arc Part of Vocation falling exactly conjunct the 5th house of 'creations' in the pre birth eclipse, and his natal 5th house cusp is conjunct the eclipse itself on the exalted Moon. This plugged him into the power source of the eclipse.

The natal arc Part of Vocation is calculated by using the Moon – Sun arc from the nativity and projecting it from the Midheaven of a separate chart. This can be done with the other major parts as well, following the same method; take the natal arc of the planets the Part is derived from and project it from the respective point in the separate chart rather than the natal. It seems to show a deeper working out of things in time – almost at what we would call a 'Soul' level.

His natal Fortuna is conjunct the eclipse Ascendant, focusing its power to earth, the Ascendant being the horizon, and his Sun is conjunct the eclipse 9th house, the house of both Art and God. This was no ordinary artist, he was working for his generation and beyond, as Vasari quoted him when asked by a priest, a good friend of his why he never took a wife so as to leave all his work to his sons, said: 'I've always had too harassing a wife in this demanding art of mine, and the work I leave behind will be my sons.' How right he was, and how long they would live, his natal 5th cusp, 'his offspring' is conjunct the fixed exalted eclipse Moon.

Looking at some momentous episodes in Michelangelo's life ...

The Medici Gardens

In 1508 Francesco Granacci took Michelangelo to the gardens of the Medici of San Marco. Here he met Lorenzo the Magnificent, father of Pope Leo, as Condivi says, 'a man renowned for every excellence'. Lorenzo had so many beautiful antique statues and decorative sculptures that Michelangelo resolved not to return to the workshop he was apprenticed to and instead study in the gardens of the Medici princes. His progressions for this year show his Moon progressing onto royal fixed star Aldebaran a magnitude 1 powerful star signifying a new beginning for Michelangelo, 'with those who will bestow many badges of honour upon him,' (Lilly). The Moon then moves onto his progressed 5th cusp and natal Part of Vocation. This pattern is confirmed by the solar return for this year. Venus is conjunct the Midheaven of the pre birth eclipse, and falls into the natal 4th house: 'the garden'. Saturn, Michelangelo himself, is exalted, conjunct the benific North Node, and an exalted Moon is in the sign of Venus entering the 9th house of study: It seems that he was never happier.

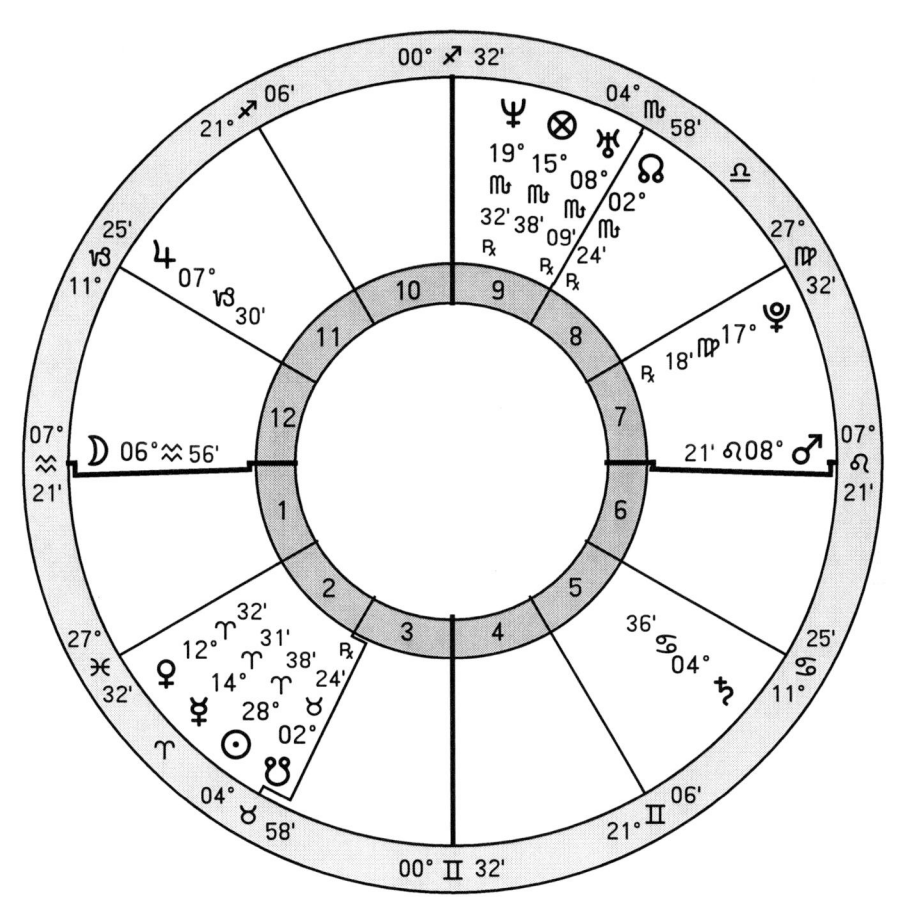

(Fig 4) Michelangelo, Secondary Progressions, 7 Mar 1508 AD JC

As happy as he was in the gardens of the Medici, he would become equally unhappy in the painting of the Sistine Chapel and yet this was to be one of the triumphs of his career.

The Painting of the Sistine Chapel

Michelangelo did not consider himself to be a painter at all; he ends his 'Sonnet 5' with the words: 'this is no place for me, and I'm no painter.' Neither did his rivals consider him to be one. In light of this, how much more remarkable the painting of the Sistine Chapel is.

The painting of the Sistine Chapel ceiling was begun in 1508 and completed in 1512, in which, Michelangelo, 'has depicted the creation of the world and then almost the whole of the Old Testament' (Condivi). The work was unveiled on All Saints Day 1512 and all Rome came to admire it.

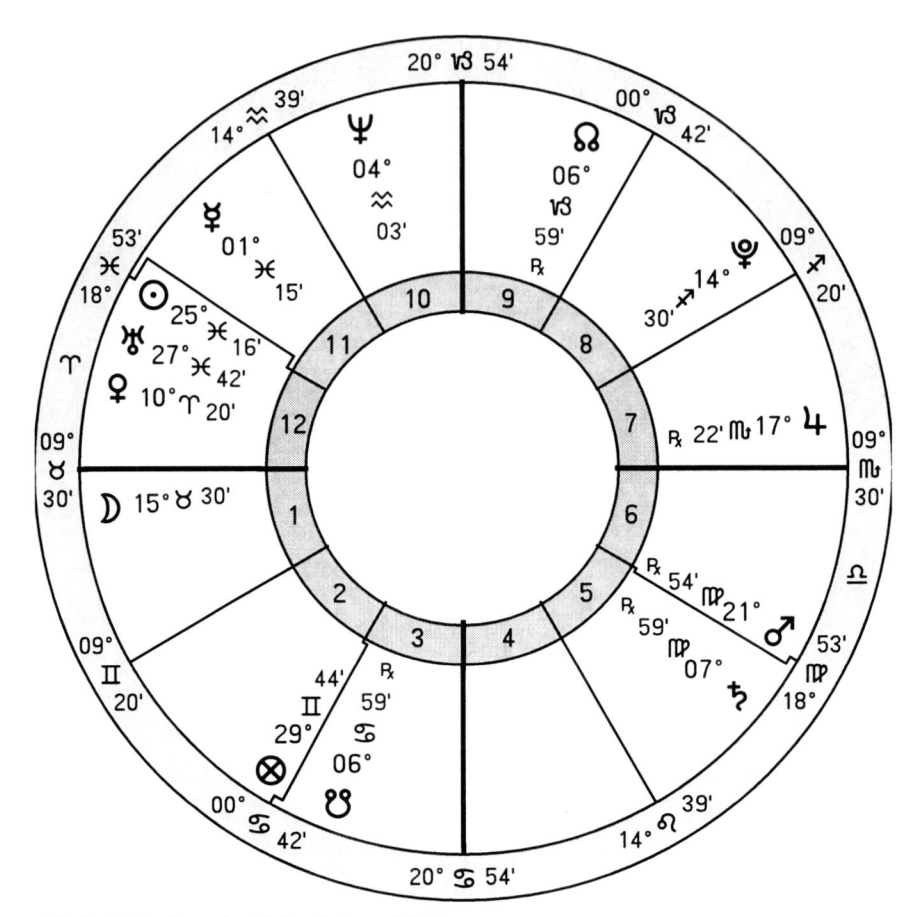

(Fig 5) Michelangelo, Solar Return 1508

As the 'Benign Ruler of Heaven' had sent him, who better to depict the Creation than Michelangelo? Though a look at his progressed Sun for 1508 separating but still opposed to his MC, soon to leave its exaltation and lose all its dignity and then conjunct the unfortunate South Node, one can see it was not a commission he was looking forward to.

In fact his rivals, the architect Bramante and the artist Raphael were plotting in secret. Judging that his principal art was sculpture they had put him forward for the job, convincing Pope Julius, that Michelangelo was the man. Then they waited in the wings for him to fail as they were sure he would, thus destroying his reputation and his friendship and patronage of the Pope. Jupiter is Lord 12, his 'secret enemies', and is in Michelangelo's 1st house influencing him and opposing his Lord Ascendant in the 7th. Jupiter also rules his Arabian Part of Fame. There is mutual reception between them, and between Jupiter and Venus, ruler of his career: his enemies would be influential in his fame.

The Divine Michangleo

Michelangelo protested. Condivi tells us: (He) '... as yet had never used colours, and knew the painting of the vault to be a very difficult undertaking and tried with all his power to get out of it ...' Pope Julius was not moved and despite Michelangelo's protestations he insisted. And so Michelangelo set himself to do the work.

Instability, troubles and contentions are shown by his Ascendant progressing onto fixed star Armus, as he is called to exercise his knowledge and art: progressed Ascendant is in early Lord 9 Mercury terms, in humane Aquarius, with his Sun sextile natal Mercury. He is called to 'voyage' as his 9th house of 'long journeys' progresses onto fixed star Acrux, a magnitude 1 Jupiter star, the brightest star in the Southern Cross, traditionally bringing religious beneficence. As his natal Lord 9 is in a fixed air sign, and with his contemplative nature and artistic gifts this was to be a voyage of imagination and stunning vision, and his Ascendant had also progressed onto the Descendant of his pre birth eclipse: it was time to capture everybody's imagination, it was time to capture the zeitgeist.

His enemies would play their part: the solar return for 1508–09 shows an exalted Moon in mundane conjunction with the Jupiter that sits inside Michelangelo's Ascendant, Jupiter being ruler of his Part of Fame and of the 12th house of enemies. It is also opposed to the Jupiter in the return chart.

His gifts are called into play to describe a cosmic drama for all to see: the return Mercury is conjunct his natal Venus and the return 9/3 axis is conjunct his natal Ascendant/Descendant thus bringing his art into the world, or images of Heaven (9th) down to earth (3rd) for both himself and others, the 3rd traditionally being seen as the flowering and manifestation of the imagination of the 9th. The 3rd house is also where we see the return's Fortuna, which is conjunct natal Lord Ascendant, Michelangelo himself and is ruled by a strong exalted return Moon.

The return Mercury conjunct his natal Venus brings to mind the Mercury/Venus conjunction in the pre birth lunation (in fixed Aquarius and ruled by Saturn). This time the conjunction is ruled by Jupiter in a fluid, mutable, water sign: it would be paint and not stone that this religious vision would be created with.

This was filled with problems though: natal arc Fortuna falls at 17 Degrees 10 Sagittarius in the return in the 8th house of fear and anxiety. At one time the Pope threatened to throw Michelangelo off the scaffold; the 8th house is also the house of death. This natal arc Part falls into the natal 12th house where Michelangelo felt trapped, the 12th being the 'place of confinement' and was in the power of his secret enemies, also shown by the 12th, Bramante and Raphael et al. And trapped he was. When he finished the picture of the Flood the work grew mouldy, again he protested: 'I have told your holiness that this is not my art; all I have done is spoiled; if you do not believe it, send and see.' The Pope sent architect Sangallo to inspect it, who said the lime in the fresco was too wet thus causing the problem. 'Informing

The Pattern of Time

Michelangelo of this he made him proceed and the excuse was unavailing.' (Condivi)

Michelangelo continued to finish the work, without assistance, and 'not even anyone to grind the colours.' (Condivi)

The progressions for 1512, the year the Sistine Chapel was completed show his Sun conjunct the South Node, between progressed South Node and natal South Node a very unfortunate place to be. William Lilly tells us this progression brings the native, 'grief and pains in his eyes, many obstructions in the body'. Michelangelo's progressed Sun is also opposed to his natal Moon, for which Lilly says will bring the native, 'dangerous infirmities in the eyes and sickness in other parts of the body, many times sore eyes and a violent fever.' He was in a right state. He couldn't even bring his eyes downward to see, he had to hold letters above his head to read them.

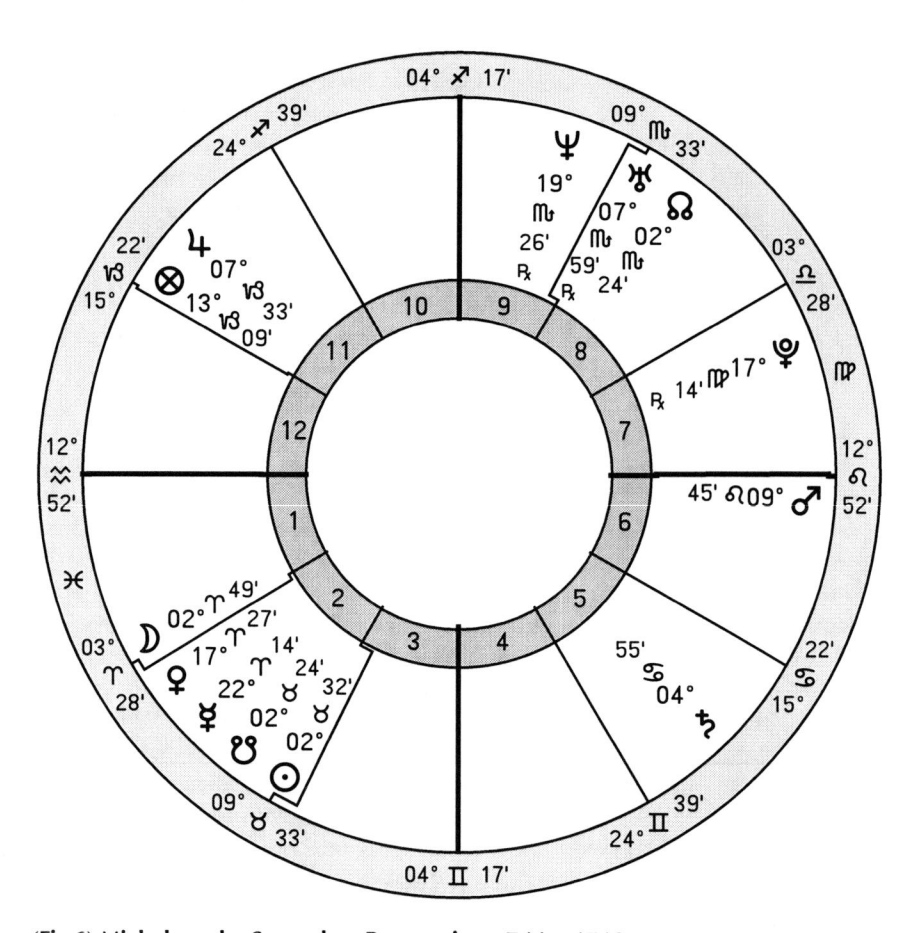

(Fig 6) Michelangelo, Secondary Progressions, 7 Mar 1512

The Divine Michelangleo

His 1512 solar return shows the return Ascendant/Descendant axis falling onto his natal Midheaven, and this conjunct the Midheaven of the pre birth eclipse, and so links all the way back to the eclipse as a flowering of the seeds planted there. Return Saturn (natal Lord Ascendant) is loosely conjunct return Moon and both are conjunct natal Moon and natal North Node in the 10th house of career, there is also a mundane conjunction with natal Saturn. It was this painting that lifted him above and beyond any living artist. His enemies must have been beside themselves.

'And all Rome came to see it …' (Condivi)

Raphael and Bramante had lost and Michelangelo was honoured as the greatest of all living artists.

The lunar return for the completion, it was unveiled on the feast of All Saints 1512, has its Midheaven conjunct Michelangelo's Part of Vocation

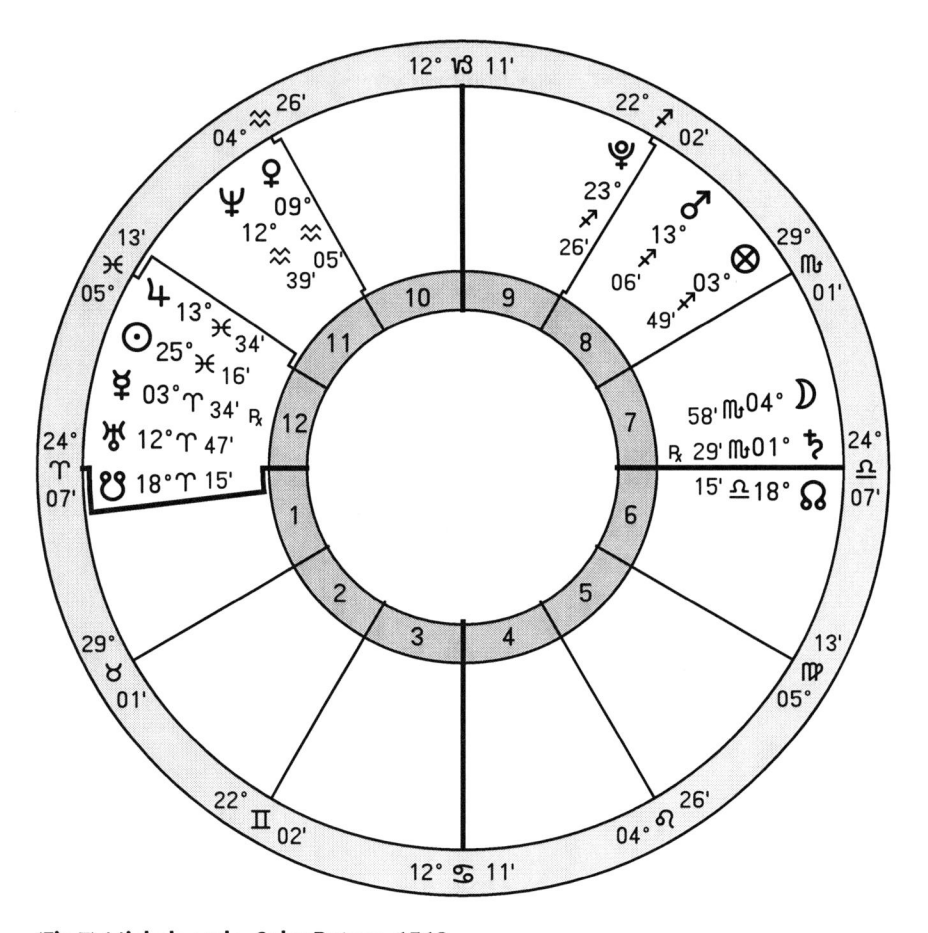

(Fig 7) Michelangelo, Solar Return, 1512

and royal star Aldebaran. Return Lord 9, signifying his art, is conjunct fixed star Wega, traditionally said to bring visions from Heaven, and is exalted in the 5th house of the return signifying his creations at that time. It is also conjunct natal Jupiter in his 1st house.

'It was such to make everyone speechless with astonishment.' (Vasari). Return Lord 7 is in a mute sign exalting Venus who is art and beauty conjunct Michelangelo's natal Sun, in other words, Michelangelo himself.

He was lifted up above all other living artists: return Mercury natal Lord 9, his art and knowledge also ruler of his Part of Vocation is conjunct the North Node and Fortuna.

His fame was mighty indeed, and yet there would be another fresco, later in life, in which he 'excelled the masters,' and even 'outstripped himself.' (Vasari). This was the painting of *The Last Judgement*.

The Painting of *The Last Judgement*

Michelangelo started work on *The Last Judgement* in 1536. This fresco was painted on the end wall of the Sistine chapel. It was during this time he also composed 'Sonnet 104' which as we can see in this excerpt, is laden with astrological imagery:

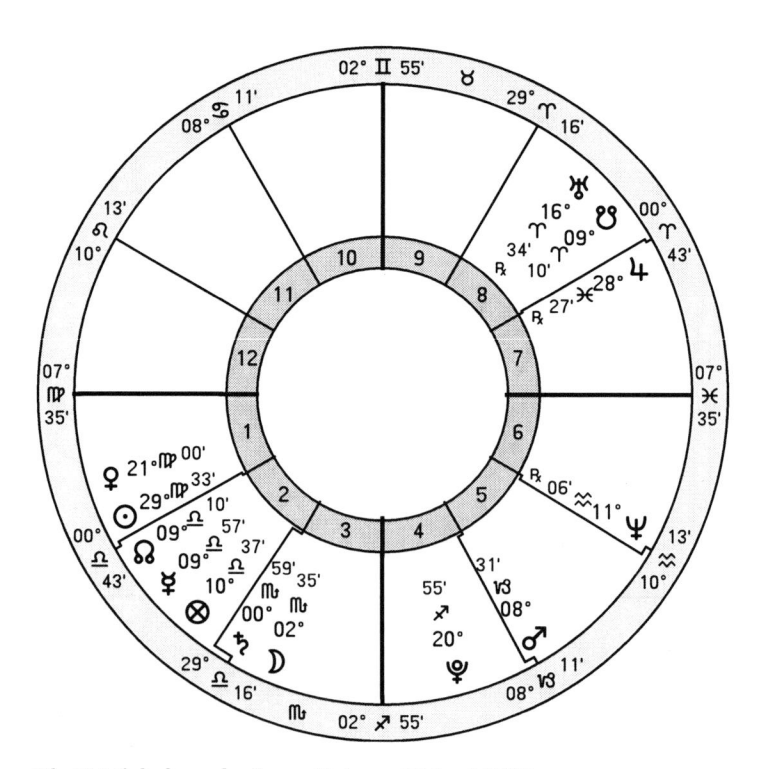

(Fig 8) Michelangelo, Lunar Return, 13 Sept 1512

The Divine Michangleo

> He who created time from nothingness
> (but after man's creation, only then)
> split time in two: one half held high the sun,
> the other had the moon that's near to us.
> From these were born, before the moment passed,
> the fortune, fate and chance of every man;
> I was assigned the dark time for my own,
> as what my birth and cradle suited best.
> I copy what I think fate says I am …

Michelangelo's painting; *The Last Judgement* was uncovered on the 31st of October 1541 (private view). His Midheaven had progressed onto his Ascendant and his progressed Moon conjuncts the pre birth eclipse Midheaven. His Sun has just progressed into Gemini showing a new phase and his Fortuna is on royal fixed star Fomalhaut, 'changing material to a spiritual form of expression,' (Robson). This star is associated with the winter solstice and the birth of Christ. How fitting that this painting would be unveiled to the public on Christmas Day.

His solar return for this year shows return Saturn, natal Lord Ascendant, Michelangelo himself, exalted. It is retrograde, going backward, thus showing a return to painting, on his natal Midheaven; at the highest point, in glory, for all to see. A nice fertile return Moon conjuncts natal Saturn, bringing bounty

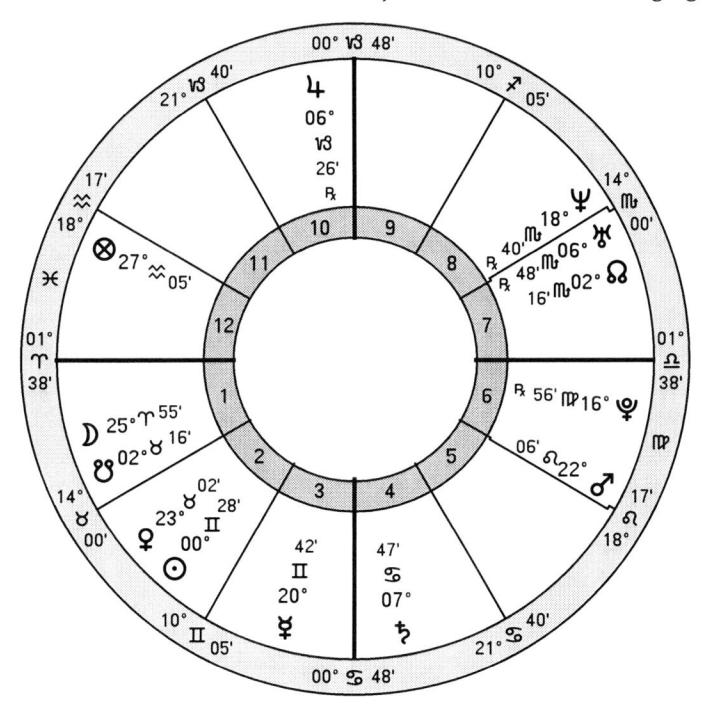

(Fig 9) Michelangelo, Secondary Progressions, 7 Mar 1541

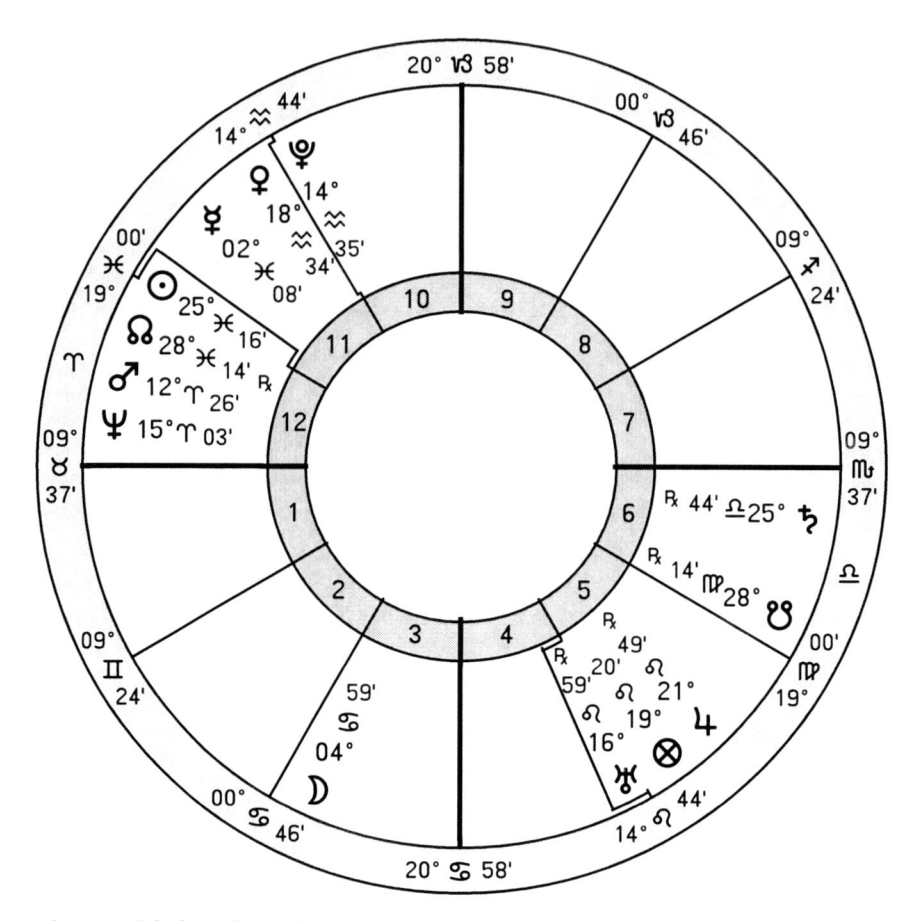

(Fig 10) Michelangelo's Solar Return, 1541

with it, and yet is opposed to natal Jupiter showing the tension and opposition in the work. Natal arc Fortuna is conjunct natal Sun and the return North Node, suggesting his soul's search to bring his visions of God's power and majesty was achieved in this, and this all happening on the natal 3rd, again, bringing these visions into manifestation, down to earth, as Vasari, Varchi, Condivi and others would later say. With return Jupiter, ruler of his natal arc Fortuna and natal Part of Fame conjunct powerful royal fixed star Regulus, which leads straight to the throne, we can see this was indeed the work that propelled him in the eyes of his peers, beyond all others living or dead.

The lunar return for the uncovering shows return Sun conjunct Michelangelo's Moon/North Node natal conjunction. This is powerful; as the Sun is on Acrux, brightest star in the Southern Cross, even more so. We have seen this star before: it is the same star his 9th house had progressed onto with the painting of the Sistine Chapel. Acrux brings him religious beneficence.

Return Jupiter though in its detriment is conjunct Fortuna conjunct return Ascendant which is, in turn, conjunct natal 9th house. Many, like Biagio da Cesena, the master of ceremonies, and so naturally ruled by Jupiter, were unhappy: Jupiter is in its detriment, about Michelangelo's art: Jupiter is conjunct Michelangelo's natal 9th house of art. This was because of the nakedness of the people he had depicted, "exposing themselves shamefully," they felt it was unseemly: Jupiter is in the fall of Venus.

But, despite this, the return Ascendant, Fortuna and Jupiter are all conjunct the full Moon of the pre birth lunation, marking this time as highly significant. This was to be unlike anything else.

'... to the wonder and astonishment of the whole of Rome, or rather the whole world.' (Vasari)

The public came to see this work on Christmas day, December 1541, and were, 'stupefied by what they saw.' (Vasari)

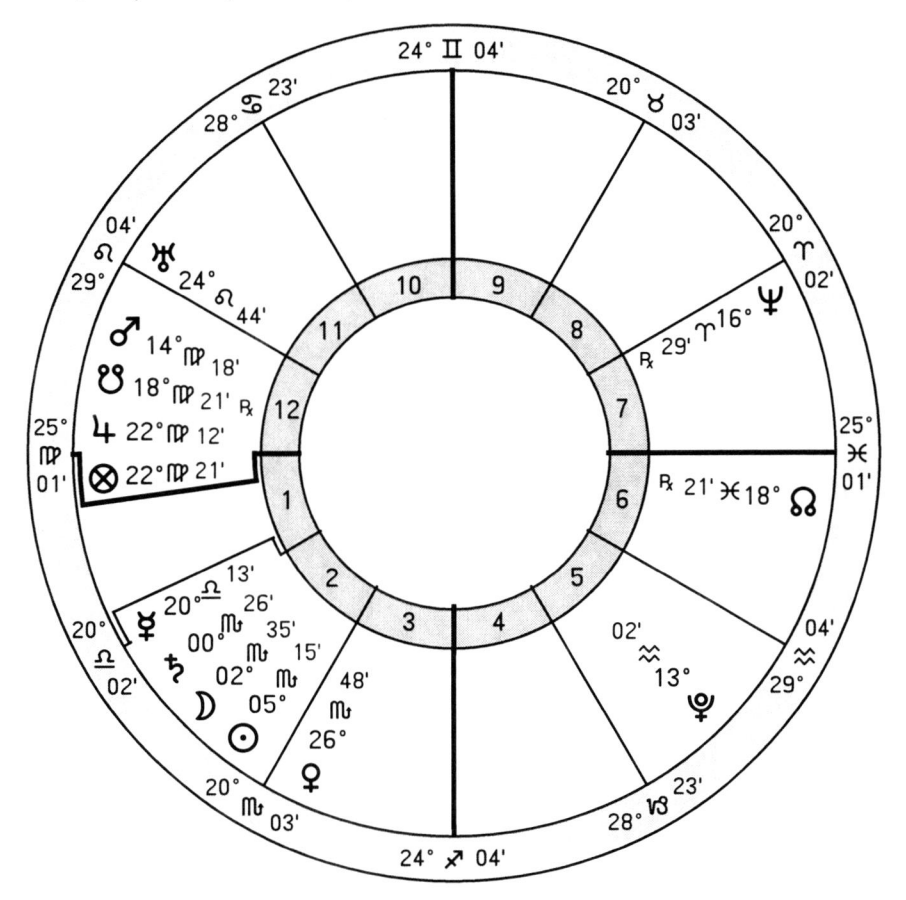

(Fig 11) Michelangelo's Lunar Return, 19 Oct 1541

The lunar return preceding this event shows the return Ascendant conjunct natal Mars, appropriate, given the power that shocked the populace and not surprisingly, many again, did not receive it well at first. But the return Mars is conjunct fixed star Spica, associated with The Virgin Mary, strongly protective and bringing success and renown. The return North Node is on the return 9th house. A humane Venus, showing Michelangelo's decorum in painting humanity, is in the 7th house in mundane conjunction with natal Saturn who is natal Lord Ascendant, Michelangelo himself. Return Sun is conjunct natal Ascendant: shining light on Michelangelo and the light of God shining through him, as Vasari and others would later say. His natal arc Part of Vocation is conjunct the return North Node, showing it was part of his vocation to be once again lifted up: natal arc Part of Vocation/North Node conjunction lifts him up, that this is via his art is shown by it being conjunct the return 9th house, to show the world, the 7th house of other people, how to do it.

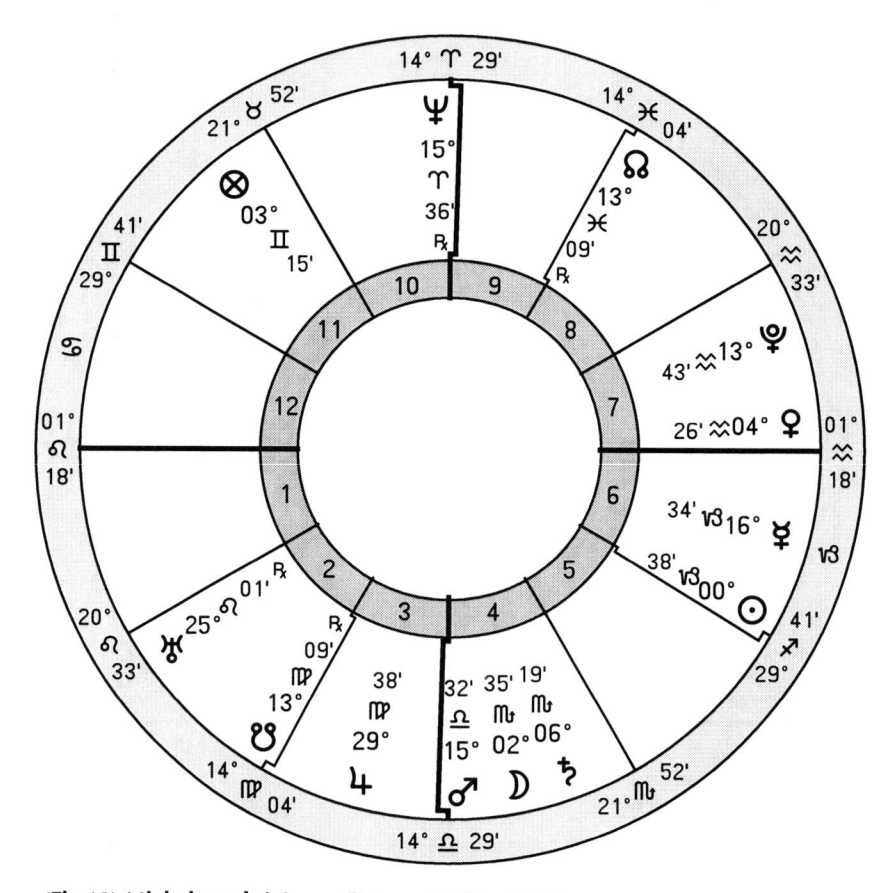

(Fig 12) Michelangelo's Lunar Return, 12 Dec 1541

The Divine Michelangleo

On Christmas day at 12 noon, with the Sun at it's zenith, exactly opposite, on the IC, traditionally seen as 'the end of things' was Michelangelo's natal arc Part of Fame: *The Last Judgement*. The Moon shows the populace and is square both his Part of Fame and the Sun, so showing the tension between them, and yet exalting the Sun, symbol of God on the Midheaven. To be in square aspect as Ibn Ezra said in his book *The Beginning of Wisdom*: is a sign of 'each party seeking control for his self', in this context the battle between human free will and God's destiny. Terrified by the square but exalting God, the populace are captured by this tension and power, while the vision, the ruler of natal arc Part of Fame, exalts God Himself. And this noon chart's Ascendant/Descendant axis falls on the Midheaven of his pre birth eclipse and on the Venus of the Medici gardens, through the Sistine Chapel charts and onto Michelangelo's natal Midheaven, linking them all through time, like a line between God and man thus bringing vision of the Heavens down to earth, or as Vasari would later put it: 'enabling mankind to see the fateful results when an artist of sublime intellect infused with Divine Grace and knowledge appears on earth.'

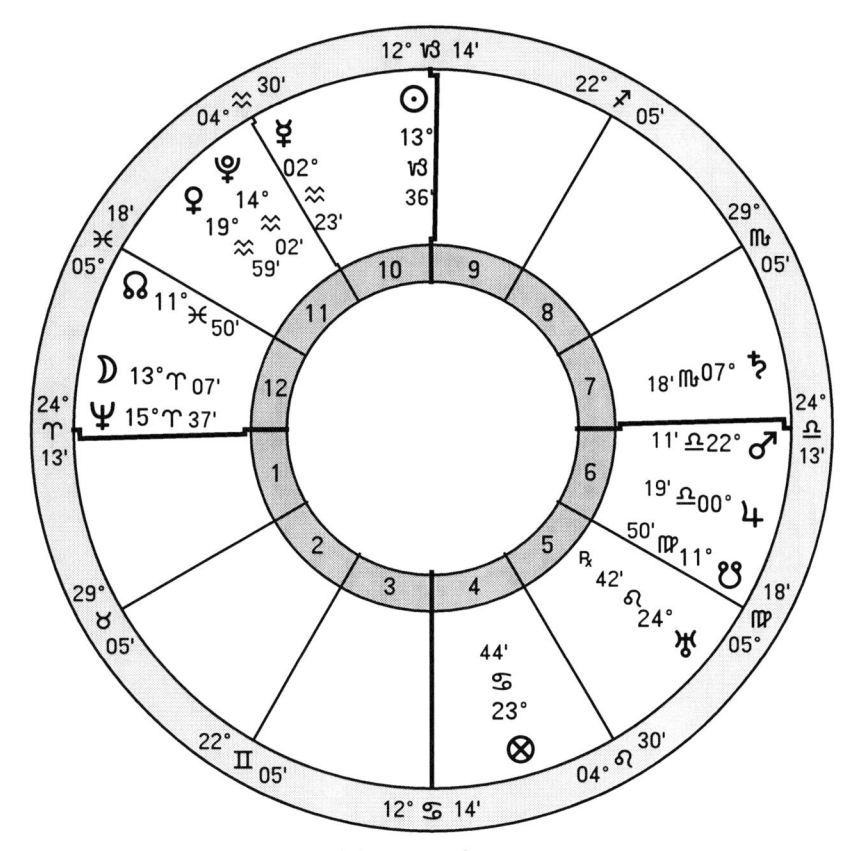

(Fig 13) The Public Unveiling of The Last Judgement

2

When Will I Find My Next Job?[1]

As I write this essay the media are busy watching another financial crisis unfold. World leaders gather to attend important sounding 'summits' and the media cheer and boo from the sidelines. While they marvel at the beauty of one president's wife and gossip over another's fashion choices, many of the rest of us face the mundane and not so simple task of finding another job in financially uncertain times. As the growing legions of unemployed wonder what to do next, it might be instructive to see what astrology has to say on the subject, indeed to see if it can point us in the right direction and help us navigate through troubled waters.

The approach in theory is clear and simple. The practical application is, like all things practical, not quite so simple. Lord 10 will signify the job and the Lord Ascendant and Moon will signify the querent. Connect Lord Ascendant or Moon with Lord 10 or vice versa and we have new job and querent coming together. Fail to do this and we do not. Take the distance between them, figure out the time units, count the degrees to perfection and we have the timing of the event.

Now a lot of time this is exactly what we will see or rather, things being what they are, what we won't see. Usually our attempts to force the chart into contortions to connect querent and job show simply a large dose of wishful thinking about a job that is, at least in the context, not essentially available. Yes you can apply for it, yes you are simply perfect for it, but no, you're not going to get it.

It will be helpful to look at some examples, to see how the reality and the intricacies of the matter and method play out ...

'When will either I or my wife get some work?'

The querent was in financial difficulty and worried; Lord Ascendant is Jupiter which has just turned retrograde in the 8th house of anxiety. Lord 2 signifying his money is also in a precarious situation inside the 12th house of self

---

[1] When the world financial crisis unfolded in 2008 Saptarishis Astrology asked me to write an article about the difficulties of finding work. *When Will I find My Next Job* was that article. It reappears here in a slightly edited form.

When Will I Find My Next Job?

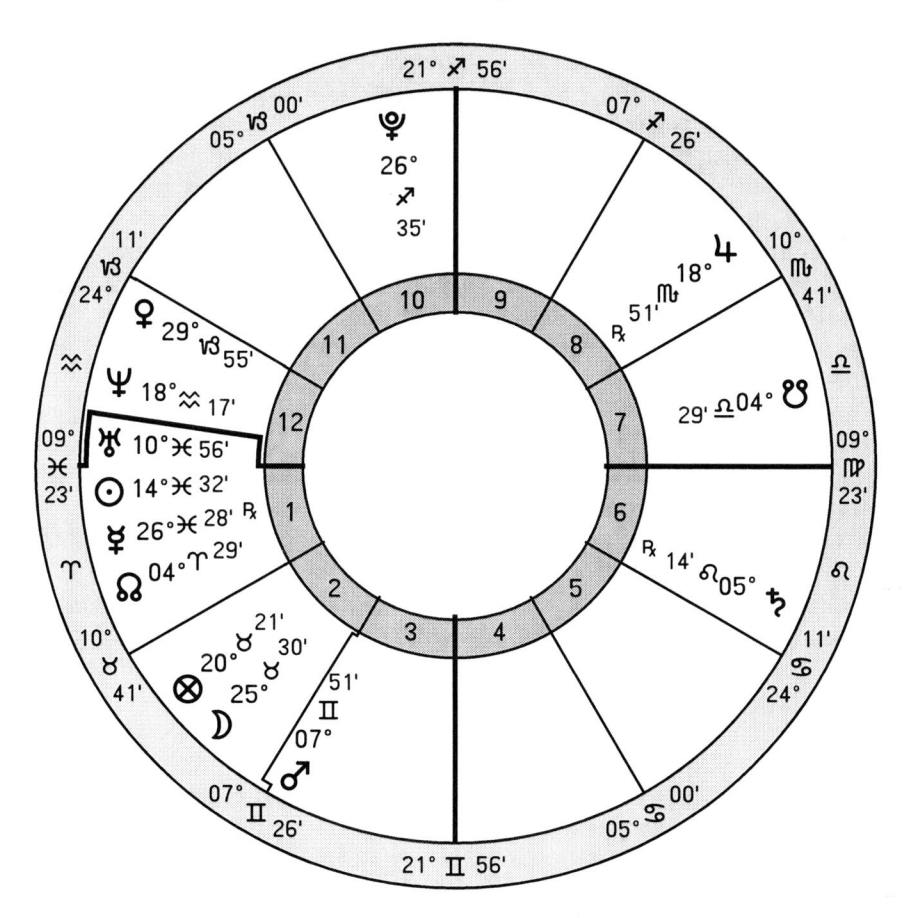

(Fig 14) 'I/Wife get some work?' 6.34 am, 5 Mar 2006, London, England[2]

undoing and about to change sign and lose all its dignity by triplicity.[3] Mercury, Lord 7, is the querent's wife and this planet is also retrograde and in its detriment and fall, so she too is not in a good way. With Mercury also about to back onto the malefic South Node by antiscion this situation looks quite precarious indeed. The querent is also signified by the Moon who being close to malefic fixed star Caput Algol shows that emotionally he is losing his head in the situation.

As I said earlier, ideally we'd want a connection between Lord Ascendant, Lord 10 or Lord 7 and Lord 10 – but here there is neither. One apparent

---

[2] All horary charts are set using Regiomontanus cusps.
[3] Lord 2 Venus is in Capricorn and so is dignified in it's triplicity by day. This is a day chart even though the Sun is not quite above the horizon as it would have already been light outside. Always give the day a few degrees leeway at sunrise and sunset as the Sun's light is visible just before it rises and just after it sets.

problem is that Lord 10 and Lord Ascendant are the same planet. But when the querent is self employed, as in this question, this can be quite common showing that in this sense; person and job are one and the same. We can look for other significators of the job usually the ruler of the next sign on the 10th, in this case Saturn, but before we jump to this let us see what we already have in front of us.

There is an aspect, showing something is about to happen, and this aspect is Moon to sextile Mercury in 1 degree. In context of the question the Moon, natural ruler of wives, to aspect Mercury turned[4] Lord 10 could show wife getting some work (also note that Saturn will retrograde onto antiscion of Moon).

To figure out the nature of the time units involved we consider only the applying planet and the sign and the house he is in. A fixed sign indicates a slow time unit, mutable a medium and cardinal a fast time unit. We add to this the house, with angular house equalling slow, succedent /medium and cadent/fast. This gives us the following combinations: fixed and angular gives us slow, fixed and succedent is medium, fixed and cadent again gives us medium. Mutable and angular gives us medium, mutable and succedent is medium, mutable and cadent also gives us a medium unit. Cardinal and angular is medium unit, cardinal and succedent is also medium and cardinal and cadent gives us fast. As you can see this weights the medium unit heavily, but none the less this system works very well and is quite capable of showing fast if the event is fast and slow if it is slow. Try and you will see. The number of degrees to perfection of the aspect gives us the quantity of time units i.e. ten degrees to perfection equals ten hours, days, weeks, months or years or whatever unit we've judged to use. For a further detailed exposition of this method I refer you to John Frawley's masterful and remarkably clear work *The Horary Textbook*.

As with all things in astrology it is vital that we apply this timing method within the context of the situation. We still need to weigh the testimonies carefully and most of all, we must remember that this is not a mechanistic tool and it cannot be applied in the manner of one.

So in this context the applying planet is in a fixed sign and so suggests a slow time unit but it is also in a succedent house suggesting a medium unit of time. Slow and medium together gives us medium. As there was no hint of any upcoming work at all to the knowledge of the querent and his wife we could safely say that the most obvious unit would be weeks, using days/fast, weeks/medium, months/slow. But with the knowledge that due to the nature of her business she would normally hear on the grapevine about any upcoming work coupled with the fixity of the Moon slowing things down we may well decide to push up the time unit to a month.

---

[4] Mercury is ruler of the 'turned 10th' his wife's 10th house, and so is significator of her job. We find the turned 10th house by counting from her 1st house (the 7th in the chart) and 'turning the chart' until we come to her 10th (the 4th in the chart).

When Will I Find My Next Job?

And so the judgement was that the querent's wife would get some work most likely in one month's time.

And so it proved – querent's wife started work on the 4th of April – a month later from the chart.

'Take job?'

During times of financial difficulty we are often tempted to apply for or take on a job that is most certainly not the best thing for us. This next chart shows this exact situation. In this instance, thankfully for the querent, he looked before he leapt.

Querent was worried and very unsure about taking a job that had been offered to him. He was, 'worried that it might be a nightmare'. Lord Ascendant the Sun has just lost all his dignity and is now in the detriment of Lord 10 showing he really doesn't want this job.

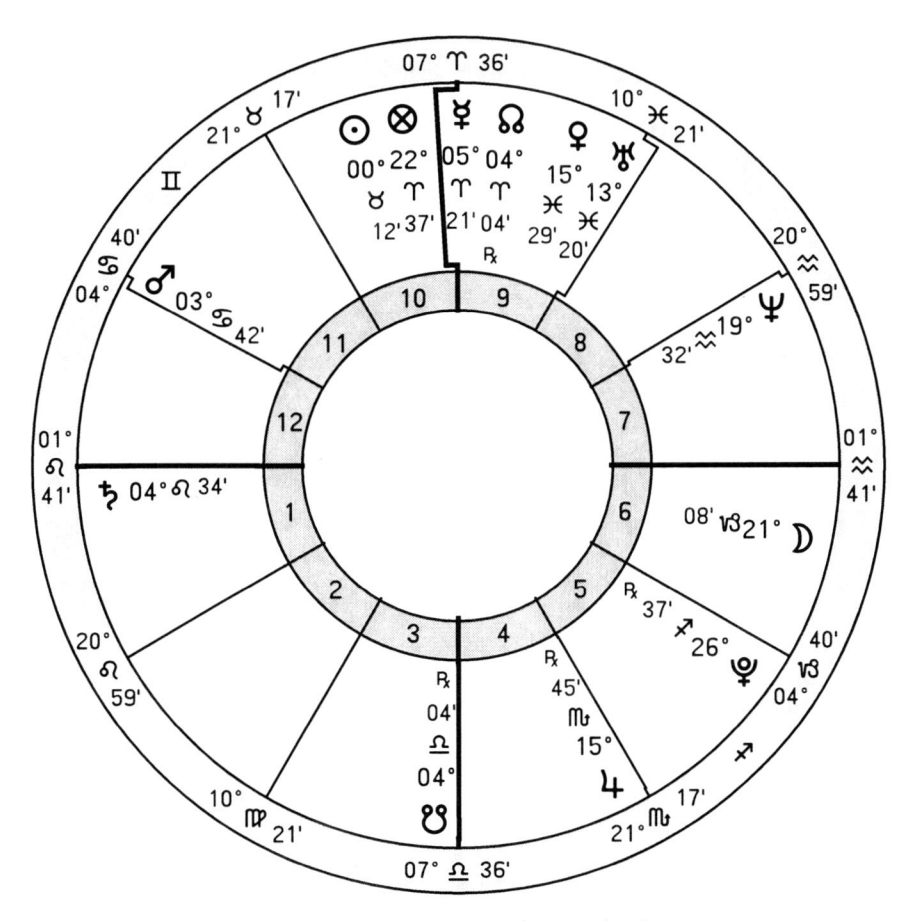

(Fig 15) 'Take Job?' 11.35 am, 20 Apr 2006, London, England

The Pattern of Time

Mars is Lord 10, the job. He has dignity by triplicity and term but more importantly is seriously debilitated in his fall close to the querent's 12th house of self undoing, as if it were leaning on his self undoing. This screams out 'don't take it' and in the context shows the possibility that the job will undermine the querent and cause him problems.

We can go a bit deeper into the chart …

Lord Ascendant has recently lost his dignity and is now ruled by Venus Lord 11, or rather 2 from 10, the jobs money or wages. This is what he is now interested in. The wages are in their exaltation and so very good indeed and the benific North Node is near the 10th house cusp showing increase and beneficence which is of course, also promising. The Moon is Void of Course and is in its detriment exalting the job and in mutual reception with the job. This shows that the querent is emotionally exalting the job, putting it on a pedestal. That the Moon is also in its detriment shows that this is a debilitated Moon, it is not as it should be, and its love for the job is reciprocated by the job itself, meaning they both want to be together. This is cause for concern: He may be blindly drawn into this – With the Moon Void of Course the querent would be unlikely to ruffle the status quo and so if he has committed to the job and now is just having second thoughts, then things would very probably continue as they are, and he would be drawn into it. Hopefully he has not committed in any way. Saturn is also in its detriment inside the 1st house, the weight of Saturn weighing down on the querent, which doesn't bode well generally. This can be quite common in situations like these.

Querent thought about the situation some more. He had not yet committed himself to the job, and explained that though he somehow felt he wanted the job, shown by the Moon exalting it, that he also didn't want the job, shown by Lord Ascendant the Sun, in the detriment of it. This is a classic heart (Moon), head (Lord Ascendant) split. Of the type usually seen in personal relationships, but as you can see, not limited to them.

The querent decided not to take the job. Looking back at this chart we can see that he made a good decision as the job, though well paid, would probably have been the nightmare that he imagined it would.

'Is my job safe?'

In difficult economic downturns we may still have a job, but if we work for a company that is restructuring, downsizing, or randomly contorting in order to stay afloat we may also be urgently occupied with the question of 'will my position in this company last?'

A querent contacted me with this worry as her employer was changing over to what she had been told was 'a new system', and she had serious doubts whether or not this new system had a place for her.

The job is signified by Lord 10, Mercury, who is accidentally very strong inside the 10th house and being in his own sign and exaltation, is very

When Will I Find My Next Job?

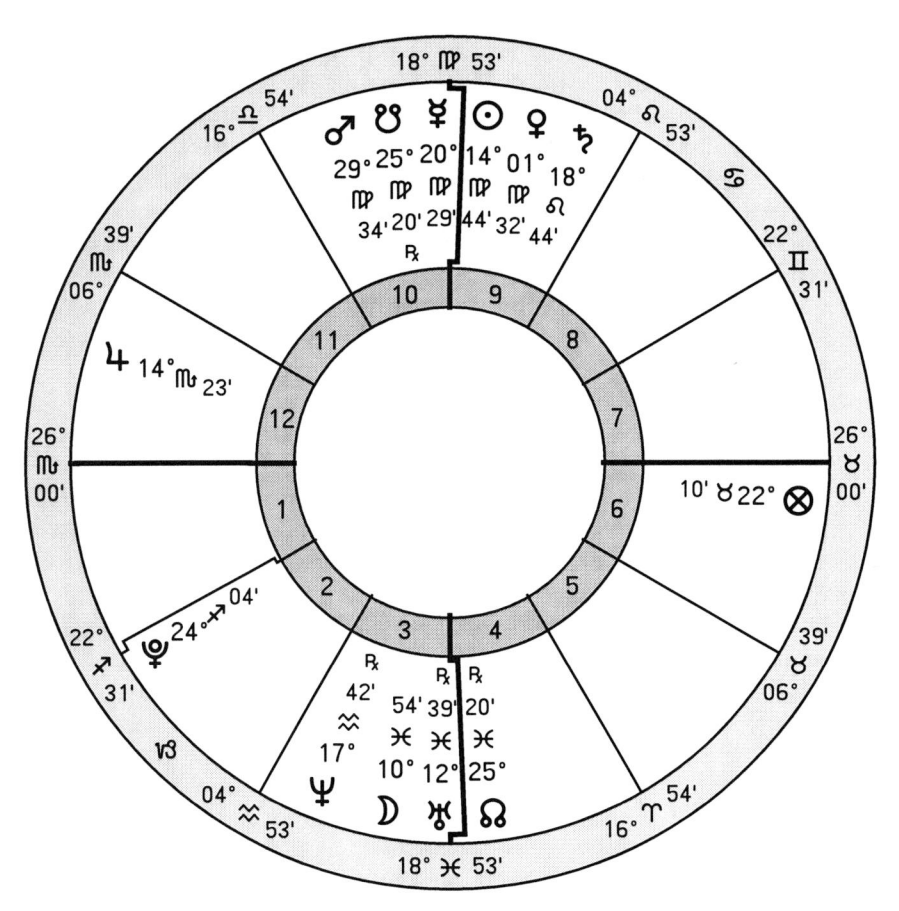

(Fig 16) 'Is my job safe?' 1.14 pm, 7 Sept 2006, London, England

strong essentially. It certainly looks on the surface as if all is well. But we can also see that Mercury is heading towards the malefic South Node: there is trouble ahead.

Mars is Lord Ascendant and has a little essential dignity by term but he is about to lose even this small amount and enter his detriment hence the querent telling me that she felt like she was looking over the edge. Lord Ascendant is also leaving the sign of the job. This is all strongly indicative of change. So we could see, in this context, the querent getting fed up with her work and leaving. The Moon is in the detriment and fall of Lord 10 showing that our querent's emotions strongly dislike this job situation and her bosses who are also signified by Lord 10. The Moon is applying to an opposition with the Sun, natural symbol of high authority, pointing to a run in or an argument with the people in charge, of which the querent said there was great potential! Thankfully there is also a trine with the great benific Jupiter, also a symbol of authority but not an authority that is as high as the Sun, maybe a benific manager might intervene and warn her off tackling 'the powers that be' head on. This Jupiter aspect happens before the opposition with the Sun, and so traditionally it will prohibit this aspect, it is as if the opposition will not happen, as if it is prevented somehow. We could see the friendly executive having a word in the querent's ear warning her away from a confrontation with the people in charge. The querent later mentioned to me that her line-manager did indeed do this.

I judged that her job would still exist. Lord 10 had too much dignity and was not about to lose it. Mercury's position in its own sign and exaltation so close to the Midheaven was very strong. Yes it would hit the South Node and things would go downhill but it would still maintain its dignity and not essentially change. The querent would probably lose heart and interest in the job herself shown by the dire impending situation of the Lord Ascendant and so she could be in danger of quitting rather than being laid off. But there is also a fixed sign on her Ascendant and even though her Lord Ascendant was entering a cardinal or 'movable sign' the fixedness of the horizon I felt would help hold things together even though her heart was not in it as shown by the Moon in the detriment and fall of the job and also opposing the Sun.

And yes things did change – A supposed 'new job' was created as a result of her company 'rebranding' but as the querent told me her job remains technically exactly the same – shown in the chart by Lord 10 essentially maintaining its dignity and so it does not in essence change even despite the accidental debility of heading to the South Node. It nonetheless became more difficult for the querent to execute the tasks that she has to do: essentially it would remain good but it would be debilitated by the conjunction with the South Node. Lord Ascendant moves into its detriment and so, losing heart, the querent begins to look at her work as just 'a job' also shown by her significator moving out of the dignities of Lord 10 – literally, she fell out of love with her job. And despite this falling out of love, she still remained working there and did not quit, therefore showing the fixedness of the horizon and that the job remained essentially the same.

Let us move on from such difficulties and trials and end on a hopeful note. Here is a nice well behaved chart that shows the timing of the 'next job' beautifully ...

'Will this job come through? Will it happen? When?'

Querent had repeatedly and unsuccessfully tried to contact by telephone the person offering him the job. This person had previously offered the querent work that had failed to materialize and the querent wondered if this would be the same story.

Moon trine Sun is generally a positive testimony but this is now separating and the Moon is heading into the Via Combusta, showing a period of

When Will I Find My Next Job?

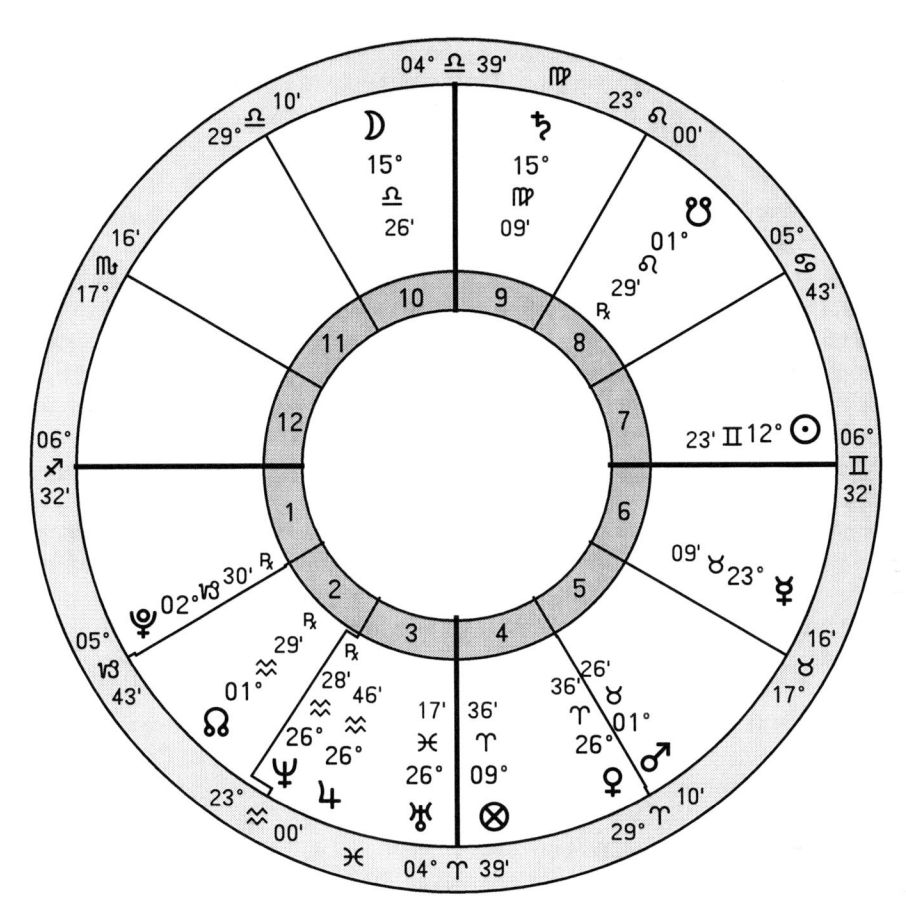

(Fig 17) 'Will this job come through?' Will it happen? When? 8.32 pm BST, 2 June 2009, London, England

emotional turmoil, in the 10th house of work thus indicating querent's worry over the job and his feeling that it might not happen. The Moon is also opposing the antiscion of Saturn and so maybe showing the client's frustration and inability to get hold of his potential employer by telephone as Saturn is Lord 3 – messages/telephone calls.

But the job is signified by Venus Lord 10 who is thankfully in an applying sextile aspect with the querent, signified by Lord Ascendant Jupiter. This will perfect in less than a degree – in fact in about 10 minutes of arc. Venus is in a movable sign and so it is a fast time unit, but she is in a succedent house which gives us a medium unit. Together they point to a medium unit. Again a realistic option within the context of the situation was days/fast, weeks/medium and months/slow. This would give us a week as our basic time unit. The aspect is almost perfected and so if our time unit for the

29

degrees to perfection is a week and the aspect perfects in around 10 minutes of arc and so, very, very soon, 10 minutes will probably show a day.

The judgement was that yes the job will come through within a day from now.

And so it proved much to the querent's amazement: the man with the job called him within an hour of the chart being set to see if he could indeed start work the very next day.

These charts, and many others, continually show us that things happen in their own time, despite what we may think or want. Contrary to opinion, the knowledge of this does not condemn us to wandering around like doomed fatalists waiting to be showered with largesse or lightning. No, far from it, it demands instead that we do what we can, what is within our power to do, in fact what it is our 'job' to do. We must try to make sure that we are ready when the opportunity knocks, hone our skills and develop our vision so we can spot an opportunity when we see it. We can nurture our hope and expand our horizons to take in possibilities that we may not of considered and remember that our unfortunate circumstances may provide the opportunity for better things to manifest. We may simply find that we are looking for opportunities in the wrong place, a bit like looking for a jar of sweets in an empty cupboard – no matter how hard we look we won't find what we are looking for. Or equally, we may be looking at the wrong time – the cupboard has not been restocked – mum hasn't returned home from the shops yet. These things can be clearly seen in the horary chart. And so the idea behind all of this is to bring us and our will into harmony with the larger will that is out there, which is shepherding and guiding us towards our next opportunity, which again, contrary to received opinion, is also out there waiting within the threads of time, waiting till we finally meet. Let's hope we are ready.

3

The Colour of the Spheres

'*Sol* is put for gold, the colour of which is yellow.
Luna for silver, the rust of which is azure.
Mars for iron, the rust of which is violet, rather inclining to blackness.
Mercury for quicksilver, of which are made sinopia and minium, which are red.
Jupiter for tin.
Venus for copper or brass, the rust of which is green.
Saturn for lead, the rust of which is a white colour.'

Experimenta de Coloribus[1]
Jehan Le Begue

To look at the remarkable images of planets and stars beamed from NASA'S telescopes is to be transfixed by a profusion of colour. It is as if God had a brush and a palette of the most vivid of hues ... purples and orange, vibrant greens and reds, yellows, blues, pinks and everything in between. And yet when next looking up into the night sky who can't help but feel a twinge of disappointment that the stars do not blaze with the colour seen in NASA images. Having seen these colours we could even be forgiven for feeling sorry for our ancestors, who without the aid of powerful telescopes had to be content with simply looking into the sky. Not for them the purple and orange super nova – there was no glossy Technicolor space calendars to show them how things *really* are.

This type of thinking is similar to us looking at old black and white film footage while unconsciously imagining that back then everyone lived in a black and white world. Of course they didn't – and neither did our ancestors see only black and white in the skies above them.

As there was a harmony of the spheres so too was there a colour of the spheres. And as the harmony of the spheres is composed of music we can no longer hear, so too, is the harmony of colours composed of colour we no longer see. The 15th Century manuscript on painting, *Experimenta de Coloribus*, tells us of the associations between planets, metals and pigments. From this we learn that the harmony of colour does not stop with each planet; instead it runs through all of creation. It is present, regardless of

---

[1] *Experimenta de Coloribus* is a manuscript Jehan Le Begue compiled in 1431. It is contained in Merrifield *On the Arts of Painting 1849*

The Pattern of Time

whether we can see it or not and the thread of associations can be traced and followed. We can begin with the planet or the pigment and we can follow the connections like strands of light. Each colour has its own particular significance and each colour will give us insight into the nature of the stars themselves.

The Colours of the Watchers of the Heavens

When we look up to the sky most of what we see are the fixed stars. Sitting majestic and silver-white they barely give a hint of the colours they contain. The Edwardian astrologer Vivian Robson collected the traditional descriptions of these colours in his book, *The Fixed Stars and Constellations,* and colours there are aplenty.

The Watchers of the Heavens, the royal stars of the Persians, were used to mark the four corners of the sky. Aldebaran is the Watcher of the East. It is a pale rose colour as befits a powerful, but generally benific, Martian star.

Why the colour pale rose?

The rose is beautiful, benific even, but it has thorns, just like sharp Mars. The pale pink tells us that its nature or origin is in the red of Mars, but this nature is mellowed, somewhat 'pale'. This paleness means it is 'greyed' a traditional term for bringing a complementary neutral tint together with an intense colour, the colour will remain what it is and yet the intensity of its hue is tempered.

Opposite Aldebaran is Antares, the Watcher of the West. Antares is fiery red and emerald green as befits this powerful Martian and Jupiterian star, the fiery red being ruled by Mars and the emerald green by Jupiter. Antares is also called, Cor Scorpio: the Scorpion's Heart.

Regulus, the Watcher of the North, is flushed white and ultramarine. Ultramarine was the most expensive colour on the palette of the traditional artist. Ground and processed alchemically from Lapis Lazuli, ultramarine, meaning from over the seas, was truly the king of colours. The 15th Century Florentine artist, Cennino d'Andrea Cennini, tells us that, 'Ultramarine blue is a colour illustrious, beautiful, and most perfect, beyond all other colours; one could not say anything about it, or do anything with it, that its quality wouldn't not still surpass.'[2] As Regulus is the king of the stars, situated on the lion, the king of the beasts, so too is ultramarine the unrivalled king of the colours.

Fixed star Fomalhaut is the Watcher of the South, and for the Persians it marked the winter solstice. Fomalhaut is the star in the mouth of the southern fish. Robson tells us its name is from, Fum al Hut, meaning the fish's' mouth. It is a reddish star, as befits a star in the mouth of a fish.

But, if we want to hear the music of the planets, the harmony of the spheres, we must bring our attention to rest upon them. As beautiful as the

---

[2] Cennino d'Andrea Cennini, *The Craftsman's Handbook 'Il Libro dell' Arte'*

fixed stars are, for us to see the harmony of the colours, it is to the planets that we must turn.

The Colours of the Planets

The 17th Century English astrologer William Lilly, following tradition, gives a list of colours for each planet.[3] These traditional associations of colours and planets are often confusing or contradictory to the modern mind. It can seem as if a mish-mash of colours has been thrown together. But it is not a mish-mash of colours at all and it has not been thrown together. It is all perfectly logical. I am not suggesting Lilly knew the origin of all these often obscure colour connections. It is likely he compiled his lists from traditional sources that he had in his possession in a manner not dissimilar to what Robson would do for the fixed stars centuries later. Lilly and Robson were reporting or handing on the tradition, compiling, organizing and repeating what they had discovered in their studies. Therefore they did not give reasons for the particular associations of colour with planet. But, with the knowledge of traditional colours and their associations it is possible for us to piece together some of the more obscure astrological connections. If we can do this we will expand our understanding of the traditional nature of each planet.

Lilly's Colours

Saturn, Lilly says, is 'not very bright or glorious, nor doth he twinkle or sparkle, but is of a pale, wan or leaden, ashy colour.' Pale, as we have seen, does not always mean light in colour, but depending on context it often means neutral grey, lacking intensity of colour, or simply 'wan and leaden' exactly as Lilly follows it with. Saturn was also connected with pure black as can be seen by the things that traditionally artists made black paint from: burnt bones and burnt ivory.

Jupiter is 'bright, clear, and of an azure colour'. Azure is like a dull Mediterranean blue and stems from a colour made from Azurite. Azurite was a stone that medieval painters ground into powder to make a blue pigment for their paintings – it is beautiful, though not as beautiful or expensive as the ultramarine blue that was processed from Lapis Lazuli. Also for Jupiter Lilly gives, 'Sea green or blue, purple, ash colour, a mixed yellow and green. In this context, 'ash colour', likely refers to a dull but beautiful blue, like the later batches of ultramarine extracted from Lapis Lazuli at the very end of the alchemical process. As Cennino Cennini tells us, good Lapis Lazuli stone was processed up to eighteen times and produced different grades of the colour. The later yields of Ultramarine are heavy with calcite giving it a grey

[3] William Lilly, *Christian Astrology*

ash blue colour and not at all as pure, brilliant and vibrant as the first two yields of pure Ultramarine.[4]

Mars, Lilly tells us, '... delights in red colour, or yellow, fiery and shining like saffron. To the modern mind yellow and red do not seem related at all, yet traditionally many reds were made by alchemically heating and burning yellow earth – burning being of course a very Martian attribute. Hence the beautiful red of Burnt Sienna is made by heating and burning the yellow colour of Raw Sienna. Mars also rules iron, traditionally heated and hammered into a glowing fiery red in the blacksmiths forge. In the excerpt from the manuscript of Jehan Le Begue's, quoted at the beginning of this chapter, Le Begue tells us the rust of iron is 'violet, rather inclining to blackness'. Anyone who has seen a nail left in the rain will know that iron's rust is also red, as is the blood that is shed in war by the Martian weapons of iron.

In regards to the Sun Lilly first says, 'it's needless to mention his colour, being so continually visible to all mortal men ...' Yet later he lists the Sun's colours as '... yellow, the colour of gold, the scarlet or the clear red, some say purple.' The Sun is traditionally the symbol of the divine, sustaining all life on earth, and Gold being the most precious of metals is also the very thing that cannot be destroyed – it can only be transformed. The scarlet or clear red colour Lilly mentions is likely referring to the heart, as the Sun is the natural ruler of the heart. When Lilly says, 'some say Purple' he is referring to the regal colour of Murex Purple. This colour was a dye made in classical times. Extremely expensive and very labour intensive to produce it was made by crushing the glands of thousands of carnivorous Murex water snails. As Daniel V. Thompson tells us[5], 'There are seashores piled high to this day with the carcases of whelks which died to provide stripes on Roman togas, the family name of *Porphyrygenetos* (born to the purple), and the luxury writing material of the Emperors. '... Millions and millions of Mediterranean whelks gave each a little drop of liquid which produced the purple of the ancient courts, the purple of Byzantium ...' The fluid extracted from the snails was clear and colourless, but when exposed to the sun it turned a beautiful purple. From that point on, light would not diminish its colour – Murex Purple was the colour that did not fade.[6]

For Venus Lilly says, 'in colours she signifieth white, or milky sky-colour mixed with brown, or a little green'. Here we have the colours of milk, blue sky and fertile earth and so we have the colours of fecundity as befitting the nature of romantic Venus. Let us not forget that traditionally romance is not just wine and roses it leads, by its very nature, to babies. Brown copper is also ruled by Venus and its 'rust' is green. This green is called Verdigris. As

---

[4] Cennino d'Andrea Cennini, *The Craftsman's Handbook 'Il Libro dell' Arte'* See also *Alchemy of Paint*, Spike Bucklow

[5] Daniel V Thompson, Jr, *The Materials and Techniques of Medieval Painting* (1956)

[6] For an informative in-depth look at traditional colour from a traditional perspective I recommend *The Alchemy of Paint* by Spike Bucklow

Cennino Cennini tells us, this colour is, 'manufactured by alchemy, from copper and vinegar'.[7]

Mercury, Lilly tells us, '... is of a dusky silver colour' '... mixed and new colours, the grey mixed with sky-colour, such as is on the neck of the stock-dove, linsie-woolsie colours, or consisting of many colours mixed in one.' Grey is a colour mid-way between black and white as befitting Mercury's nature of being neither male nor female. As Lilly says, 'We may not call him either masculine or feminine, for he is either one or the other as joined to any planet; for if in conjunction with a masculine planet, he becomes masculine; if with a feminine, then feminine ...' A dusky silver colour takes on the colour of those around it, not like a mirror but more like the dull hint of a reflection. The sky-colour modifying the grey, Lilly mentions, 'such as is on the neck of the stock dove', points towards the Mercurial nature of modifying and mixing. This modifying colour on the stock dove's neck is a band of iridescent bottle green. Iridescent green, again depending on the context of light and its surroundings, will often reflect change and appear like a mixture of colours. The term, 'linsie– woolsie', refers to a cloth whose warp and weft is woven from a mixture of linen and wool. Though linen and wool are very different, they come together in Linsie Woolsey and this mixing, this combining and duality, is very Mercurial. Also when Linsie Woolsey is dyed each different thread takes on the colour of the other much as Mercury mimics those planets it finds itself near. Therefore Lilly's, 'linsie-woolsie colours' analogously refers to very different colours woven together; very Mercurial.

The Moon, Lilly tells us is, '... white, or pale yellowish white, pale green, or a little of the silver colour.' White signifies the maternal milk as the Moon is the symbol of maternity and mothers. When Lilly mentions, '... a little of the silver colour' he is referring to the reflective quality of the Moon. This silver and its reflecting quality are of a different nature than the 'dusky silver colour' of Mercury. Mercury reflects things via articulating them and expressing them whereas the Moon reflects things as they are – like a mirror – without the articulation and modification that Mercury would, by its nature, be impelled to add. The 'pale yellowish white' and 'pale green' are simply the beautiful luminous colour's of moonlight.

Like opening up the rusted shutters on an old and partly forgotten window, peering through these colour associations, we can begin to see the landscape that lies beyond. Next time we look up to the sky or at an astrological chart we shall have these colour associations as part of our awareness and never quite see in black and white again. Able to see each planet shine with its own, sometimes surprising colour, we can better understand its nature and the materials associated with it. And just when we believe we can see clearly, we will begin to notice other connections. As if the landscape opens out onto rolling hills where first fields come into view and then

---

[7] Cennino Cennini, *Il Libro dell' Arte*

trees and forests and a mirror-like lake in which we will see the reflection of the Sun that sustains it all. How each is connected to the other and how the planetary colours can seemingly contradict or overlap becomes clearer. And no matter how much we begin to understand, there is always more. For instance, though William Lilly didn't mention it, both Mars *and* Mercury are associated with red. Mars is the natural ruler of iron, and iron's red rust and Mercury is a core ingredient in the alchemical preparation of Vermillion, the traditional red from the past. If Mercury is alchemically transformed it will release its redness. This transformation hints at the hidden depths of potential within things. Red may be associated with Mars, but a hidden stream of red will still pour forth from Mercury. To find something where we least expect it shows us that with colour, as with life, things are not always as they seem.

4

Starry, Starry Night

The Dutch painter van Gogh, practically unknown to the art world of his time, continues to capture the imagination of contemporary art lovers. An exhibition of his work is guaranteed to sell out with lines of people winding around the block desperate for a glimpse of paintings familiar to them. This familiarity is due to the existence of a virtual empire of merchandise of van Gogh prints, books, tea towels, cups, plates, calendars and t-shirts. Critics remain divided over his work but somehow he seems to resonate with the modern mind. Whether this is more to do with the myth of the tortured soul who would sacrifice all for his art, or more to do with an appreciation of his undeniably powerful paintings, it is interesting to cast an astrological eye over the creator of these multitudes of images who signed his work humbly, and quite simply, 'Vincent'.

Though forever connected with swirling visions of the French countryside, Vincent van Gogh, as mentioned above, was born in the Netherlands, in Groot-Zundert at 11am on the 30 March 1853.

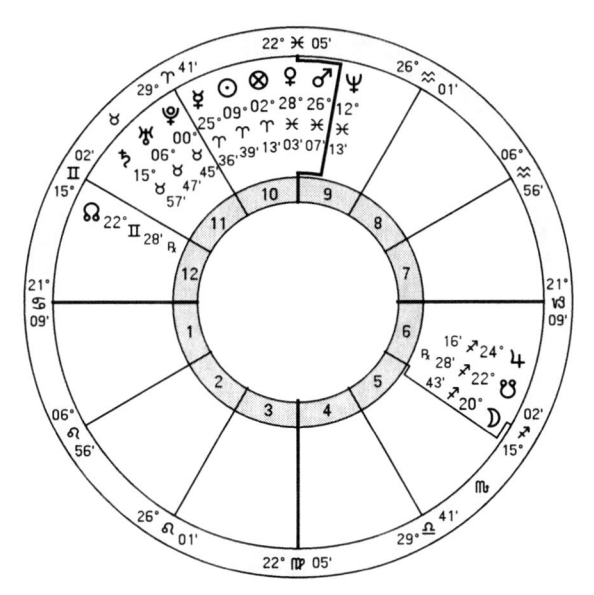

(Fig 18) **Vincent van Gogh, 11.00 am LMT, 30 Mar 1853, Zundert, Netherlands**

The Pattern of Time

Temperament

To build our astrological picture we traditionally start with the temperament. 'The cloth from which we are cut', this is the foundation of all else that will follow. It is most important that we do this.

The temperament is similar to the support of a painting – is this on a heavy weave canvas or the finest linen? A heavy weave canvas will rule certain things in and certain things out. It is not that the finest strokes are not possible on a heavy weave – they are – it is just that no matter how finely and delicately painted the image, the heavy weave will always be there, making its presence felt, the background and material context on which all else is painted.

To find the temperament we look to the condition and placement of the Ascendant and Lord Ascendant, the season of the year determined by the sign the Sun falls into and the phase of the Moon. Also we have to take into account the Lord of the Geniture, the planet which has the most accidental and essential dignities in the nativity. (For an explanation of essential and accidental dignities please refer to chapter 1, *The Divine Michelangelo*).

We have a choice of 4 temperaments: sanguine which is hot and moist, choleric which is hot and dry, melancholic which is cold and dry and phlegmatic which is cold and moist.

Vincent's temperament though reasonably balanced is cold and moist: phlegmatic. He will approach and experience life through his emotions and will be driven by his desires. If we bring in his Lord of the Geniture here then there is also a competing sanguine streak which will probably become more apparent as his life develops. The sanguine temperament will approach life through their mind. Nevertheless, Vincent is first and foremost, phlegmatic.

Manner

Next we look at his manner; this is the way he is in the world, or the way that he will express himself through the medium of his temperament. All planets have a hand in this but especially prominent angular planets will make themselves felt.

This is where we begin to sketch in the main lines of our picture. This is 'une esquisse', a basic sketch, but without it, we will find ourselves straying. This will lead into 'un croquis' a more developed sketch leading to the full picture. If we do this right then the development of our astrological portrait will appear seamless. There will be no need for fancy tricks.

Vincent's predominant significator of manner is Venus in conjunction with Mars. They are also in mutual reception. We have an artistic, passionate, sensitive and intense manner with impetuous Mars, traditionally the ruler of the turbulent water element, driving and intensifying this passionate Venus. That this happens inside the Midheaven tells us his manner will be clear for all to see. As Vincent was an artist, this is also visually manifested in his swirling tempestuous paintings, with Venus being his Lord 5, his creations.

The Moon is Lord Ascendant and is ruled by Jupiter and this dignified Jupiter also has a large role in his manner. It rules the Venus Mars conjunction and squares it from Sagittarius, it is also trine his Mercury: His passions are worn on his sleeve with an expansive and deeply sincere religious manner. Generous, caring and altruistic, as can be seen in many episodes in his life, such as the time he tried to rescue, out of pity, a street woman called Sien who was pregnant, struggling and downtrodden by life. She modelled for him and he tried to give her the understanding and kindness she desperately wanted but others had not shown her. He tried to put her on the straight path. It was not to be. His Moon, natural ruler of maternal things, caring, philosophic and religious in a Jupiter sign, is sailing towards the South Node thus signifying loss.

Phlegmatic with such a strong Venus Mars conjunction close to the Midheaven shows he is ruled by a powerful aesthetic sense with Mars adding intensity and recklessness. He could also be pugnacious and unruly, the Mars spilling out as it were, in an expansive Jupiterian fashion.

In light of all this, Vincent's Moon heading for the deep dark hole that is known as the South Node, is depressing and does not look good at all – his emotions are dangerous, as the Moon is also Lord Ascendant, the danger is to himself. There is a tragic-ness to this position in context with everything else.

Quality of Mind

We next look at his quality of mind. For this we have to investigate the condition of his Mercury and Moon and the planets that are influencing them.

His Mercury is above the horizon inclining him more towards oratory, putting his intellect to work out in the world. With Mercury in trine to Jupiter and exalting the Sun this would be a religious kind of oratory. Vincent certainly preached in church many times in his life and he worked as a lay preacher in England and a missionary to the mining population of Borinage in Belgium.

His Mercury is 'Under the Beams' – within 17 and a half degrees of the Sun – though not super close it is close enough and this 'incites the wit to meddle in impertinent matters' as Lilly[1] says. Mercury is ruled by Mars who in turn is conjunct Venus on the Midheaven. This shows he is passionate and impetuous in his communications. With his Moon trine Mercury he is ingenious and as this Mercury is influenced by being 'Under the Beams' exalting the Sun, and with the Moon also in the triplicity of the Sun, he is most definitely ambitious.

[1] William Lilly, *Christian Astrology*

But his Mercury is isolated. With no planets in Air signs, no planets in any Mercury dignities and 4 planets in the detriment or fall of Mercury this oratory would only ever leave him isolated, lonely, frustrated and unfulfilled and it was after he had given up his theological studies in Amsterdam and left the miners at Borinage that he would turn to his Lord of the Geniture Venus – who is in mutual negative reception with his Mercury, and so doesn't want any truck with it – and decide to become an artist, thus attempting to reconcile things through the medium of paint.

Yet still this lack of Air and isolated Mercury is problematic. Problematic in itself, but within context of what we have seen so far, this spells real trouble – His fierce cardinal Mercury, and a underlying sanguine strand in his temperament could turn out to be quite a problem. Indeed it was – when later in life van Gogh began to experience health problems it was in experiencing and approaching life through his mind, Mercury, to attain knowledge, the sanguine path, and attempting to reconcile this with his emotional nature that would become so very difficult for him to bear. Both the phlegmatic and the sanguine temperaments are moist – it was as if he was simply flooded and carried off by this excess moisture with only his melancholic Moon in the cold dry third quarter of the Moon's cycle that gave him anything solid to cling on to. That, and of course, his Saturn, peregrine and so wandering, in a fixed cold dry sign; wandering over the same things again and again. Clinging to such a Saturn is, though stable, utterly sorrowful, exalting the emotional philosophic Moon, which of course is Vincent himself, loving Venus, his creations and paintings, while in the detriment of, and so hating, the most influential planet in Vincent's chart the Mars – the engine room that drives him.

While he was a missionary among the mining people in Borinage in Belgium Vincent interpreted the Gospel literally and gave all his possessions away and lived in poverty – Lord Ascendant Moon heading towards the poverty of the South Node, while the generous Jupiter moves away from the South Node, giving his things away. He had a deep understanding of the poor and downtrodden which he attempted to portray in his paintings in the most truthful way he could – this again being shown by Moon, Lord Ascendant and natural significator of the common people, near the South Node, he understands them emotionally, also helped by a reception between his Lord Ascendant and Saturn as Lord 7 other people. Though perhaps this reception is more of a problem than it first seems as Lord 7, in the detriment of Mars, can't stand his intensity and passion, while expecting far too much of him, Lord 7 is in exaltation of Lord Ascendant. The Miners of Borinage did not appreciate Vincent's display of sincerity.

Mercury is in trine with Jupiter which also rules the Moon. This dignified Jupiter can help his two sides, his Mercury and Moon, to work together but at the expense of Mercury – Jupiter is in the detriment of Mercury, and the Moon, as we know, is heading for the South Node; poor Vincent.

Venus is the natural ruler of art and van Gogh's Lord of the Geniture. It is very dignified inside the Midheaven and being Venus its great virtue is to reconcile or bring reconciliation to things. This is also ruler of Vincent's Lord 5 his creations, his offspring, his paintings and as such could show a possible path through which this reconciliation that he is driven towards can be made manifest – Mars is the most influential planet in the chart, with more planets in Mars dignities than any other, conjunct his Venus inside the Midheaven and passionately driving and influencing him.

But, though the aesthetic freedom promised by this Jupiterian/Venusian Mars is in fact his heart's desire, as Mars is ruler of Fortuna, it was again not to be – as it and Venus, Lord 5, his paintings, his attempt to reconcile his internal and external conflicts, oppose Fortuna by antiscion.[2] By doing this they are at war with his deep desire. Yet we must also remember that this is an artist that we are looking at here; this underlying tension, in the right hands can produce great and powerful work.

There is a theme of forever coming together and falling apart underlying his quest for freedom thus mirroring this antiscial opposition with Fortuna.

Vincent's Starry Night

Vincent's night time paintings contain skies that are full of vibrant, swirling intensely painted stars. As anyone who has ever looked up to a sky full of stars will quickly realize these twinkling lights cannot only be the 7 visible planets. They are known as the 'fixed stars', they are of extreme importance and are very powerful in colouring a natal chart and crucial in the building of our astrological portrait.

Traditionally fixed stars can be approached either through the myths associated with them or by their planetary nature or, indeed, both[3]. This can be a subtle act. It is not a case of somehow 'decoding the myth'. It is, instead, simply a case of seeing what is there.

The approach via the planetary nature of stars is always related to the stars within the natal chart in question. If it is a Venus and Saturn star that we are looking at in Vincent's chart then it is coloured by the nature of *his* Venus and Saturn not someone else's Venus and Saturn or indeed an abstract Venus and Saturn. Having said that, the stars still have their own individual personalities and qualities and one must remember that these methods are only a workable approach towards an understanding of what these natures are.

Looking at Vincent's fixed stars we can see how keenly he must have felt them, and how they still resonate for him, even down to our time …

---

[2] See Chapter 1, *The Divine Michelangelo*, for an explanation of the traditional technique of antiscia.

[3] Vivian Robsons' book, *The Fixed Stars and Constellations in Astrology*, is the authoritative compendium of traditional information on the Fixed Stars.

Vincent's Venus Mars's conjunction falls on the fixed star Scheat. This is on the left leg of Pegasus and is an irregular, variable, deep yellow star. This is a nasty star indeed, according to Robson it points toward 'extreme misfortune', and among other things 'suicide'. This is just the star in general, if Venus is conjunct Scheat, which it is here then we have the potential for such things as, 'evil environment, suffering through own acts, danger of imprisonment or restraint.' Vincent was restrained several times and was a voluntary patient at the Asylum at Saint-Remy-en-Provence. He certainly suffered through his own acts, and whether by accident or deliberately, he very sadly died due to self inflicted gunshot wounds.

Vincent's Lord Ascendant is the Moon. It is near the star Rasalhague, a sapphire star on the head of Ophicius, the head of the Serpent Charmer. This is a star of Saturn and Venus nature bringing among other things misfortune through women. Even more so here, as it is on the Moon, natural ruler of women and as it is also Vincent Lord Ascendant signifying Vincent himself. Theo, Vincent's brother, always felt that if Vincent could have found a woman to love and to care for him, then he would not have suffered in the way that he did. This is probably very true but again this was not to be.

The Moon is natural ruler of the poor and downtrodden which as subjects Vincent felt desperate to paint. But this was not from a so called 'objective' position, no, he wanted to paint their spirit and their dignity, he was painting from a position of empathy as his Moon heading towards the South Node and on a Saturn and Venus star would show: He knew all about difficulties and struggles himself. With 4 out of 7 planets in fixed signs and within context of what we have seen points towards an artist who is relentlessly dedicated to exploring all that he can or is possible for him to explore about the subjects before him.

Ramon Lull in his *Treatise on Astronomy*,[4] points out that the Moon is the planet through which the 'impressions of colours are made below more strongly than through another planet'. He points out how water, which is ruled by the Moon, takes on the colour of whatever is poured into it i.e. ink or wine. As Mercury articulates things from above 'so the Moon is the planet through which water is converted into many colours'. Vincent felt the colours of this world very keenly and did his best to translate these through the liquid medium of paint. Containing them in images would be helped by his Moon being on a star of the nature of Saturn and Venus. Situated on the head of the Serpent Charmer Rasalhague can also bring mental problems, even more so here as the Moon, Vincent's Lord Ascendant, is the planet that falls on it.

He can bring his Mercury into play only through his Moon, which is in trine to it and is united in its search for Truth with a capital T, or what is known as 'objective truth'. This is shown by both Mercury and Moon in Sun

---

[4] Ramon Lull, *Treatise of Astronomy*

dignities, natural ruler of truth, and the Moon ruled by the expansive and religious Jupiter. That the Sun, visible symbol of Truth, is also in its exaltation shows just how high he is trying to reach. But Mercury is also close to the fixed star Vertex on 'the great nebula to the north of Andromeda's head'. This star is of the nature of Mars and the Moon and is unpleasant. It can bring 'blindness, injuries to the eyes, sickness and a violent death'. (*Robson*).

Regulus is a royal star, meaning among other things, that it leads to the throne. It is a triple star, flushed white and ultramarine on the body of the Lion. It is also called, Cor Leonis: the Lions Heart. It is very powerful, of the nature of Mars and Jupiter, and Vincent's third house cusp falls very close to it.

So the road to fame and recognition could somehow be through the 3rd house. The 3rd house is associated with bringing the visions of the 9th house down to earth. Here we see Vincent's searching for a technique to articulate his images, eventually settling on a Jupiterian expansive and Martian assured swift yet deliberate calligraphic brush work. This was very unusual at the time, and is forever associated with him, coming from him cutting a reed pen and using this to draw with directly, inspired by the approach of the Japanese print artists that he admired so much and then translating that into brushwork when painting. His 3rd house is ruled by the Sun in its exaltation, by antiscion it falls on the 4th house – the very bottom of the chart – The exalted Sun come to rest by antiscion on the very earth itself. This brings to mind Vincent's famous and much loved paintings of sunflowers which seem to be a perennial favourite of the public, and so, of course, modern merchandisers. Also as Vincent was born in the day, the Sun is his Light of Time. Painters work with light, and Vincent looked for the most powerful way he could to make this light visible on canvas and it was eventually first and foremost his physical technique of applying paint that captured and also repelled the public.

The 3rd house also signifies the native's letters, Vincent was prolific and eloquent in his letter writing, and his letters have become almost as famous as his paintings.

Copula is the spiral or Whirlpool Nebula under the tail of the Great Bear; it is on Vincent's 4th house, the place of home. It is of the nature of the Moon and Venus. It brings: 'Blindness, defective eyesight, strong passions hindrances and disappointment' (Robson).

This would affect greatly Vincent's very deep and enduring desire to found a community of artists. Also with the ruler of the 4th house being his isolated Mercury in a Cardinal sign, his desire to found a home for artists did not bode well.

When Vincent was living in Arles in the South of France he moved into 'the Yellow House' where he felt that he might actually be able to realize his dream of founding the artist community he so desperately wanted.

The French painter Gauguin had agreed to join Vincent in Arles, and Vincent was very excited, he saw this as a beginning. But after a couple of months they quarrelled and fell out and Vincent had a mental breakdown; he cut off part of his own ear and was hospitalized the next day. Vincent's Brother Theo visited him in hospital but the day after that Theo returned to Paris. Sadly for Vincent, Gauguin returned to Paris also. Copula can be very cruel with the disappointment that it can bring.

Vincent was always restless, as shown by his influential Jupiter and Mars and could be unruly and reckless but he was still very ardent and practical in his work, he had taught himself to draw and then when he could draw he had taught himself to paint. He was outspoken and critical of himself and others, again the Jupiterian Mars, and yet he still remained magnanimous, which is an example of using this Mars and Jupiter to their very best. And this combination of Jupiter, Mars and Venus in context of everything else meant that Vincent's passionate, religious manner was prevalent in all things.

Jupiter is on fixed star Aculeus – the sting of the Scorpion – which often points towards where life will hurt us the most. Here it is on his Jupiter. Yes, this is his Lord 10 and so this would be indicative of hurt in his career, after all he certainly was not lucky there in many ways, but also this is Jupiter qua Jupiter and so Aculeus is afflicting the deep sense of optimism that is part of his nature and that is struggling out from the influence of the South Node, and it is this, his optimism, which later in life would suffer too.

The Fixed star Markeb is on The Midheaven, Vincent's work or career. This is the white star on the wing of Pegasus signifying great aspiration. It is a Mars and Mercury star and it can indeed bring honour and fortune but it can also bring 'cuts and blows stabs, fire and a violent death'. If it is culminating on the Midheaven as it is here in Vincent's chart, it can bring, as Robson says, 'disgrace and ruin and often a violent death'. Poignantly Vincent remarked very near the end of his life in a last letter to his brother; 'Ah well, I risk my life for my work and my reason has half foundered in it – very well…'

The Twins

On Vincent's Ascendant is the star Pollux, this too is a royal star, one of the 'six kingly stars of signification' as Lilly calls them. These royal stars, as I mentioned previously, will within the context of the native's life and potentials, lead to 'elevation to the throne'. That this elevation did not happen within Vincent's lifetime can also be seen as part of the tragedy.

According to Greek mythology Pollux is one of the Dioscuri, the 'sons of Zeus', one half of the twin brothers Castor and Pollux. When Castor is fatally slain in battle, Pollux is wounded, but is borne up to heaven by Zeus. Due to his love for his brother, Pollux is unwilling to accept the immortality conferred upon him while his brother Castor is left to remain in the underworld. And so Zeus allows Pollux to share his immortality with Castor. Together the brothers spend half their time in the underworld and half their time with the gods on Mount Olympus.

Starry, Starry, Night

This theme flowed throughout Vincent's life. His brother Theo was hugely influential in all areas. It was under Theo's encouragement that Vincent had decided to become an artist. Theo supported him emotionally and financially throughout his life. Theo also supplied him with paints and canvas, whatever Vincent asked for that was within Theo's power to provide he did. And the letters back and forth between them are a testament to an incredibly tender relationship of brotherly love and support. And as can be seen by the hugely successful van Gogh exhibition at the Royal Academy in London[5], this theme of lending immortality to the other continues as Vincent's letters to Theo were displayed side by side with his paintings.

Vincent and Theo died within a few months of each other and are buried side by side in the little graveyard in Avers-sur-Oise.

---

[5] *The Real van Gogh: The Artist and His Letters*, 23 January–16 April 2010 Royal Academy London

5

The Nativity of a Lady

Some time ago I came across a facsimile of an unusual little book called, *A Collection of Remarkable Nativities*[1]. On the title page the author, John Worsdale tells us his book is aimed at, 'proving the truth and verity of Astrology in its Genethliacal part'.

Worsdale was an English astrologer who practiced his art in Lincolnshire in the late 18th and early 19th century. He was also the author of a much larger work, *Celestial Philosophy or Genethliacal Astronomy*[2], which is aimed at much the same end as his *Collection*.

The *Collection* was published in 1799, a time when, as Worsdale notes in his introduction, 'the study of the motions of the heavenly bodies, and their influence on the human race, be deemed unfashionable, in some degree, by a certain description of men'.

And so, against such things, in his little book he takes, 'four curious nativities,' which he feels, 'will be of sufficient importance to convince every reasonable man of the truth of this ancient science; for which purpose, alone, these nativities have been collected and combined.'

The four nativities selected for this quite considerable task were: 'The Nativity of Robert Twelves', 'The Nativity of George Hill', 'The Nativity of Jonas Stavely' and 'The Nativity of a Lady'.

It is to the last of these nativities that we shall turn our attention ...

The Nativity of a Lady

In his introduction to The Nativity of a Lady, Worsdale tells us:

> 'The time of this person's birth was communicated to me by a gentleman of Italy who is very well versed in the astral science; and, as the genethliacal figure and aspects of the stars are of so very extraordinary a nature, I shall take the liberty to examine the same and every part thereof in rotation as concisely as possible; and also to consider every occurrence, worthy of notice, through the whole period of the natives life; that the reader may observe that all important events may be known in a general way, independent of calculation, from a short inspection of the nativity only ; but the precise time of each momentous event can only be known by directional motion.'

[1] John Worsdale, *A Collection of Remarkable Nativities*
[2] John Worsdale, *Celestial Philosophy of Genethliacal Astronomy*

So, while maintaining one eye on Worsdale, let us also take our own look at this enigmatic lady ...

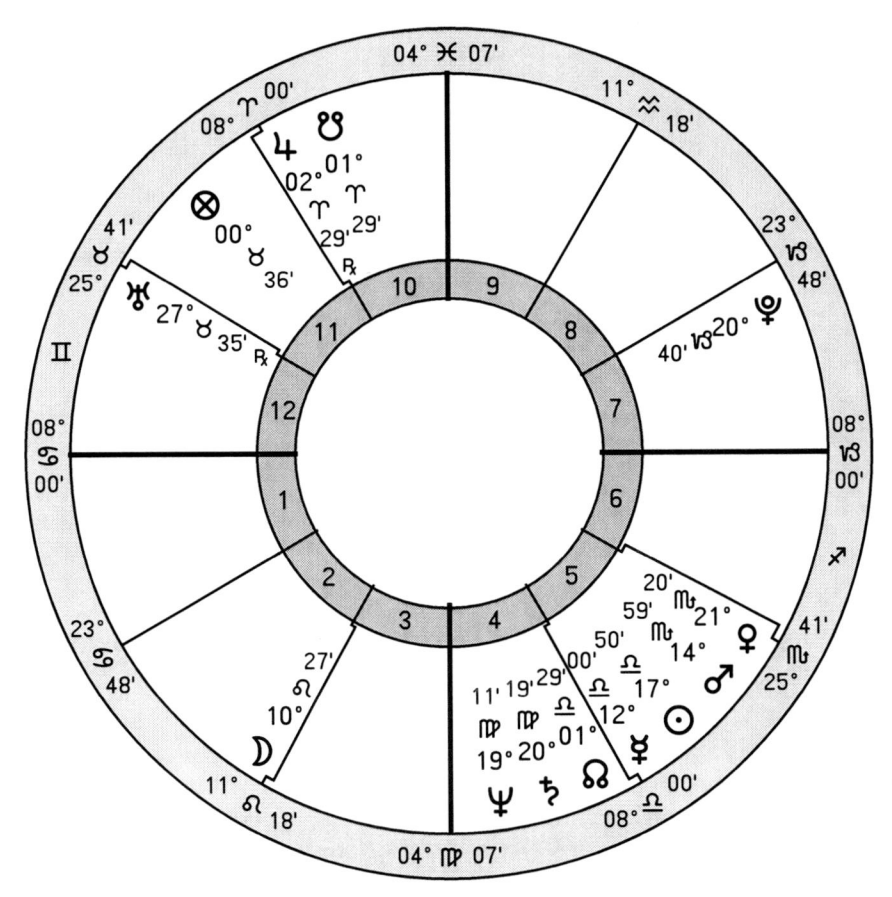

(Fig 19) The Nativity of a Lady, 21.05.05 LMT, 10 Oct 1773, London, England
This chart is a close enough computer match of Worsdale's original chart.

Temperament

As I have mentioned in previous chapters the first, most vital step in the assessment of a natal chart, is to delineate the temperament; the foundation of the nature. In this case the native is extremely cold in temperature and this coldness is predominantly moist. The cold and moist temperament is known as phlegmatic. A phlegmatic person will be driven by their desires.

Worsdale does not mention the lady's temperament but instead starts his assessment by looking at her appearance. He mentions that as Cancer rises in the chart and the Lord Ascendant Moon is in Leo, sextile to Mercury and the Sun, this will show the Lady to be,

'... of a fair complexion, round face, light brown hair, with large eyes, of short stature etc'.

This sounds about right and there is little to quibble about here, except experience tells me that small eyes rather than 'large eyes' could be likely in such a configuration.

The affliction to Lord Ascendant by a square from a strong Mars could certainly show as some kind of mark or blemish and Worsdale also points this out:

'... as the Moon is afflicted by the quartile of Mars, and both under the earth, it declares that the native would be subject to some wound or hurt in the face, the truth of which is verified beyond the limits of contradiction'.

And later we shall find out why this is so.

The Quality of the Native's Mind

Worsdale points out that the quality of a native's mind is a most important enquiry to make;

'... since the success of our worldly pursuits depends on our mental endowments to a considerable degree'.

He recommends following the method of Ptolemy in this pursuit:

'... observe chiefly the disposition of the Moon and Mercury, in the celestial constitution, and how they are beheld or afflicted by the other planets'.

Mercury is below the horizon and oriental thus giving our lady a liberal nature. This is liberal in the traditional sense of being more free and outgoing. Mercury is placed in the 5th house; in the context of her phlegmatic temperament, this might manifest as a little too liberal in the modern sense of the word.

The connection between Mercury and the Sun shows an ambitious nature and the sextile from the Moon to Mercury in an air sign could show her to be quite clever. But Mercury is also combust, which will bring problems with her understanding and she could also become obsessed or involved in matters that are hidden from the eyes of others. The Moon is afflicted by a square from a strong Mars making her manner quite sharp and argumentative and with the Sun combusting Mercury in a Venus sign she may even have the potential to be arrogant and proud.

With her phlegmatic nature, Mercury combust and Lord Ascendant the Moon on fixed star Acubens, 'The Claw of the Crab', we could have someone who doesn't always tell the truth, someone who in pursuing her ambition might be somewhat unscrupulous in her methods. Vivian Robson in his book, *The Fixed Stars and Constellations in Astrology*,[3] gives Acubens as showing 'Liars and Criminals'.

[3] Vivian Robson, *The Fixed Stars and Constellations*

Worsdale thinks that as the Sun, in its fall is ruling the Moon and combusting Mercury and Mars in Scorpio afflicts the Moon by square, this combination will,

> 'be productive of more evil than many will imagine' causing the native to 'chiefly employ her mind to follow those pursuits, in this sublunary world which will ever prove injurious to her character and reputation; their being once lost, can never be regained'.

Despite all this Worsdale still hopes that she will take his judgement as a warning, he adds, rather thoughtfully, that she,

> '... will I hope obtain a friendly admonition from the forgoing premise'.

Family Background and Inheritance

A very important thing for a lady is her family background and inheritance. We look to the 4th house, the very bottom of the chart, for information on the father in particular and the home life and parents in general.

For a rough idea of the wealth of the early part of her life, we can also look at Jupiter, the first triplicity ruler of her Light of Time.

Jupiter, the great benific, is retrograde, but has essential dignity and is in a succedent house. In context this tells us that at least in the early part of her life she will have wealth.

But it seems that this might change; Worsdale points out that, 'she would have no inheritance from her father.' This loss Worsdale blames on afflictions from Saturn in the 4th house and, 'Mercury, lord of her father's ascendant, being in reception with Saturn but combust of the Sun, and Venus posited in her detriment, afflicted by Mars, declare no inheritance left.'

We might note that Mercury, her father, is inside the cusp of the 5th house, which is the fathers 2nd house, and so signifies his finances. He is combust, burnt up, and placed inside his 2nd house, in his pocket so to speak; it is as if he has burnt through his money. Saturn, night time ruler of fathers has some essential dignity; he is not a bad father, maybe he is simply a victim of circumstance. Her mother, Lord 10, has money on her side, as shown by Lord 11, the 2nd house of the Mother being very dignified and Jupiter, also with some dignity close to the 11th cusp. But Jupiter is Lord 10, the lady's mother, and though it has dignity, showing she is decent; it is retrograde near the 11th cusp and so afflicting it somewhat. It is also close to the South Node, signifying loss, all this is congruent with a fall or backsliding in her financial affairs and by the time the money becomes the legacy from the parents, lord 5, it seems that it might all be gone.

The family finances are not in good shape, Lord 5 ruled by Venus in her detriment, with Venus ruled by Mars who also squares the Lord Ascendant: the family financial situation causes grief to their daughter.

It looks like there is no inheritance for this lady.

The Pattern of Time

Friends in High Places

Worsdale begins his considerations of the lady's, 'worldly riches and preferment', by pointing out that in her nativity the Moon, and Fortuna are, 'the superior significators of wealth and prosperity'.

The Moon is Lord 2 in its joy in the 3rd house. It is also peregrine[4], ruled by the Sun in its fall close to Mercury. The Sun and Mercury are ruled by Venus who is in the 6th house, in her detriment and in the fall of Lord Ascendant. As far as worldly riches and preferment is concerned, this doesn't look too good at all, and with the square from Mars also, one might wonder, as Worsdale seemed to; how this Lady, if she no longer has an inheritance, might ever acquire enough capital to still be considered a lady.

Nevertheless there is certain truth in the old saying that money does not buy you class, and so if this is a lady then one hopes that she has some lord or lady friends, who can lend a hand.

Worsdale points out:

> 'Jupiter, having exaltation in the ascendant, is conjoined with the dragon's tail, in its own dignities, in the medium caeli, and, consequently, in platic trine aspect to the Moon; which configurations argue that the native (in some part of her life,) would prosper considerably under the protection of a person of quality ...'

He might be stretching things a bit here; Jupiter is so far from the Medium Caeli itself, almost in the 11th house. For some reason Worsdale also places Fortuna at 25 degrees 41 Pisces, instead of around 0 degrees 36 Taurus, where it would be if he was indeed following Ptolemy. Nevertheless he uses this Fortuna in Pisces in his assessment, it is ruled by Jupiter, and so adds to his testimonies.

Yet, we needn't look to a Piscean Fortuna, as Worsdale himself also notes; her rich friends are primarily shown by the nature of the planet ruling the 11th house, 'which signifies friendship and friends etc.' this is Mars in Scorpio.

So she does have rich friends – Mars, Lord 11, is in strong essential dignities and also ruling Jupiter who, rather than being in the Medium Caeli, is as I mentioned, close to the 11th cusp.

Worsdale notes that she,

> '... would prosper considerably under a person of quality', 'for when the respective benevolent directions were operating, which forbode[5] prosperity, she then lived in the greatest of splendour, having no less than five servants at her command, and a coach likewise'.

---

[4] A traditional term meaning a planet, that due to the position it occupies in the chart, is in no 'essential dignities' of its own. It is thus like a homeless wanderer, literally it is peregrine: wandering. For further explanation on traditional terms and dignities please see earlier chapters especially *The Divine Michelangelo*.

[5] Promised or foretold

The Nativity of a Lady

The greatest of splendour! Not bad for someone with an afflicted Lord Ascendant, Lord 2 and dispositer of Fortuna, and a salutary reminder to present day astrologers that a quick glance at a natal chart is often wrong.

Fixed star Procyon, a star on the Body of the Little Dog, is on the lady's 2nd house cusp. A binary yellow and white star of the nature of Mercury and Mars; Procyon can indeed lead to preferment but this preferment is usually accompanied by problems. Robson gives 'sudden preferment by exertion' and 'elevation ending in disaster', as some typical manifestations of the influence of this star. 'Saucy, giddy and petulant', are other manifestations, but, as with all things when looking at a natal chart: everything must be read in context of everything else. This is vital and must always be kept in mind.

My calculation of this lady's Fortuna[6], at 0 degrees 36 Taurus, falls on fixed star Sharatar; a pearly white star on the Horn of the Ram. Robson gives, among other things: 'bodily injuries and unscrupulous defeat'. Of the nature of Mars and Saturn, this is a generally unfortunate star.

To close his section on the lady's wealth and prosperity, Worsdale notes, that due to the afflictions of Mars and Venus:

> '... it is certainly very evident, beyond dispute, that the riches which this native may accumulate, will be obtained by dishonourable means',

Which in light of what we have seen so far is quite possible, and that,

> '... the native will never again have the honour to possess that splendour which she has hitherto attained; for most of the important directions which operate hereafter, will be of a malefic nature and tendency.'

It appears that all may not go well for the Lady.

The Passions and Loves of a Lady

Worsdale draws our particular attention to the 5th house, which will, 'yield us information concerning the native's issue, whether she shall have children or the contrary.'

He points out the, 'remarkable congress therein', and bids us to sit up and pay attention.

Venus is Lord 5 and is in a fertile sign and there are a stack of planets in the 5th house. Worsdale wants to show, that again, the unwary astrologer could fall into a trap here, this time of believing that this lady will have a mighty brood of children.

He mentions that the 5th house is also the house of 'pleasure and delight'. Bearing this in mind, and the knowledge that we have a very phlegmatic lady on our hands, who is not so much led by desire as driven by it, we could have

---

[6] Moon – Sun projected from the Ascendant. I do not reverse Fortuna for a night time chart, nor do I reverse the Parts derived from her.

a lot of pleasure and delight going on here, but with this pleasure and delight not necessarily resulting in children.

As Worsdale points out, though Venus lord 5 is in a fertile sign, she is also in her detriment. Venus rules Mercury and the Sun, who along with Mars are all in the 5th house. He also notes that the Lord Ascendant Moon is in a barren sign,

> '... with her dispositer in his fall, in conjunction with Mercury', and he concludes that, 'it is therefore very obvious, from these considerations, that the native will have no issue'.

We might also note that the Sun and Mars who are traditionally the natural significators of men in a woman's natal chart are located in the 5th house, and what do they love? They are both in major Venus dignities and so they love Venus herself – ruler of the 5th and the planet which governs her pleasure and delight. And what does the ruler of her pleasure and delight love? She is in major Mars dignities and so she loves Mars, one of the natural rulers of Men in a woman's chart, and also the turned Lord 5 of Lord 7: The Lord of pleasure and delight of any prospective partner.

Worsdale remarks that to derive knowledge of, 'whether she shall marry or not',

> 'we must chiefly regard the position of the Sun and Mars, the seventh house, and lord thereof, which are this lady's significators of marriage, on viewing which attentively, I conceive it would be deemed needless and even absurd, to trouble either myself or my readers on this subject, having before disclosed the natural inclinations of the native.'

He points out that,

> 'Saturn in this figure is the lord of the seventh house, posited in the fourth, aspected by Mars and Venus from the occidental part of heaven; the Sun is also very unfortunately placed in the fifth house, in the exaltation of Saturn, and consequently, in no aspect with Mars or Saturn; from which consideration, and others of a similar nature sufficient may be gathered to assure us that, the native will always give herself up to lustful pleasures and have a natural aversion to the married state.'

We might add that her Lord Ascendant the Moon is in major Sun dignities – so showing that she loves the Sun, and all he stands for. This Sun is in its fall, so he is probably not a good guy and he only has eyes for her frolicking, both loving Lord 5 and also placed in her 5th house. With a strong Mars squaring the Moon also, commitment is not on the menu. Despite her having fixed star Caphir on her 5th house; a nice Venus and Mercury star, showing her to have the potential to be courteous, refined and lovable in her 5th house activities.

Caphir is also known as 'The Submissive One', and is also a binary star – I have noticed the 'more than one' element of binary stars sometimes[7] show-

---

[7] I repeat: *sometimes*.

ing itself with more than one character appearing in a particular scene, of whichever drama we may be looking at. With her Venus on magnitude 1 fixed star Agena, on the right foreleg of the Centaur, a star traditionally bringing a passionate poetical nature but rashness in friendships, we can see that this drama has all the signs of a tragic romance. Saturn is Lord 7; he is in a double bodied sign, which, within context of everything else, also shows the possibility of more than one sweetheart.

The lady's Part of Marriage is located at 24 degrees 40 Leo. This falls on fixed star Alphard an orange star on the neck of the Hydra, also known as The Hydras Heart. This can manifest in strong passionate relationships and a lack of self control, Robson gives, 'admired by the opposite sex', but, 'sorrow through love affairs if female'. The ruler of the Part of Marriage is the problematic Sun, which we have looked at already and which simply confirms what we have seen.

The Part of Marriage also falls quite close to powerful fixed star Regulus. Royal star Regulus could show that in context she wants to or does indeed, 'marry above her station', after all she only has eyes for the Sun, symbol of royalty and rich people, and she has Jupiter, significators of lords and ladies, in essential dignity near the 11th house of friends also exalting, 'looking up to' the Sun. However, she does not seem the marrying kind, and Robson gives 'many disappointments, violent attachments and trouble through love affairs', when Regulus is connected with Venus, and Venus is of course, the planet from which we derive the location of the Part of Marriage from.

Maybe there is always a good guy on the scene somewhere, and maybe, just maybe, if she only looked to Lord 7 itself for a beau, then things might be so different.

On the cusp of the 7th house we have fixed star Pelagus, an aspirational star situated on the vane of the Archers Arrow. According to Robson this will show as 'truthfulness, optimism and a religious mind'. This sounds much more promising, especially if she is looking for a 'nice guy'. And, as Lord 7 is Saturn, we know that at least he likes her, as shown by Saturn being in Moon dignities.

But this is a passionate lady, and this is no grand romance; Lord 7, Saturn, is only in the triplicity of the Moon: he only wants to be her friend. And she, if we bear in mind the portrait we have been building of her, does not seem the type who would want such a man – as is shown by her Lord Ascendant in the detriment of Saturn Lord 7: Thanks, but no thanks – she doesn't like him at all.

Why? He simply is 'not man enough', as while he, Saturn, is fussing around in Virgo, she, the Moon, only has eyes for the Sun, and the Sun, in a woman's chart, is of course, natural ruler of *Man*.

With Mars occidental and in square aspect to her Lord Ascendant and lord 7 Saturn, in a double bodied sign and located in the 4th house – this lady has no great desire to marry, and the lack of mutability in her chart coupled with her nature shows she has a difficulty in saying goodbye, in ending things, in finally saying enough is enough and moving on.

In a Carriage from the Opera House

Worsdale mentions an unfortunate accident in the lady's life:

> 'When the native was somewhat more than twenty three years of age, as she was returning from the opera house in a carriage, it broke down; in consequence of which, she received a very violent wound on the left cheek, which confined her to her bed for a long period of time.'

Worsdale mentions that at the time of the incident, 'the Sun was directed to the body of Mars', exactly describing the circumstance,'

Which of course the Sun directed to the body of Mars does.

Unfortunately he did not care to mention which method of direction he used in his calculation, and as Worsdale was quite fond of many different methods we could spend quite some time checking them all.

But, instead, if we look at the progressions for 1796, 'when she was somewhat more than twenty three years of age', we can see that progressed Sun is square natal Moon which is of course also her Lord Ascendant. The Sun is also natal Lord 3, ruler of short journeys, and the natal Moon is also placed on the 3rd house cusp.

This does seem descriptive of the accident in the carriage with the progressed Sun squaring Moon traditionally showing troubles in journeys, unhappiness in travels and hurts to the eyes – Moon and Sun being rulers of the eyes. In this lady's case, the Moon is also her Lord Ascendant, and so an injury to the face is congruent.

A square from the Sun is usually pretty unpleasant, in the light of the potentials of her nativity, even more so.

Progressed Sun still has 3 or so degrees to travel to conjunct natal Mars but the Square from progressed Sun to natal Moon is just as descriptive, and as Moon is Lord Ascendant it fits the situation well.

If we also check the Solar Return for the same year we have the Ascendant of the return falling on Martian fixed star Antares. Fiery red and emerald green Antares is very often malefic and violent, and does, in context of the progressions, seem to point towards the same event, with return Mars also strong in its exaltation, a few degrees inside the return Ascendant by antiscion and square the Sun, sextile natal Venus and trine natal Saturn. Return Mercury is close to the natal Mars that is afflicting in the nativity and so he is also square the natal Moon.

Honour and Preferment

Looking at the significators of the lady's preferment Worsdale points us toward,

The Nativity of a Lady

'... the benevolent planet Jupiter'.

He continues, by saying that Jupiter is,

> '... very favourably posited in the medium caeli, in his own dignities; which is an argument of preferment and considerable honour, particularly, as Jupiter is lord of the tenth: but, the effect of this eligible position of Jupiter, in the present case is, we find, considerably reduced by his being in conjunction with the dragons' tail and also retrograde, and his dispositer afflicting the Moon, lady of the Ascendant; the Sun her general significator of preferment, is posited in his fall, disposted by Venus and she in her detriment, which are so many infallible testimonies of loss of reputation and dignity that the fortunate position of Jupiter in the midheaven, cannot be of any avail in reducing the efficacy of the before mentioned discordant configurations.'

As I mentioned earlier, I certainly wouldn't consider Jupiter as 'posited in the medium caeli', the Midheaven, as it is only about 6 degrees from the 11th house cusp. Maybe Worsdale is using 'medium caeli' as meaning the top of the chart as well as meaning the actual Midheaven itself, also, as Jupiter is retrograde, he may see Jupiter as moving away from the 11th cusp thus staying in the 10th house. Still, we need not worry too much about these things; there are plenty of other testimonies.

He then remarks:

> '... when the medium caeli[8] in this nativity was directed to the tail of the dragon, this native was imprisoned; the like effect with its consequences will happen again, when the same point is directed to the opposition of Mercury and the Sun which is several years distant.'

Again, he does not mention how he is directing the Midheaven, and we are not just talking about Primary and Secondary directions here, Worsdale had a whole host of directing techniques that he employed, often simultaneously, and not always mentioning which one he happened to be using or referring to at the time.

Despite this cornucopia of directions, if we look at the progressions, which have already worked well for the earlier incident in the carriage home from the opera house, we can see that the progressed Midheaven conjuncts the South Node, the 'tail of the dragon', in 1798. The progressed Sun to Mars conjunction is closing in and the Solar return for that year puts a debilitated Saturn, natural ruler of prisons and restriction, inside the return Ascendant, conjunct and afflicting the natal 2nd house cusp of money and resources. This Saturn is also conjunct the progressed Ascendant. The return Moon is in its detriment and in mundane conjunction with the combust natal Mercury and the return Mars is conjunct the natal Midheaven itself.

Why, one might ask, did this lady end up in this way? Worsdale points to the 12th house, that place of, 'malignant private enemies', and of 'the

---

[8] Here he is referring to the angle of the Midheaven itself.

misfortune of adversity and imprisonment'. Venus, in her detriment is ruler of this house, as Worsdale goes on,

> 'very malignantly seated on the cusp of the sixth, in quartile with the Moon, lady of the ascendant; all which tend to show that the private enemies of the native, as are such as follow the same remarkable pursuits in life, which does not seem proper to mention in this place.'

> '... this native has suffered imprisonment, which is very aptly denoted by the Moon's position in quartile of Mars, and the Sun in his fall, conjoined with the lord of the twelfth, together with the position of the Pleiades and Aldebaran in that part of the heaven also signifying captivity.'

Aldebaran is far too far away from the cusp for me to consider it but fixed star Alcyone, the brightest star in the Pleiades, The Seven Sisters, is on the 12th cusp. The Seven Sisters are the virgin companions' of Diana, forever weeping with grief at the fate of their father Atlas who was sadly destined to carry the weight of the heavens upon his head and hands. This carries echoes of the lady's own family background, Mercury, ruler of the 4th house of the father, utterly debilitated, combust by the Sun yet also sextile to the Moon, reaching out to her Lord Ascendant on the third cusp of sisters and siblings and by antiscia sitting on the 12th house of sorrow. The Pleiades on the 12th house is a sign that in light of what we have seen, this particular tale could, like the 'weeping sisters' themselves, very well end in tears; Alcyone traditionally bringing such things as wantonness and turbulence, disgrace, exile and imprisonment. We don't know what eventually happened to the lady, Worsdale only tells us that at the time of writing she was in good health, but as the antiscion of afflicted Lord Ascendant Moon is hovering close to the cusp of the 12th, and in light of all that we have seen, whatever did happen, self imprisonment would also be a likely theme running like a thread through the Nativity of a Lady.

The Nativity of a Lady

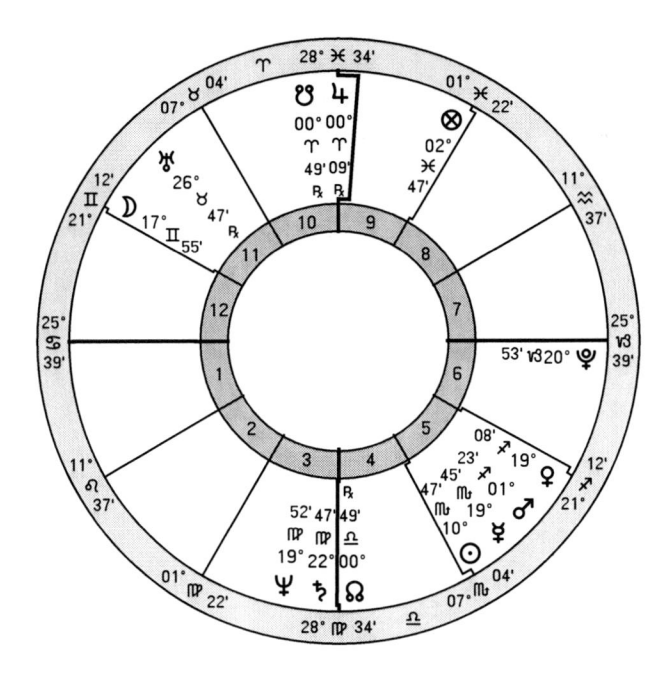

(Fig 20) Secondary Progressions, 10 Oct 1796

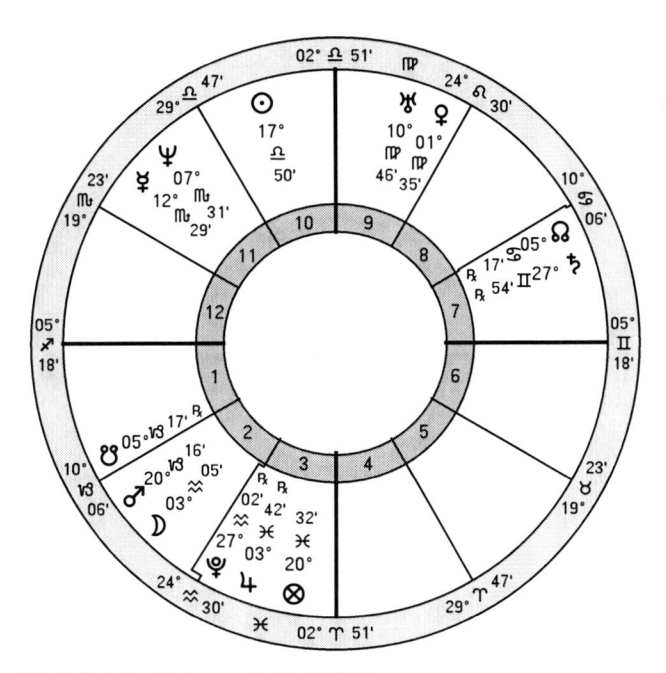

(Fig 21) Solar Return, 10 Oct 1796

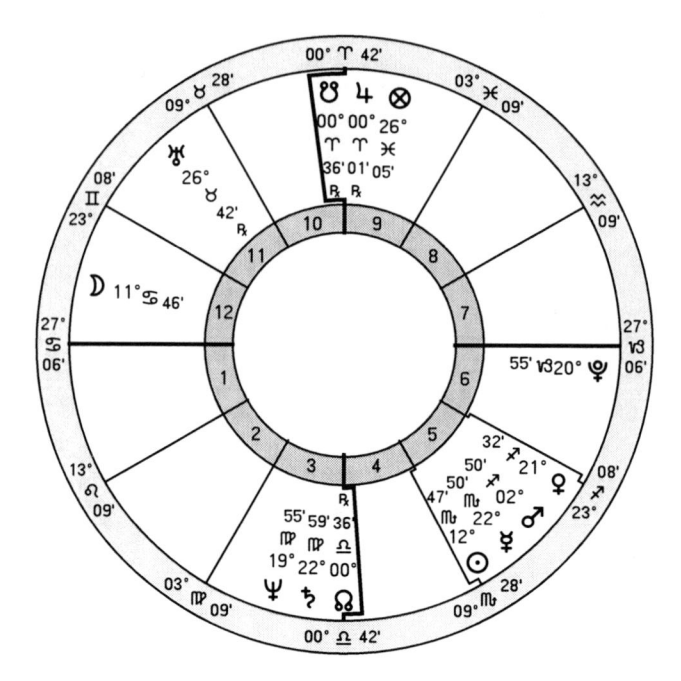

(Fig 22) Secondary Progressions, 1798

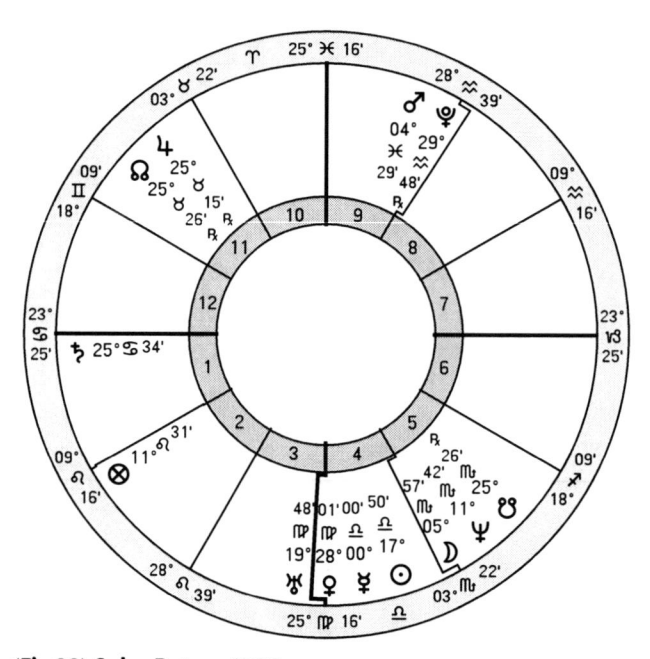

(Fig 23) Solar Return 1798

6

Fate, Freewill, Fortuna and the Soul

> *With domineering hand she moves the turning wheel,*
> *Like currents in a treacherous bay swept to and fro:*
> *Her ruthless will has just disposed once fearful kings*
> *While trustless still, from low she lifts a conquered head;*
> *No cries of misery she hears, no tears she heeds,*
> *But steely hearted laughs at groans her deeds have wrung.*
> *Such is the game she plays, and so she tests her strength;*
> *Of mighty power she makes parade when one short hour*
> *Sees happiness from utter desolation grow.*
>
> Boethius. The Consolation of Philosophy

If there really are such things as crossroads in time then Boethius, the Roman philosopher and theologian, stands at one of them. At the meeting point of the ancient world and the early middle ages we shall find him, erudite and visionary, and only too willing to teach us a thing or two about fortune and fate.

Born around 480 AD into an aristocratic Roman Christian family, Boethius worked for the Ostrogothic king Theodoric. Initially Boethius was commissioned to design and build a water clock and sundial, but by the time he was thirty he held the high office of Consul without Companion. Later King Theodoric made Boethius, Magister Officiorum – a very responsible and powerful position. A man of high principles, a politician due to his sense of duty rather than desire for power, Boethius was also a scholar and philosopher. He'd planned to translate the entire works of Aristotle and Plato into Latin but did not complete this before his death. Boethius wrote commentaries on Porphyry and Cicero, five of his own works on logic, books on music, arithmetic, geometry, astronomy and theology, including a highly influential book on the Christian Trinity. He was a busy man, and thank God he was, as it was largely through him that the logic of the ancient world was transmitted to the middle ages.

Due to political machinations with the Eastern Empire of Byzantium he was accused of treason. Boethius protested his innocence, but nevertheless, he was arrested and condemned by King Theodoric and later by the Senate. Boethius was imprisoned, and in time, he suffered torture and execution. During his imprisonment he wrote what was to become an extraordinarily influential book: *The Consolation of Philosophy*.

In the *Consolation*, Boethius is pictured, pondering his fate, comforted by the Muses of poetry. He wonders how on earth he could have ended up like this after being so successful in life; how could he fall so low that he is now imprisoned and awaiting execution? Suddenly the muse Philosophia appears and promptly sends the Muses of poetry, in her words, 'hysterical sluts' out of the door!

Philosophia then proceeds to tell Boethius the answer to his question and in so doing she introduces him to Fortuna.

Fortuna tells him, 'Wealth, honours and the like are all under my jurisdiction. They are my servants and know their mistress. When I come, they come with me and when I go they leave as well.'

Boethius learns the hard way: it is the inconstancy of fortune that is its essence.

Fortuna in Astrology

Fortuna also makes an appearance in astrology. The Arabic Part of Fortune is traditionally called by its Latin name Fortuna and it too, like its namesake, is a mysterious thing. Derived from the relationship of the Sun, Moon and Ascendant, the cheapest astrological software will show its position, as will a traditional square chart in a 500 year old manuscript. Like Fortuna herself, it has been with us for a long time.

The Roman Macrobius, in his compilation of traditional lore, *Saturnalia*, recounts a tale that seems to hint at a very early appearance of Fortuna. Macrobius tells us, 'The Egyptians use the caduceus' significance to explain people's horoscope ("genesis" it's called), saying that four gods attend a human being as it's born, Deity (Daimon), Chance (Tyche), Love (Eros), and Necessity.'

Deity was traditionally associated with the Sun and Chance was associated with the Moon. This picture of Sun, Moon and Horoscope, alerts the astrologer to the possible presence of Fortuna.

Macrobius explains further,

> 'The first two they mean to be regarded as the sun and moon, because the sun as the source of breath, warmth, and light is the begetter and guardian of human life and so is believed to be the Daimon, or deity, of the one being born; whereas the moon is Tyche, because she is in charge of our bodies, which are buffeted by various chance circumstances. Love is signified with a kiss, Necessity by a knot.'

Whether or not this is a veiled early instance of the Part of Fortune it clearly reminds us how our lives are often, as Macrobius says, 'buffeted by various chance circumstances'. It shows the awareness of the mysterious power of fortune and chance in our lives and suggests that as well as this indeterminateness, we are all still constrained by necessity.

Fate, Freewill, Fortuna and the Soul

These days such simplicity of approach is no longer in vogue, and in astrology, the talk of chance and indeterminateness is virtually unheard of. Fortuna, as her name suggests, hints at fortune and chance but the Part of Fortune has also acquired a host of other meanings. Much like the modern idea of freewill, these meanings are often confused and bear little resemblance to what Fortuna, or indeed freewill, has meant for most of history.

Yet when Fortuna explains her nature to Boethius she is quite clear:

'Inconstancy is my very essence; it is the game I never cease to play as I turn my wheel in its ever-changing circle, filled with joy as I bring the top to the bottom and the bottom to the top. Yes, rise up on my wheel if you like, but don't count it an injury when by the same token you begin to fall, as the rules of the game will require you must surely have been aware of my ways.'

So, before rushing ahead, it might be helpful to continue to cast our eyes back into the past to see what Fortuna meant for those before us.

The Classical Meaning of Fortune

The Oxford Companion to Classical Literature tells us that Fortuna was an, 'Italian goddess, perhaps originally the 'bringer' of Fertility but identified with the Greek goddess Tyche and so the goddess of chance or luck.' Tyche was chance, good or bad fortune, the part of life that could not be pinned down, that which, no matter how much we might attempt to scrutinise it, will still resist explanation and calculation. Fortuna was usually portrayed as seated and generally shown as blind. She held the cornucopia, 'the horn of plenty' and a rudder to symbolize her power in steering the courses of men's lives. Classically, she pointed towards chance, the indeterminate cause. But the image of blind Fortuna and her wheel also suggests necessity, those things in life that could not be any other way, in other words, Fate.

There's a general confusion between Fortune and Fate; are they simply the same thing?

When we look back on events in life, there are some things that seem to have happened randomly, without any intent, or certainly without any intent on our part. Traditionally, these unforeseen events were given a cause. Fortuna caused the inexplicable; it was something independent from reason and nature, something mysterious that accidentally controlled an event. If we change our focus and see the accidental event as divinely controlled, then the effect rather than the cause is emphasised and the distinction between chance and fate blurs and disappears. Fortune becomes the outcome of an event rather than the cause of it.

In astrology we can see fortunate events indicated by things like the natal progressions of Fortuna. The temptation for the astrologer is to make the hidden, or not so hidden, assumption that things proceed from absolutely determined causes. Because they can see astrological patterns unfolding in a chart the astrologer often unconsciously assumes that it is by necessity that things happen.

It is also common for the astrologer's client to make this assumption. However, the whole concept of a consultation contradicts the idea of all things happening by necessity. If everything is happening unfailingly, from absolutely determined causes, then why bother via a consultation to try to understand what might be the best way forward? If all happens in this world by necessity, very quickly freewill and reason go out of the window. Yet if in seeking a consultation you try to find an astrologer, modern or traditional, who still believes in the concept of chance, you'll probably have a long and fruitless search in front of you. Chance as an indeterminate cause has also been slung out of the window and it too has been replaced by necessity.

But are these astrologers right?

You won't find the answer to that question in an astrology book. To find out the truth of the matter you need to leave the astrology books on the shelf. Instead, let us dust off our volumes of Aristotle and Aquinas.

I. ARISTOTLE AND ST THOMAS AQUINAS

First we turn to Aristotle whose thinking sits beneath astrology like a mighty foundation stone.

The Hidden Causes

In book II, chapter IV of the *Physics,* Aristotle calls chance and fortune, *The Hidden Causes.*

He mentions those who deny the existence of chance and spontaneity:

> 'Some people even question whether they are real or not. They say that nothing happens by chance, but everything that we ascribe to chance or spontaneity has some definite cause, e.g., coming, "by chance" into the market and finding there a man whom one wanted but did not expect to meet is due to ones wish to go and buy in the market.'

> '... it is always possible they maintain, to find something which is the cause; but not chance.'

He also wonders why people who do not believe in chance or fortune in the world still try to make use of it in their lives or assign chance or fortune to the stars or accept it as a cause but say 'that it is inscrutable to human intelligence, as being a divine thing, and full of mystery'.

He suggests for us to find the truth we need to distinguish between causes.

> 'First then we observe that some things always come to pass in the same way and others for the most part. It is clearly neither of these that chance is said to be the cause, nor can the "effect of chance" be identified with any of the things that

come to pass by necessity and always or for the most part. But as there is a third class of events besides these two – events which all say are "by chance" – it is plain that there is such a thing as chance and spontaneity ...'

He gives his own example.

'A man is engaged collecting subscriptions for a feast. He would have gone to such and such a place for the purpose of getting the money, if he had known. He actually went there for another purpose, and it was only incidentally that he got his money by going there; and this was not due to the fact that he went there as a rule or necessarily, nor is the end effected (getting the money) a cause present in himself – it belongs to the class of things that are intentional and the result of intelligent deliberation. It is when these conditions are satisfied that a man is said to have gone there by "chance". If he had gone of deliberate purpose and for the sake of this – if he always or normally went there when he was collecting payments – he would not be said to have gone there by "chance".'

Therefore, he says,

'It is clear then that chance is an incidental cause in the sphere of those actions for the sake of something which involve purpose'

And our need to distinguish between causes is paramount. For if we do this we shall see that,

'... the causes of the man's coming, and getting his money (when he did not come for the sake of that) are innumerable. He may have wished to see somebody or been following somebody or avoiding somebody or may have gone to see a spectacle'.

'... these causes are indefinite, chance is indefinite'.

Chance is an incidental cause, a per accidens cause; it is a cause that happens without intention, it is a cause that happens by accident.
What is it a cause of?

The External Goods

Chance and fortune are the cause of the external goods. These are the goods of the outside world. As Aristotle explains, in Book I of *Rhetoric*, 'By Fortune I mean good birth and wealth and powers and their opposites and in general good fortune and misfortune'. And in Book I chapter 8 of the *Nicomachean Ethics*, he divides these external goods into two groups, 'friends, money and political influence' and 'noble birth, good children and physical beauty'.

In order for something to be an effect of fortune it cannot be something that happens by necessity, normally or regularly, as Aristotle said above, it must be accidental. For example a person digging a hole to plant a tree finds a pot of gold by accident – 'per accidens' – because it was an accident of digging the hole. He was digging a hole to plant a tree; he was not seeking gold. A fortunate, chance occurrence will have this peculiar purposeless quality.

And this accidental nature Aristotle illustrates nicely, in book V, chapter 30 of *Metaphysics* where he says,

> 'Nor does an accident have any determinate cause, but only a contingent or chance cause, i.e., an indeterminate one. For it was by accident that someone came to Aegina; and if he did not come there in order to get there, but because he was driven there by a storm or was captured by pirates, the event has occurred and is an accident; yet not of itself but by reason of something else. For the storm is the cause of his coming to the place to which he was not sailing, and this was Aegina.'

This example of an indeterminate cause, where the storm or pirates drive the sailor to 'the place he was not sailing ...' perfectly captures the accidentality of fortune.

As well as fortune as a cause of fortunate events we also have fortunate people. A fortunate person is someone that something good happens to apart from and aside from any intention they may have had.

Fortunate People

In Book VIII of the *Eudemian Ethics,* Aristotle wonders, 'Whether it is by nature or otherwise that one man is fortunate and another unfortunate ...'
He states,

> 'That there are some people who are fortunate is a matter of observation. For people who lack wisdom succeed in many things where luck rules ...'

> 'That they succeed is obvious, though they are lacking in wisdom in the very things they are fortunate ...'

But he also wonders if some people are fortunate because they are guided by something outside of them? As he says, 'Just as a badly constructed ship often sails better, not on its own account, but because it has a good helmsman ...'

He concludes there are two types of fortunate people – 'two kinds of good fortune'.

Aristotle believes that fortune in the first sense is an irrational impulse a sort of hunch or instinct that guides them to do something at the right place, the right time and in defiance of what is thought. Even though this hunch or intuition is irrational Aristotle still considers it natural because it comes from within the person.

But others attain a desirable end that is not even considered by them. And this kind of luck has nothing to do with an intuitive impulse or hunch. It is not natural as it does not originate from within the person; it comes from outside the person as Aristotle suspected. Where does this impulse come from that guides them to do something at an opportune moment that then turns out well?

To explore this he suggests we follow each of our thoughts back to each preceding thought. If we do this we will eventually come to something that is higher than thinking. And we will realise that, '… intelligence is not the starting point of thinking, nor is counsel the starting point of deliberation.' He then wonders if there is some originating principle, with no other principle external to it.

> 'That is what we are looking for' he says, 'what is the starting point of motion in the soul?'

He concludes,

> 'The answer is plain: as in the universe, so here, God moves everything by intelligence. For in a manner the divine element in us moves everything. Reason is not the originator of reasoning, but something superior.'

That something is God, 'who moves everything by intelligence' and who guides us from the outside when we succeed despite our irrationality or lack of judgement. The fortunate or lucky person is the one whose desires are prompted and guided by God. And therefore the cause of luck that makes us desire the right thing at the right time is God.

We can now turn to St Thomas Aquinas whose thinking runs like a secret river taking us right to the very heart of what we are doing in astrology.

St Thomas Aquinas on Fate, Chance and Providence

In the *Summa Contra Gentiles* and *Summa Theologica* Aquinas agrees with Aristotle on the existence of chance as a cause and he argues against determinism, absolute necessity and all those people who deny the existence of chance. And, as Aristotle before him, he also believes that fortune has something to do with divinity. In order to know more we need to be clear about what is meant by providence and we need to understand the difference between primary and secondary causes.

Providence

St Thomas tells us, 'Providence, properly speaking is the plan of ordering things to an end …'[1]

He explains, 'There are two elements in providence, the plan and its execution, which is called government. As regards the former, God's plan is immediate to everything, for in his mind is the reason for everything, even for the very least. As regards the latter there are intermediaries, for the divine rule governs lower by higher, not from any defect of power but from an abundance of goodness endowing creatures with the dignity of causing.'[2]

---

[1] St Thomas Aquinas *Summa Theologica*, I Q22 1
[2] St Thomas Aquinas *Summa Theologica*, I Q22.3

This 'dignity of causing' enables us to freely bring our powers to bear upon the world.

Our world is coherent because it is ordered to an end. Providence extends to everything, as God is keeping everything in existence, for every moment of time – like a singer singing a song. There is nothing outside, nor is there any escape from God's providence, as anything outside of it would no longer exist. As St Thomas says,

> 'Everything is provided for in the scheme of the universal cause; nothing can evade it'.[3]

This is because if it were outside of God's providence then it would be outside of the universal cause of existence on which everything *depends* for its existence.

There is chance and necessity within providence because, as we have seen with Aristotle, chance and necessity can be led back to a higher cause. Therefore, when things occur by chance, say by some cause failing or by one cause being stopped by another cause, the cause that interferes and is doing the stopping will still depend upon the first cause for its existence.

Also, as Aquinas tells us,

> 'When a master sends two servants to the same place, their meeting may seem to them a chance encounter. So a happening may seem haphazard or casual with respect to lower causes when it appears unintentional, but there is nothing fortuitous about such events with respect to a higher cause.'[4]

The chance encounter is indeed fortuitous for us but it still remains within providence.

Primary and Secondary Causes

Understanding the difference between causes is the route to understanding how and why chance is contained within providence. It is because providence includes secondary causes that providence also includes freedom.

A primary cause is the first cause in a series of causes. A secondary cause is a cause that is dependent upon the first cause. It is a cause that can fail in its effect. Primary or secondary is in order of importance and not in order of time – one does not necessarily come before the other. The important thing to remember about secondary causes is they are contingent. This means they can fail. Aquinas gives the example that for a plant to bear fruit is a contingent effect; it may or may not bear fruit because of the proximate cause that is the power of germination. A remote cause, say the sun shining on the plant, is a cause that acts by necessity. Many proximate causes can fail. Not all the effects under providence will be necessary; many of them will be contingent.

[3] St Thomas Aquinas *Summa Theologica*, I Q 22, 2, ad I
[4] St Thomas Aquinas Opusc, XII *Compendium Theologiae*, 137

That some causes are contingent and some are necessary also explains why the stars cannot be an unfailing cause of our choice in things.

Why the Stars are Not the Unfailing Cause of our Choices

In our world everything is always changing and fluctuating. It is changing in the sense that matter is always potentially lots of different things and there is a profusion of forms, all so different and contradictory of each other. Because of this, the stars cannot determine things by necessity, in a manner that absolutely must be one way.

The stars always move in the same way, if they caused things in a manner that was necessary, in a way that could only be that way and no other, then we would have no variety in our world. If we take many things that could be other than they are, or things that could be hindered and fail in their effects, and we add them all together this will not add up to or make a necessary thing. As each could fail, be hindered or stopped in their effects separately, then so too, could all of them together.

Things that happen through the influence of the stars cannot be necessary; this means there cannot be determinism via the stars. The stars are part of nature and the natural world, and therefore belong and conform to nature's laws. That they are bodily natural things tells us they need matter on which to act. The matter or bodily substance they act upon is of this world which means it is 'corruptible'. This means it can dissolve, perish or break up into parts. It can fail in its action as well as fall apart, disintegrate and go out of being. The nature of this corruptibility and change means that they should be able to do things that are not constrained by necessity, things that could be other than they are. Therefore, if the stars do cause effects on things in this world they do not cause things in a necessary manner, where they can only manifest in a certain way and not another.

This is clearly seen by the astrologer when a configuration or pattern of testimonies in a chart manifests in a way different than was imagined. In natal work, often a querent can be worried about a particular progression or return or even transit that they envisage manifesting in a certain way. Yet the reality is, that if it does manifest, then it often manifests in a different manner than the best or worst case scenario they'd imagined. The fact there is more than one way for an effect or an astrological pattern to manifest shows that astrologically things do not proceed from necessity.

In his commentary on Aristotle's *Peri Hermeneias* Book I lesson 14, Aquinas tells us,

> 'Some, not considering the difference between accidental and per se effects, tried to reduce all the effects that come about in this world to some per se cause. They posited as this cause the power of the stars and assumed fate to be dependent on this power – fate being, according to them, nothing else but the power of the position of the constellations.'

This brings to mind Dante Alighieri's powerful image of the damned, standing on the banks of the river near the gates of Hell, cursing their heritage, 'they blasphemed God and their parents; the human kind; the place, the time, and origin of their seed and of their birth.'[5] This is an extreme example of a type of thinking that underlies a lot of astrology and comes from both astrologers and their clients.

Aquinas continues, 'But such a cause cannot bring about necessity in all things accomplished in this world, since many things come about from intellect and will, which are not subject per se and directly to the power of the heavenly bodies. For the intellect, or reason and the will which is in reason, are not acts of a corporeal organ and so consequently cannot be directly subject to the power of the heavenly bodies, since a corporeal force, of itself, can only act on a corporeal thing. The sensitive powers, on the other hand, inasmuch as they are acts of corporeal organs, are accidentally subject to the action of the heavenly bodies.'

'The power of the stars does indirectly redound to the intellect and will in as much as the agent intellect and will use the sensitive powers. But clearly the passions of the sensitive powers do not induce necessity of reason and will, for the continent man has wrong desires but is not seduced by them.

Therefore, we may conclude that the power of the heavenly bodies does not bring about necessity in the things done through reason and will.'

The Stars Do Not Act On Our Intellect

Our intellect is our spiritual power related to knowledge – our power of knowing things in an immaterial way. It is our power to think that is higher than our imagination or our senses. Higher things rule lower things and the intellect is higher than material things. As the stars are material they cannot directly act upon the intellect or directly cause the intellect to choose or be the cause of those things that belong to the intellect.

No bodily thing, can act without movement or change. Things that are immovable and unchangeable cannot be caused by movement because the result of the movement of something happens when the agent – that which is doing the moving – moves the patient, that which is moved. So things outside of movement cannot be caused by the stars. The intellect itself and that which belongs to the intellect are completely outside movement.

So whatever directly receives an impression from a body must be a body or a bodily power. As the intellect is not a bodily thing the stars can't act upon it directly. But though the stars can't be a direct cause, they can influence indirectly. This is because even though the intellect isn't a body it still has to use bodily powers such as the imagination and memory to operate in the world. And when such things as the imagination and memory are

---

[5] Dante Alighieri *The Divine Comedy, Inferno Canto III*

affected by say illness or even laziness, the activity of the intellect is also affected. Also when someone is comparatively fit and well, or they have a physical or imaginative readiness to understand something, then the intellect is able to work quickly and fluently with the bodily powers.

The nature of a human body is that it can act or be acted upon in certain ways. One of these ways is via the stars. In Book III Chapter 84 of *Summa Contra Gentiles* St Thomas quotes St John Damascene,

> 'The various planets produce in us various temperaments habits and dispositions',

Aquinas comments on this and explains further,

> '… consequently the heavenly bodies contribute indirectly to the goodness of our understanding. This, even as physicians are able to judge of a man's intellect from his bodily temperament, as a proximate disposition thereto, so too can an astrologer, from the heavenly movements, as being a remote cause of this disposition. In this sense we can approve of the saying of Ptolemy: "when Mercury is in one of Saturn regions at the time of a man's birth, and he is waxing, he bestows on him a quick intelligence of the inner nature of things" (Ptolemy's Centiloquim verbum 38)'.

So the stars can contribute, albeit indirectly, to our understanding but the stars are not a cause of our choice or our will. This is because the will is a power of the rational intellectual soul. Therefore it too is immaterial, and if the stars can't directly impose themselves on the intellect, then neither can they directly impose themselves on the will or affect the will directly. All choice and willing is caused by us grasping the essence or nature of something that we think is good. And even though this process may be influenced by the senses, this grasping or apprehension is, in itself, an intellectual operation. The stars aren't the cause of our intellectual apprehension and so can't be the cause of our choice.

Whatever happens in the world through the influence of the stars happens naturally as things below are subordinate to those above them. If the stars have any influence on our choice then it must happen naturally. So someone naturally 'chooses' to do something as animals 'choose' via their instinct and as inanimate bodies are moved naturally. The stars thus only directly affect us via our bodies, so if they cause our choosing, this will be via an impression or influence on our bodies. But even so, they still cannot be an adequate explanatory or sufficient cause of our choosing one thing over another.

The simple objective presentation of something to us cannot be by itself an adequate explanatory cause of our choice. This is clearly seen when someone comes into contact with something that they like. The person whose reason has control of their appetite is not compelled by necessity to choose whereas one whose appetite is not under the control of their reason will simply grab it – *whatever it* may be. 'Passions' of varying strengths may move us but they are not a sufficient cause of our choosing. Aquinas explains that the incontinent man follows 'passions' by choice while the continent – the person who has resistance to evil desires does not. So, if the continent, the one who has control via their reason over their drives and desires is not driven to choose, the stars cannot have the power to cause our choices.

Determinists are similar to those who disbelieved in chance. They will still make a place for freewill even despite their determinism. Otherwise why bother even having a conversation – let alone an argument – if all is determined? The very fact they insist they are right shows an underlying belief in freewill and contradicts their own position, as if they are right, and all is determined then why bother to argue about it as you will not be able to change anything, not even someone's mind. Why ask anyone's advice if you cannot choose between options? Why even seek your own counsel if there is no making up of one's mind to do and no judgement to reach? As Aquinas tells us, no powers are given in vain. We have the power to judge and to take counsel and advice both from others and from ourselves in regard to our actions. This would be of no use to us if our choice in things was directly determined by the stars. So the stars cannot be the cause of our choice.

Things unfold according to their own nature. In choosing how to act we always need to make a distinction between what we can do in a situation and what we cannot. Often we find our efforts frustrated because we are trying to do something that is not within our power to do. That we do not think so does not change this. St Thomas, in explaining why honour, power, fame and money cannot be our ultimate end and so cannot truly bring us happiness, points out that these things, '… are due rather to external causes, and in most cases to fortune (chance); for which reason they are called goods of fortune'. [6]

In other words they depend on things that are mostly out of our power.

Power is the thing that most modern people erroneously equate with freewill. St Thomas quotes Boethius on why power cannot bring happiness, 'the power of man cannot relieve the gnawing of care, nor can it avoid the thorny path of anxiety' and 'Think you a man is powerful who is surrounded by attendants, whom he inspires with fear indeed, but whom he fears still more?' [7]

Guardian Angels

As we have seen, God does not act directly in everything; he makes use of secondary causes to execute his will. Some of these secondary causes can act freely, namely angels and human beings and, as Aquinas explains, sometimes our Guardian Angel can be the efficient cause of our good fortune.

---

[6] I-II Article IV *Summa Theologica*
[7] I-II Article IV *Summa Theologica* quoting Book III V *Consolation of Philosophy*

What are angels?

In Book III chapter 79 of *Summa Contra Gentiles*, St Thomas tells us that, 'Angels mean messengers and ministers. Their function it is to execute the plan of divine providence, even in earthly things: who maketh his angels spirits; his ministers a flaming fire'

And in Book II Chapter XI of *Commentary on the Sentences*, he also tells us,

> 'Gods universal providence works through secondary causes. All things are cared for, but especially rational beings, for they, born to possess divine goodness, operate from will, a principle higher than instinct or unconscious impulse. The world of pure spirits stretches between the divine nature and the world of human beings; because divine wisdom has ordained that the higher should look after the lower, angels execute the divine plan for human salvation; they are guardians, who free us when hindered and help to bring us home.'

Only God can act directly on our will and choice. But angels, messengers of God and immaterial beings, can influence our deliberation by intellectual persuasion. The stars can operate indirectly by their impressions thus influencing us towards taking certain choices. But stars can only influence us as far as they act on our bodies, by their influence we are aroused to act in the manner of weighing things up and considering reasons for doing things.

Our Guardian Angel can sometimes 'illume our mind' so we understand that something is good and we also understand the reason why. We know its relation to an end and because of this we know the end too. Therefore if we attain this end, it is not intentional but nor is it fortuitous. But, as St Thomas points out, a Guardian Angel can also illume our mind and we can just know something is worth doing but we do not know why. If asked why we acted that way we'd say we just simply didn't know. We can therefore attain an end that is unforeseen by us. Because of this unforeseen, unintentional quality our attaining of that end would be considered fortuitous.

Fate

St Thomas tells us that, 'Fate is the ordering of second causes to effects foreseen by God. Whatever therefore is subject to second causes is subject also to fate. But whatever is done immediately by God is not subject to second causes, nor is it subject to fate: e.g., creation, the glorification of spiritual substances, and the like. And this is what Boethius says, viz., that that *those things which are near God have a state of immobility, and exceed the changeable order of fate. Hence it is clear that the farther a thing is from the First Mind, the more it is involved in the chain of fate*, since so much the more it is bound up with second causes.'

Fate takes place in time, as do secondary causes. We may be in time but God is not in time; he is in eternity, he is outside of time. This is important to remember when talking of things being 'foreseen' by God. Regarding the difference between us in time and God outside of it St Thomas gives a useful analogy:

> 'In appreciating what happens in time, we should remark that a mind bound up in it is differently placed from a mind entirely outside its series. When many are travelling the same road, each of the company knows those ahead and those behind, he sees his immediate companion, he has seen those who have gone ahead, but those well behind he cannot. But he who is not part of the throng but watches from high above is in a position to take in the whole convoy. He is able to see simultaneously all who are on the march, not as met before and after, but as all together in their order.
>
> 'Because our knowledge is enclosed in the order of time, either directly or indirectly, the time-factor enters into our calculations, and our knowledge reckons things as past, present, or future. Past, in memory: present, in experience; future, by anticipation in present causes. Future events are either certainties, when they are wholly predetermined in their causes or conjectures, when they can usually be forecast, or unknown, when their causes are not yet committed to action. God however, is entirely above the order of time. He is at the peak of eternity, surmounting everything all at once. Thence the stream of time can be seen in one simple glance.'[8]

We may live in time, but we do not live in a universe that is pure chance or pure necessity. If it were a universe of pure chance there would be no order. If it were a universe of pure necessity everything would be fixed and determined. Fate is often understood to mean all is determined by necessity; everything coming to pass due to the necessary movement of the stars and planets. But as we have seen, not all can be due to this. Fate is not the primary cause. It belongs to secondary causes. The mistake the astrologer and indeed their client often make when looking at an astrological chart is to think they are looking at primary causes when in fact they are looking at secondary causes.

So there is fate in the sense that all causes come within providence, but not fate in the sense of everything being ruled by deterministic necessity. As St Thomas says, 'The effect of divine providence is not only that things should happen *somehow*; but that they should happen either by necessity or by contingency.'[9] Providence includes necessity as natural things are directed to their ends and it also includes contingency since secondary causes can fail.

After Philosophia has explained fate and providence to Boethius he is left wondering if chance and accidental things can still exist.

Philosophia points him towards Aristotle for the answer,

> 'My Aristotle's definition in his Physics', she said 'is succinct and close to the truth'.

'In what way?' Boethius asks.

[8] St Thomas Aquinas, *Commentary on Aristotle's Peri Hermeneias* Lect. 14
[9] St Thomas Aquinas *Summa Theologica* I Q 22 art 4

Philosophia explains,

'Whenever something is done for some purpose, and for certain reasons something other than what was intended happens, it is called chance. For example, if someone began to dig the ground in order to cultivate a field and found a cache of buried gold. This is believed to have happened fortuitously, but it does not happen as a result of nothing; it has its own causes, the unforeseen and unexpected conjunction of which have clearly effected the chance event. If the cultivator of the field had not been digging, and if the depositor had not buried his money at that point, the gold would not have been found. These, therefore, are the causes of the fortuitous harvest. It is the result of the conjunction of opposite causes and not of the intention of the doers. Neither the man who buried the gold, nor the man who was tilling the field intended the discovery of the money, but, as I said, it happens as a result of the coincidence that the one began to dig where the other had buried. We may therefore define chance as an unexpected event due to the conjunction of its causes with action which is done for some purpose. The conjunction and coincidence of the causes is effected by the order which proceeds by the inescapable nexus of causation descending from the fount of Providence and ordering all things in their own time and place.'

After addressing the theory behind Fortune, Chance and Fate we can now proceed with the old argument on how Fortuna should be calculated in an astrological chart.

II. CALCULATION OF FORTUNA – THE OLD ARGUMENT

Fortuna is calculated by taking the anti-clockwise distance from the Sun to the Moon and projecting this from the Ascendant. It is usually written in textbooks as Asc + Moon – Sun. The old argument I referred to is the idea of reversing the order of the Moon and Sun in Fortuna by night. The problem with this is the hidden assumption that the Moon and Sun are somehow equal. One simply the ruler of the night and the other the ruler of the day and their order in Fortuna therefore dictated by whether it is a night time or daytime chart we are looking at. And yet the Moon is the Moon and the Sun is the Sun – one may be the light of the day and the other of the night but this does not make them equal or in any way equivalent, which is what they would have to be in order to justify reversing their position by night. This is illogical and an equivocation.

Instead, if we simply revolve a chart to the point where the Sun's degree is on the Ascendant, the Moons position will then coincide with the geocentric house position of Fortuna. Simply: If we put the Sun's degree on the Ascendant the Moon's position will be Fortuna, if we put the Moon's degree on the Ascendant then the Sun's position will coincide with the Part of Spirit.

In these matters, the fact that the Moon shines only by the light of the Sun, is a reflection worth pondering.

Fortuna as the Part of the Moon

As the medieval astrologer Abraham Ibn Ezra tells us in *The Book of Reasons*, Fortuna was also known as the part of the Moon, 'Which is taken, both by day and by night, from the distance between the Sun and the Moon and added to the Ascendant. This is in order to extract a degree for the Moon as if she is rising, because the ascendant is of the Sun and in his nature.'

Ibn Ezra also calls it the Lot of Good Fortune, 'as the relation between the rising sign and the Sun so is the relation between the Lot of Good Fortune and the Moon'. He quotes Masha'allah saying that, 'the Lot of Mystery[10] by night is stronger that the Lot of Good Fortune (thus going back to Ptolemy's opinion without noticing it) because if we reverse the order by night – the lot of spirit becomes the daytime formula of Fortuna.'[11]

Ptolemy's opinion being[12], 'Take as the Lot of Fortune always the amount of the number of degrees, both by night and by day, which is the distance from the sun to the moon, and which extends to an equal distance from the horoscope in the order of the following sign, in order that, whatever relation and aspect the sun bears to the horoscope[13] the Moon also may bear to the Lot of Fortune, and that it may be as it were a lunar horoscope.'

That last phrase, 'that it may be as it were a lunar horoscope', is a secret key to the understanding of Fortuna.

That is enough about how it is calculated what on earth does it mean?

Traditional Astrological Meanings of Fortuna

In what is without a doubt the most influential book on astrology ever written, *Tetrabiblos*, Ptolemy tells us, 'What the subject's material acquisitions will be is to be gained from the so-called Lot of Fortune'. '... For when the planets which govern the lot of Fortune are in power, they make the subjects rich, particularly when they chance to have the proper testimony (aspect) of the luminaries'. Later in his book, Ptolemy also tells us that we progress the 'Lot of Fortune for matters of property'. This restates Aristotle and Aquinas's description of the goods of fortune we saw earlier.

William Lilly in *Christian Astrology* laments the ambiguousness Fortuna can display in some astrologers hands, 'I should have also showed you how to take the Part of Fortune, but that I will do in the first example, the use of the Part of Fortune being diverse, but hardly understood rightly by any author I ever met with'. He concludes later that, 'The greatest use of it, that hitherto I have either read or made of it for, is thus; That if we find it well placed in the heaven, in a good house, or in a good aspect of a benevolent planet, we

---

[10] Also called the Part of the Sun or the Part of Spirit
[11] Abraham Ibn Ezra *The Beginning of Wisdom*
[12] Ptolemy *Tetrabiblos*
[13] Ascendant

judge the Fortune or estate of the querent to be correspondent unto its strength, viz, if it be well posited or in an angle, or in those signs wherein it's fortunated, we judge the estate of the querent to be sound and firm, if (Fortuna) is otherways placed, we do the contrary.'

This is practical advice from Lilly – at certain times, and if in doubt, it is often best not to get too specific about the signification of Fortuna. In matters of one's estate – of material things – if Fortuna looks good then it is usually good and if bad, it is likely bad; sometimes this is all the precision we need.

Abraham Ibn Ezra in, *The Beginning of Wisdom,* tells us, 'The Lot of Good Fortune indicates the body, life, wealth, success, good reputation, the beginning of all action, and whatever is in the mind of the person'. In *The Book of Reasons* he states, 'The Part of Fortune is of the Moon because she signifies man's body and the bones in it.'

In *Liber Astronomiae* the medieval astrologer Bonatus goes into great detail about Fortuna:

> 'This part signifies the life, the body, and also its soul, its strength, fortune, substance, and profit., i.e., wealth and poverty, gold and silver, heaviness or lightness of things bought in the marketplace, praise and good reputation, and honours and recognition, good and evil, present and future, hidden and manifest; serves more for rich men and magnates than for others. Nevertheless, it signifies for every man according to the condition (esse) of each of those things. And if this Part and the luminaries are well disposed in nativities or revolutions, it will be notably good. This part is called the part of the moon or the ascendant of the Moon and it signifies good fortune.'

These traditional descriptions of the Part of Fortune fit the description that Aristotle and St Thomas gave of the 'goods of Fortune'.

Fortuna in a Horary and Natal chart

Fortuna in a horary chart often shows where the querent's desires lie, though the reason for these desires might remain obscure. Despite this obscurity it can still illustrate what the querent's attention is focused upon and what they dearly want in that particular situation, even if what they want is not available. In a natal chart, things are a lot more complex; though Fortuna will still tend to show what we value and what we seek, alas, even if that which we value and seek is not the best thing for us. It can still indicate what we want and in a natal chart it can often show what we will get.

To look at some practical applications of Fortuna in natal work, we turn to the natal chart of French composer Claude Debussy, a man whose star shone brightly both in his lifetime and after his death. A man, who in many ways it can be said that Fortune smiled upon, and yet with him, as with all of us, we see that Fortune's smile will not last. This should not be a cause for grief though – change and mutability are Fortuna's nature – what we must not do is put ourselves under her rule. As Philosophia told Boethius,

The Pattern of Time

'... once you have bowed your neck beneath her yoke, you ought to bear with equanimity whatever happens on Fortune's playground. If after freely choosing her as the mistress to rule your life you want to draw up a law to control her coming and going, you will be acting without any justification and your very impatience will only worsen a lot which you cannot alter.'

As will be seen by these Debussy charts although the point in the chart called Fortuna bears her name, she never acts alone, it is not some lone astro-goddess dropping largesse into the life; she is always supported by a cast of concurrent testimonies and always works in tandem with the planets; she simply plays her part in indicating both good and bad fortune.

III. NATAL FORTUNA

Claude Debussy

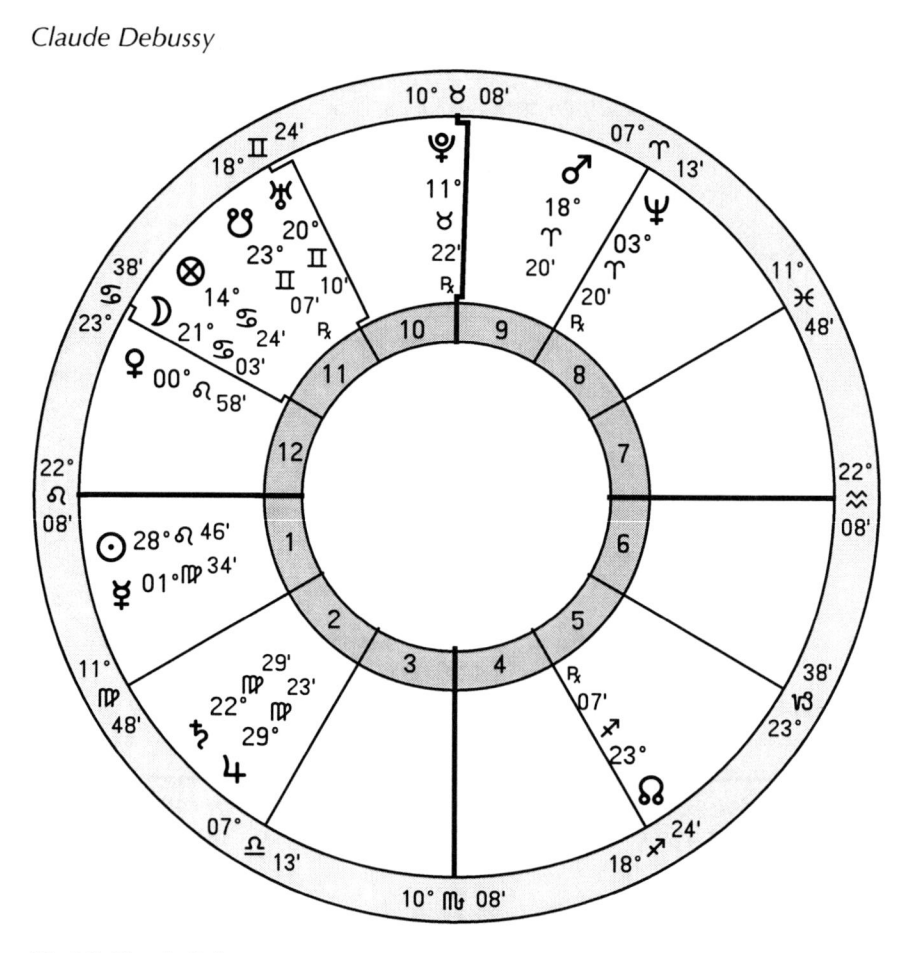

(Fig 24) Claude Debussy, 4.30 am LMT, 22 Aug 1862, St Germain en Laye, France

Debussy's temperament is very choleric. This is a man of action, a man of passion and drive. His Lord Ascendant is a very dignified Sun on a very royal star. Born at 4.30 am on 22nd August, we see the sun soon to rise at the moment of his birth thus beginning to illume and shed its dignified rays upon the world. The royal star in question is Regulus a magnitude 1 triple star, coloured white and ultramarine and located on the body of the Lion. It is connected with royalty in all its forms. Regulus is also called, Cor Leonis, the Lion's Heart and it often leads the native to the throne in whatever field they operate in. It is connected with power and honour; preferment and good fortune. And as this is material fortune we are talking about, this fortune will not last. The idea that Regulus brings fortunes that will pass away, is often overstated by astrologers, almost as if it were some kind of debility. But it is not, it is the nature of fortune; as Boethius is clearly told:

'What is it then, mortal man, that has thrown you down into the slough of grief and despondency? You must have seen something strange and unexpected. But you are wrong if you think Fortune has changed towards you. Change is her normal behaviour, her true nature. In her very act of changing she has preserved her own particular kind of constancy towards you. She was exactly the same when she was flattering you and luring you on with enticements of a false kind of happiness. You have discovered the changing faces of the random goddess. To others she still veils herself, but to you she has revealed herself to the full.'

And so too with dignified Lord Ascendant Sun on Regulus; fortune may indeed reveal herself to the full – but change is her true nature; thus even Caesar must die.

Royal Regulus often points towards pride and loftiness which brings to mind the story of how Debussy wanted to form a society to make music less accessible for the general public because he felt they were unable to fully understand it. Mercury is very strong in his chart, so too is the Moon. Oriental Mars is the rising planet and Mars is square the Moon showing that Debussy could be forceful, sharp and contentious at times. This, together with his Sun and occidental strong Mercury under the suns beams beholding the Moon by sextile, suggests he was an ingenious, arrogant, ambitious and proud man; he was also a brilliant musician.

Debussy clearly identified with his powerful Lord Ascendant but as Mercury and Mars are powerful too, they will also have their sway in his manner. He was a shrewd and thoughtful man, learned and inventive. As the interplay between his Mars, Mercury, Moon and Sun shows he was also gifted with a powerful, focused mind – in short, Debussy was very successful in attaining the ends he sought. He also had a sharp imagination and possessed power, agility and dexterity. In a review from 16th Jan 1876, when he was still only thirteen years old, we hear some of these qualities described: 'De Bussy, who carries so much courage inside such a small body. What verve! What enthusiasm! What real spirit! Never again can it be said that the piano is a cold instrument ...' 'This little budding Mosart (sic) is a veritable tearaway.'[14]

As an adult we see these qualities in full flow as the pianist, and later professor of piano at the Conservatoire, Marguerite Long reminisced, 'Debussy was an incomparable pianist. How could one forget his suppleness, the caress of his touch? While floating over the keys with a curiously penetrating gentleness, he could achieve an extraordinary power of expression.'

This 'floating over the keys' brings us to Debussy's Fortuna and to his powerfully dignified Moon – both located in the water sign of Cancer.

Debussy's Fortuna

Debussy's Fortuna is near fixed star Canopus, a white star in one of the oars of the ship the Argo. Its ruler is the Moon, conjunct fixed star Pollux. Pollux too is a powerful royal star; it is the immortal one of the twins, Castor and Pollux – it is also associated with the sea.

The ruler of Debussy's Fortuna, the Moon, is on the cusp of his 12th house exalting the ruler of the 5th house, indicative of his desire for seclusion in order to create and compose.

Debussy's natal Mercury and Venus do not behold each other. For a creative person this can cause difficulties, but his natal Fortuna is conjunct his pre birth eclipse Mercury and pre birth lunation Venus. Thus Fortuna herself powerfully brings together these two planets essential for his creative endeavours – Mercury for the skill Venus for the beauty.

Fortuna and Canopus

Canopus is a Saturn and Jupiter star. As Fortuna is close to Canopus, this star will have something to do with that which Debussy will continually seek in life. As he is a musician, and Fortuna brings together Mercury and Venus, it will also show what he seeks to express in his music. The Jupiter side of Canopus suggests him searching for expansiveness while the Saturn side can provide him with the discipline and form to give this expansiveness structure and shape. All this is filtered through his meticulous and precise mind. As E. Robert Schmitz recalled,

> 'Debussy was not a careless sensual pagan drifting wherever the wind of inspiration might blow him. He did not 'toss off' his pieces as a diamond cutter might chip off a fleck of diamond dust. He did not sit down at the piano, close his eyes, and compose a confused jumble of notes ...' (... he was) '... neat, precise, with a beautifully ordered mind and a habit of thinking clearly about everything he did.'

---

[14] This quote and all subsequent quotes regarding Debussy are from the source book *Debussy Remembered* by Roger Nichols

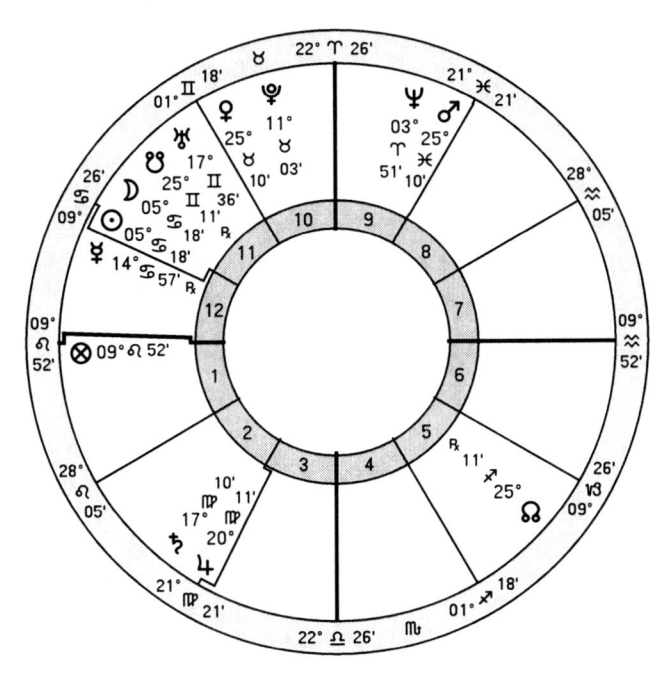

(Fig 25) Debussy's pre-birth eclipse

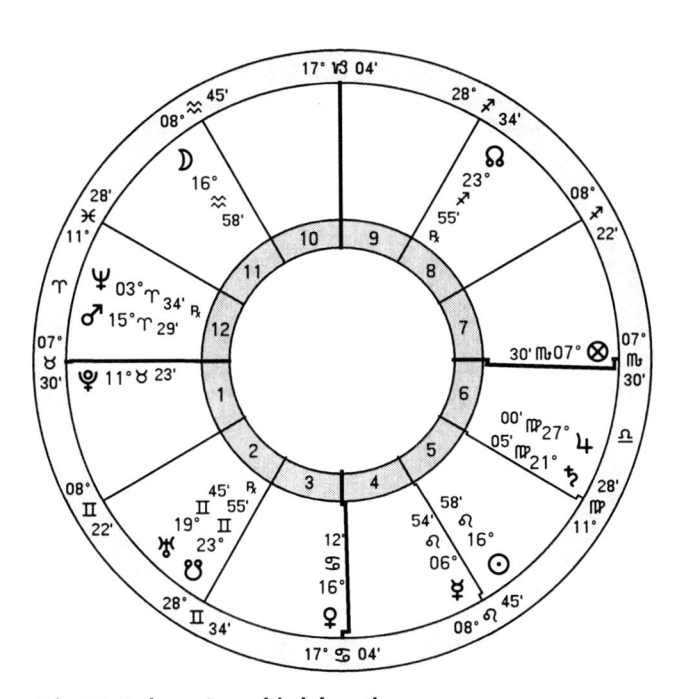

(Fig 26) Debussy's pre birth lunation

Traditionally Canopus is also said to bring the native a wide knowledge and travel. Claude Debussy was a very knowledgeable and sophisticated man and he travelled extensively, performing throughout Europe.

Canopus is situated on the oar of the ship the Argo. In Greek myth, the Argo was a ship built by Argus the Herdsman with the help of the goddess Athena. The prow of this ship was made from a piece of the sacred oak of Dodona, which Athena had cut herself. She gave it the power of speech, which it had to such a degree that it could even utter prophecies. The Argo was built for forty oarsmen and one of its crew was Orpheus, the renowned musician from Thrace.

Orpheus

Orpheus was the coxswain of the Argo, setting and maintaining the rhythm for the oarsmen. Orpheus sang while the Sirens tried to seduce the Argonauts and he restrained the Sirens with his voice, surpassing even their temptations with his sweetness and beauty. He also played the lyre and cithara, a stringed instrument, which he was said to have invented. Debussy's instrument was the piano and it too is a stringed instrument – like a harp laid upon its side, hit with tiny hammers to sound the tones. This hitting of the strings with hammers is reminiscent of Orpheus keeping the beat for the oarsmen of the Argo. Orpheus increased the number of strings of the cithara from 7 to 9 in order to match the number of the Muses thus honouring their presence and acknowledging their role in inspiring his music. Orpheus sang so sweetly that wild beasts followed him, plants and trees bowed down to him and the wildest of men became perfectly gentle.

And, as the music critic Emile Vuillermoz recalled, Debussy also had, '... a unique, unforgettable voice.'

> 'His vocal chords produced sounds that were strange, slightly veiled, articulated with a light staccato that separated the syllables, imperceptibly damped by an invisible mute.'

> 'When he moved to the piano to sing one of his works, that soft voice became cavernous and mysterious, with a variety of surprising nuances. It is the haunting quality of that voice which I chiefly remember from my first contact with the composer of Pelléas ...'

And this quality, together with Debussy's Lord 5 Jupiter in a doubled bodied voiced sign, also suggests the eloquent lyrical quality so often admired in Debussy's music.

Fixed star Canopus is forever connected with the sea and in Debussy's study he had a coloured engraving by the artist Hokusai representing the curl of a wave. Jacques Durand, Debussy's music publisher, recalled that, 'Debussy was particular enamoured of this wave. It inspired him while he was composing La Mér and he asked us to reproduce it on the cover of the printed score.'

With Venus and Mercury connected via Fortuna, his Moon so dignified and Lord Ascendant Sun in Leo, light and colour were also very important to Debussy. 'Paintings had a great attraction for him', recalled Madame Gerard De Romilly, 'he had excellent natural taste and adored beautiful things ...' And Jacques Durand tells us that, 'winter and summer', Debussy, 'worked surrounded by flowers – a symphony of colours which he used to produce music.'

The Moon, dispositer of Fortuna is conjunct royal star Pollux. Pollux is an orange star on the head of the Southern Twin. It too is a kingly star of elevation. It is the immortal one of the Twins – Among other things it traditionally gives a hatred of the vulgar – which is something Debussy definitely had. It can also show the potential for an immortal name – which is something he has too.

The IC of Debussy's chart is conjunct fixed star Alphecca promising honour, dignity and artistic and poetic ability. This is on his IC, his home, and we can see its influence in descriptions of his beautiful home. Jacques Durand again, 'His study was on the ground floor, (on the Ave Bois de Boulogne), 'with spacious bay windows which flooded it with light, and opened out on to the garden which surrounded the house. The wide table on which he used to work was cluttered with high class Japanese objects. His favourite was a porcelain toad which he called his fetish and which he took with him when he moved claiming he could not work unless it was in sight.' We are again reminded of Debussy's link with water and the saturnine toad he carried around is indicative of the Saturn/Jupiter quality of the star Canopus.

He was 'precise and pedantic to the nth degree' and his great love of precision is reflected in his music.

With his Fortuna on Canopus, Debussy's composition, *La Mér*, seems very appropriate. Fortuna is ruled by the Moon, and Debussy's, *Nocturnes*, *Claire de Lune* and *La Mér* are all reminiscent of the Moon. Debussy's pre birth eclipse Moon/Sun conjunction is in Cancer with his natal arc Fortuna falling close by. His only opera, *Pelléas*, based on the play *Pelléas et Mélisande* by Maurice Maeterlinck, also has the image of water symbolically running through it. Debussy called it dreamlike, again appropriate, as the Moon is the natural ruler of dreams and images.

Fortuna through Time

If we progress Fortuna through time we get a clearer picture of how she rises and falls.

As I said, Fortuna rarely works alone. When the desires of Fortuna are wrapped up in the career as they were with Debussy, it can also be helpful to look at the Part of Vocation. This is the same relationship between the Sun and the Moon as in Fortuna, but it is projected from the Midheaven rather than the

The Pattern of Time

Ascendant, thus showing the drives and desires of the native in regard to their career. It illustrates the desire for action, what they feel called to do.

The Beginnings of Debussy's Career

In October 1872 Debussy entered the Paris Conservatoire to study Solfege with Albert Lavignac and piano with Antoine Marmontel. At his piano examination at the conservatoire 13th Jan 1874 we have the recorded comments of his teacher Marmontel, '… charming child, true temperament of an artist, will become a distinguished musician; a great future.'

The lunar return for this period shows the return Lord Ascendant and natal arc Part of Vocation[15] dispositer Mars conjunct natal arc Fortuna, a clear

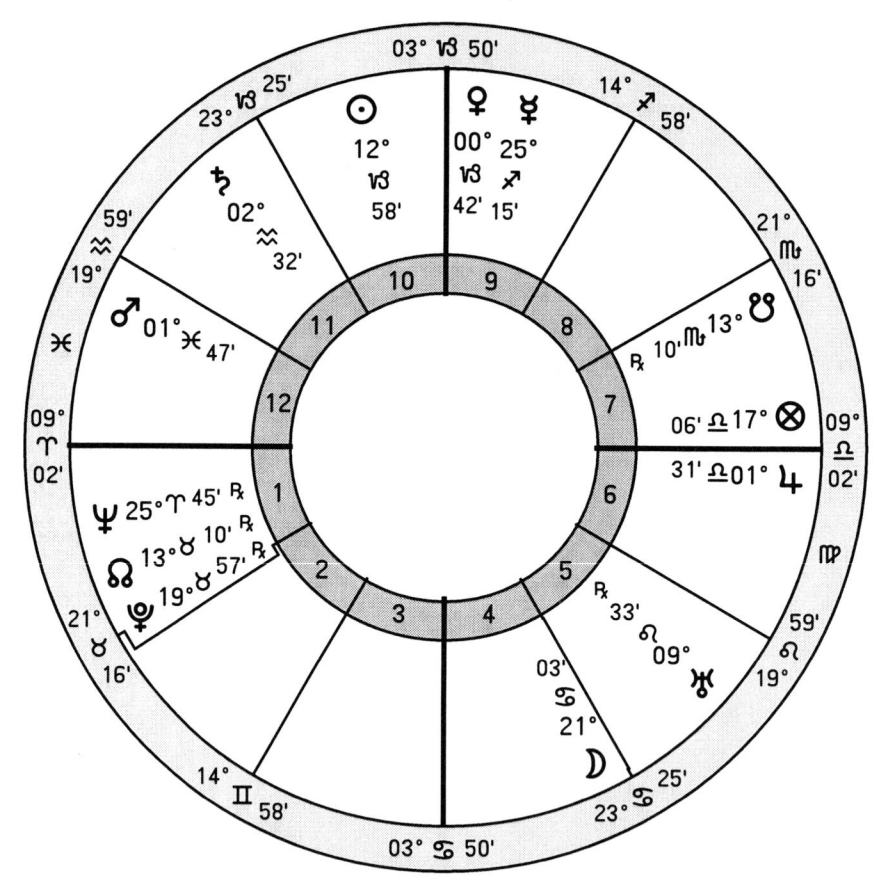

(Fig 27) Debussy's Lunar Return 3 Jan 1874

[15] A natal arc part is an Arabian part derived from the natal position of the planets but projected from the relevant cusp of a return or eclipse chart. Please see chapter 1, *The Divine Michelangelo* for more details on this technique.

82

picture of him, his vocation and his fortune coming together at this time. The return 5th house is conjunct his dignified Moon who exalts his natal Lord 5, thus showing the eloquent music of his natal 5th house judiciously flowing through his piano playing at this time.

In July 1880 he won first prize in practical harmony at the Conservatoire. Also that year, Nadezhda von Meck, the widow of a contractor for the Russian railway, hired Debussy as a pianist and he travelled with her to Switzerland and Italy. Mme von Meck was a great patroness and friend of Tchaikovsky and in a letter to him she spoke of her hiring the young Debussy,

> 'The day before yesterday there arrived from Paris a young pianist who had just won first prize in Marmontel's class at the conservatoire. I've engaged him for the summer, to give lessons to the children, to accompany Julia's singing and to play piano duets with me. The young man plays well, his technique is brilliant, but he's lacking in sensibility. He's still too young. He says he's twenty, but looks sixteen.'

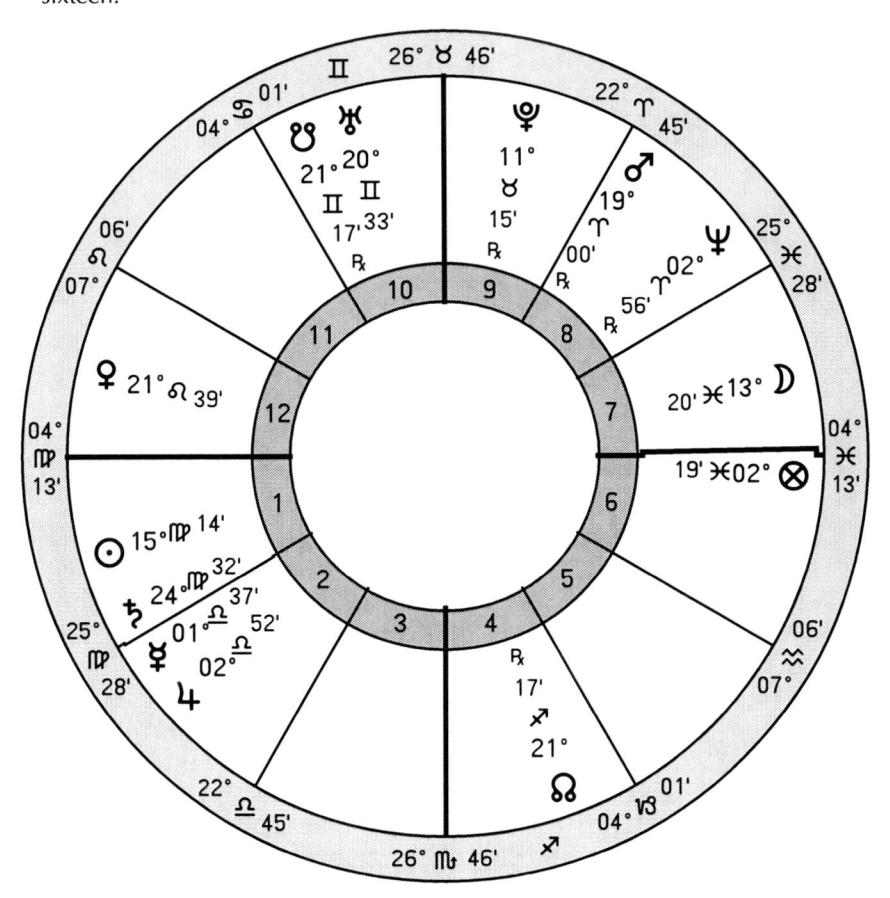

(Fig 28) Secondary Progressions 22 Aug 1879

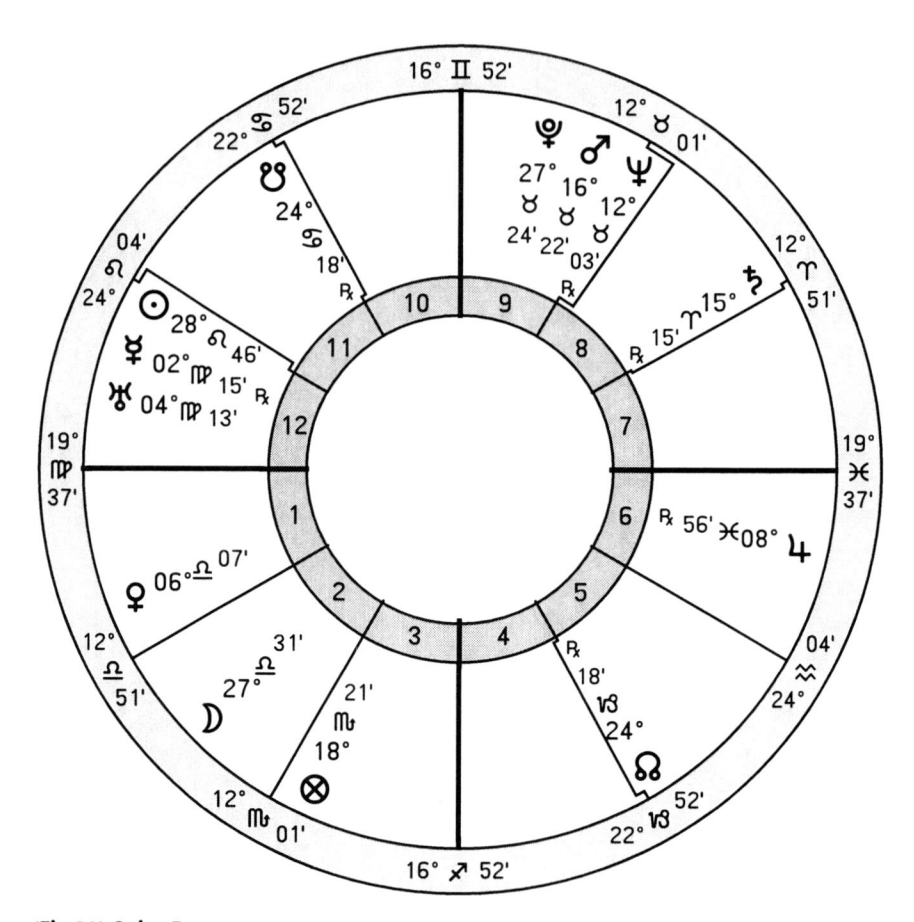

(Fig 29) Solar Return 1879

In the 1879–80 Progressions, (Fig 28), Debussy's progressed Moon trines his natal Fortuna suggesting the possibility of preferment. The solar return, (Fig 29), shows the return Mercury retrograding close to dignified natal Mercury and the cusp of the solar return 9th house, his artistry and house of Long Journeys is conjunct the cusp of his natal 10th house, his career, thus connecting his career with travel at this time.

The day he arrived at the house of Mme von Meck coincided with a lunar return, (Fig 30), in which the Ascendant is conjunct the cusp of his natal 10th house, his career. The return Lord Ascendant Venus is conjunct natal Fortuna and lunar return Fortuna is close to his natal 10th house cusp. Also, the lunar return nodes are conjunct the antiscia of the natal nodes, all these testimonies mark this out to have been a significant time in the early development of his career.

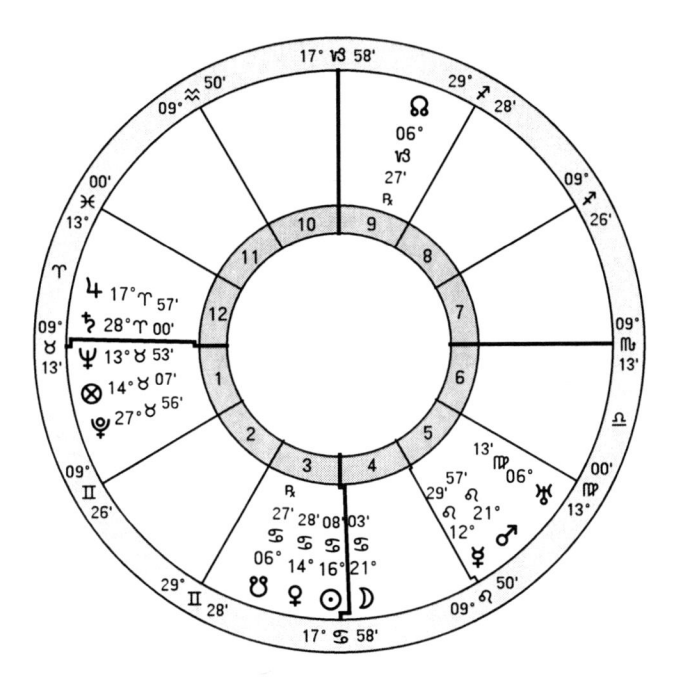

(Fig 30) **Lunar Return 8 Jul 1880**

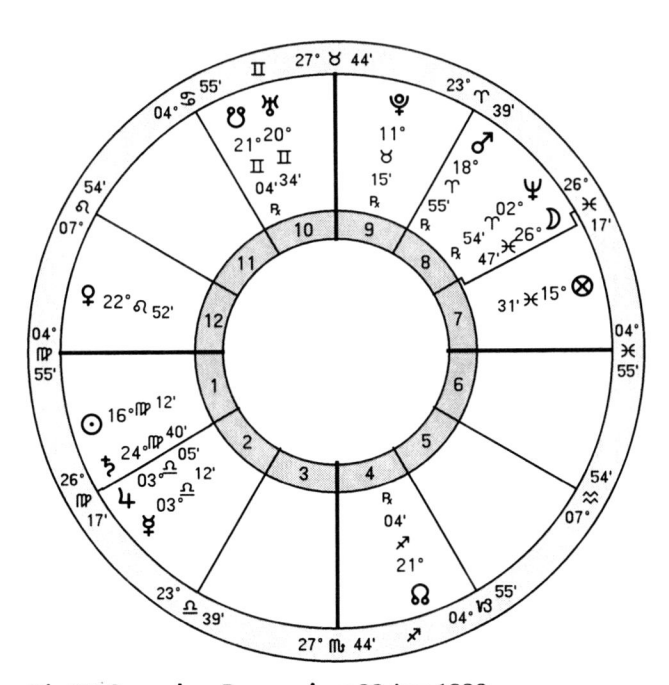

(Fig 31) **Secondary Progressions 22 Aug 1880**

The Pattern of Time

In December he entered Guiraud's composition class. Progressed Fortuna, August 1880–1881, (Fig 31), trines his very dignified natal Moon and later opposes natal Jupiter and Saturn. This suggests the release of some of the bounty of his dignified natal Moon with the oppositions to Jupiter and Saturn showing the struggle to find his own compositional voice. Progressed Moon opposes natal Lord 5 Jupiter, his piano playing, again showing struggles for expression. But it changes sign by progression and trines natal Venus suggesting the aesthetic resolution of this struggle. In May 1882 Debussy played his own music for first time in public and in July 1882 he won the certificate for counterpoint and fugue. In August 1882 he returned to Mme von Meck in Russia and then travelled to Vienna. The fruition of his search for his compositional voice are seen in the first versions of, *En Sourdine*, *Clair de Lune* and *Mandoline* that are from this time and Debussy's first work was also published. In June 1883 Debussy won the 2nd prize at the Prix de Rome. In the progressions for that year, (Fig 32), we see progressed Moon, natal ruler of Fortuna, trine the natal Sun on Regulus. Progressed Fortuna conjuncts natal Mars, Lord 9 his travels, and then squares his natal Moon.

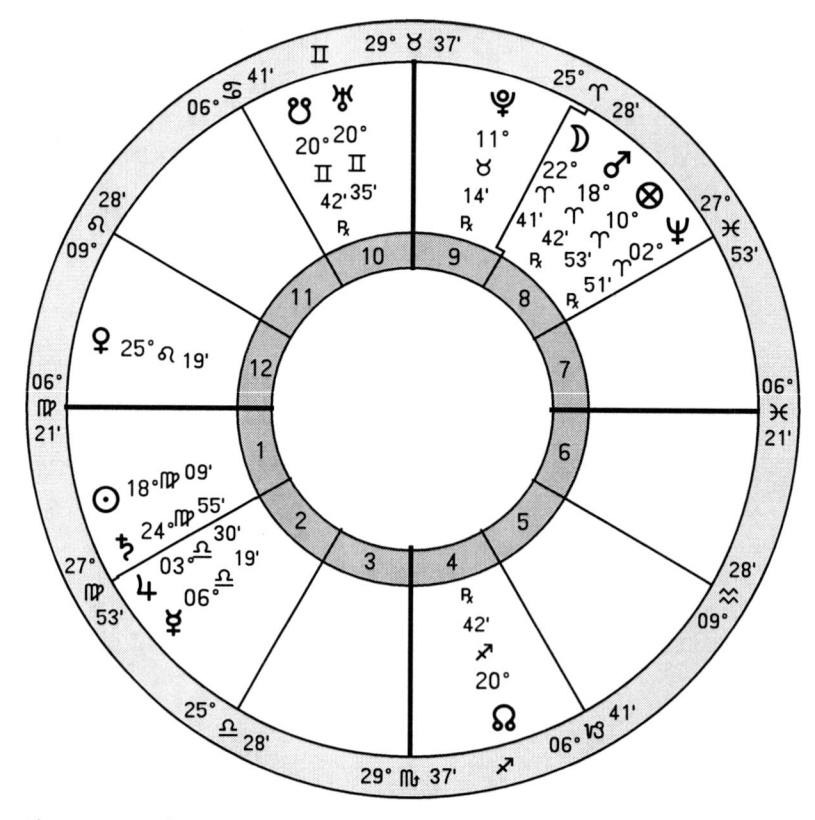

(Fig 32) Secondary Progressions 22 Aug 1882

Fate, Freewill, Fortuna and the Soul

Over this period Debussy's MC, indicative of his status and career, conjuncts fixed star Alcyone. Usually this is a negative testimony but as William Lilly says, 'it also portends in some genitures sudden preferment'. Alcyone was one of the weeping sisters; the daughters of Atlas who wept at the burden placed upon their father – that he should bear the weight of the sky upon his shoulders. It is the brightest star in the Pleiades – it is associated with water via the tears of the sisters and the associations of the Pleiades with the biblical flood. We also have the progressed Midheaven square natal Sun on Regulus, while the progressed Moon trines the Sun on Regulus both adding to testimonies that spell preferment for him.

First Prize at the Prix de Rome

From the 24 May to the 18th June 1884 Debussy was in the final of the Prix de Rome. He won first prize with a setting of *L' Enfant Prodigue*. The progressions

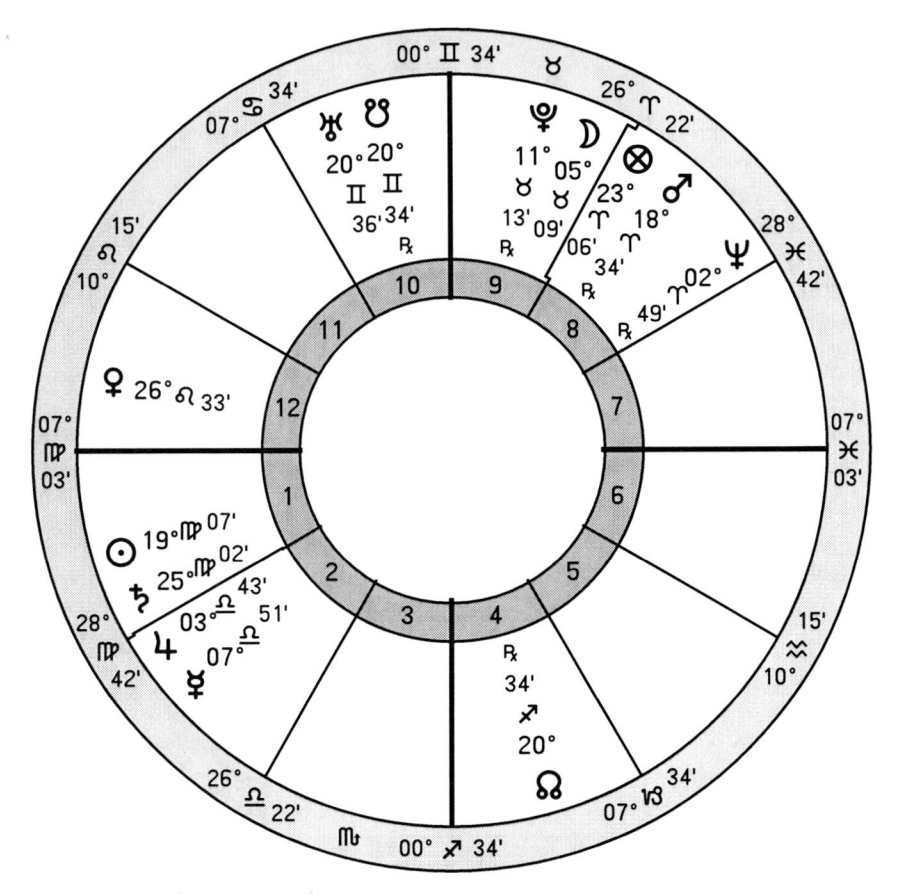

(Fig 33) Secondary Progressions 22 Aug 1883

for that year, (Fig 33), show a new sign upon the Midheaven; indicative of new beginnings in his career. The progressed Midheaven has now entered Gemini and its ruler Mercury is very dignified in the natal chart. To add to this, progressed Fortuna also trines the natal Sun on Regulus. This all suggests that the new beginnings indicated for his career are potentially very positive. Again, signs of preferment were clearly in the air for him.

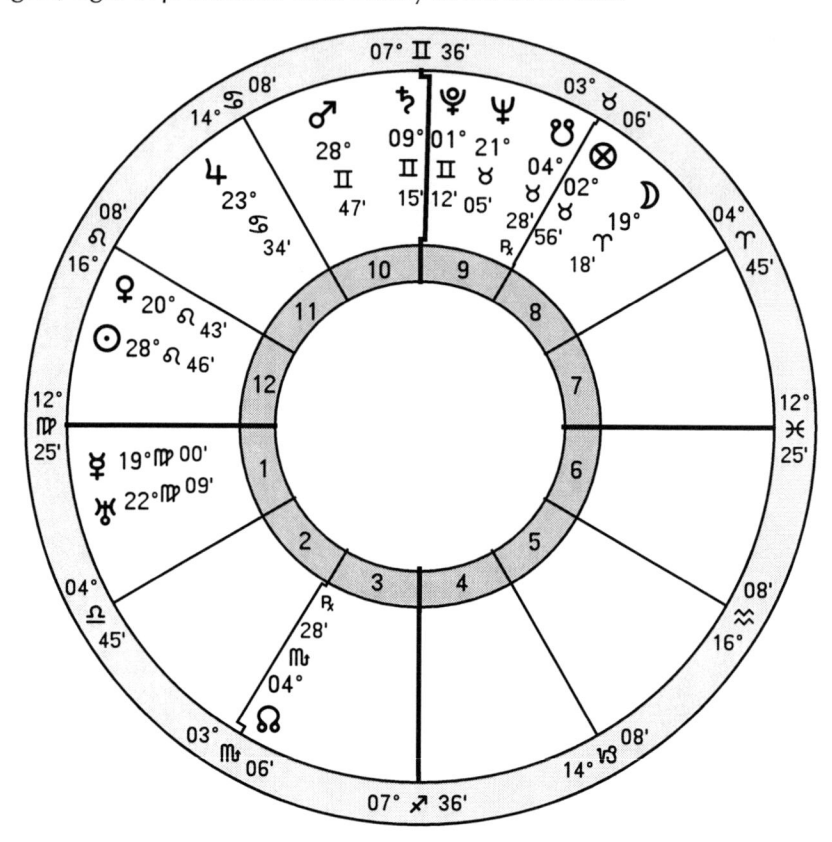

(Fig 34) Solar Return 1883

The solar return Lord 5 Saturn, his piano playing and composition, is conjunct powerful fixed star Aldebaran conjunct the return MC, again indicating a new phase in his career, (Fig 34). The solar return nodes highlight the 9th house 3rd house axis, his artistry and its expression, and the 9/3 axis is conjunct the pre birth lunation Ascendant/Descendant axis marking this time as significant. Fortuna is near the 9th, suggesting him searching for development in his art. Solar return natal arc Fortuna is close to pre birth eclipse Ascendant. Its ruler is the Sun on Regulus and natal Lord 5 Jupiter is exalted in the return, close to his natal Moon, this indicates that the fruits of his potential are truly coming to ripen.

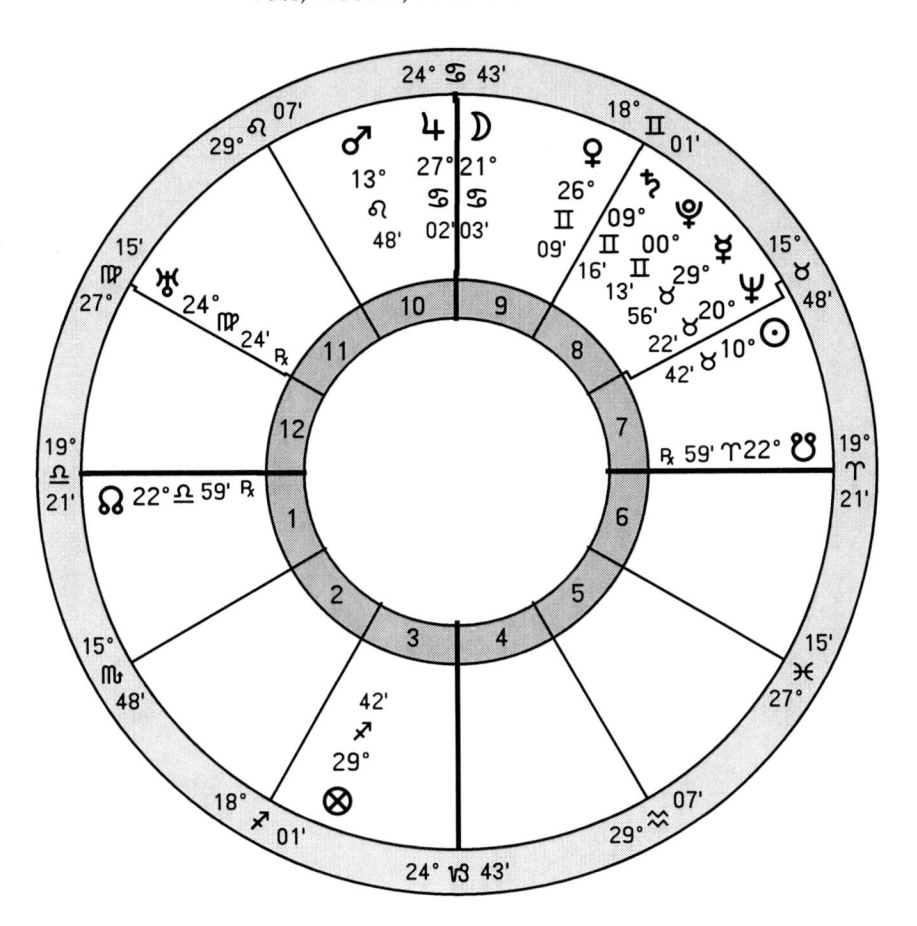

(Fig 35) Lunar Return 30 April 1884

The first lunar return for this period is the lunar return of 30th April, (Fig 35). The return MC is close to natal Moon and with return exalted Jupiter inside 10th, we have a nice 10th house clearly promising the potential for honours. Return 9th house, indicative of his artistry at this time, is conjunct natal arc Part of Vocation and return Lord 5 is conjunct Aldebaran, again showing a new stage in his playing. Return Mercury is conjunct Alcyone, conjunct antiscion of natal Venus and about to gain serious dignity – he was about to come into his own. It is also the dispositer of natal arc Fortuna and natal Part of Vocation thus showing him achieving his career aspirations. The return Fortuna is conjunct pre birth lunation 9th house cusp. And the 3rd house cusp of the return is conjunct the natal 5th cusp; thus again we see his art brought to fruition, expressed and manifested on earth. The return Ascendant is conjunct natal pre birth eclipse IC, therefore echoing the solar return.

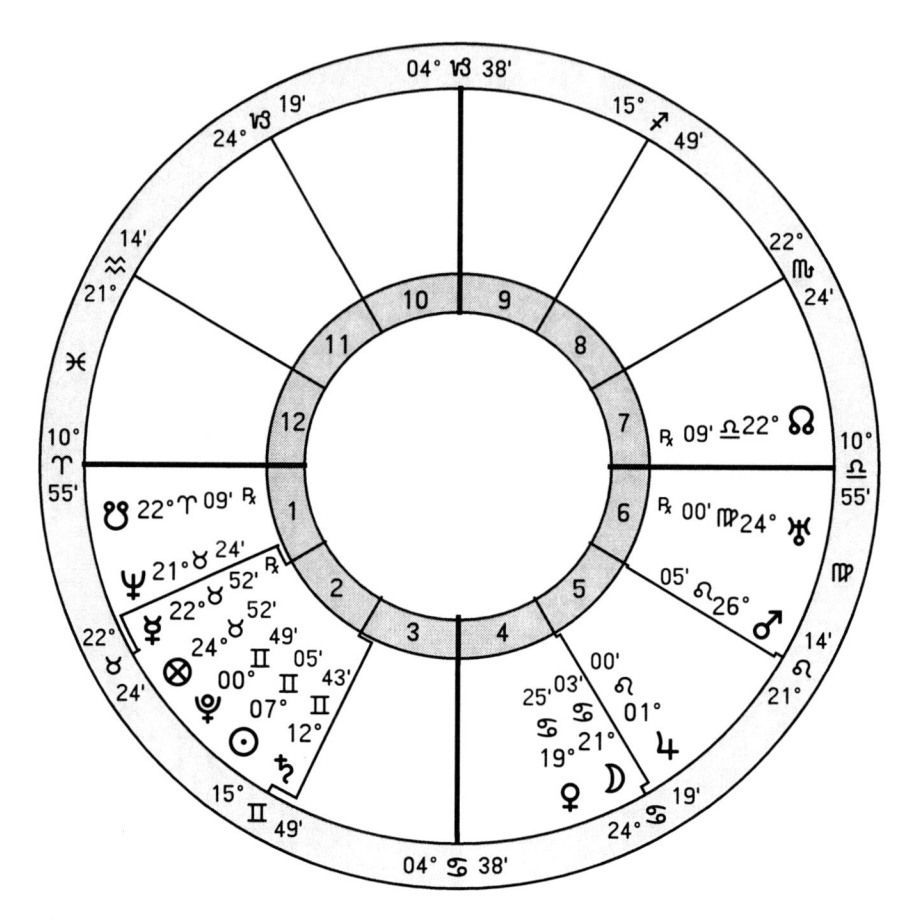

(Fig 36) Lunar Return 28 May 1884

The second lunar return for this period is the 28th May, (Fig 36). In this, return Fortuna is conjunct return Mercury and the pre birth eclipse dignified Venus. Return IC is conjunct the pre birth eclipse. Return Fortuna is also conjunct fixed star Caput Algol, which as William Lilly says, in certain cases rather than the typical calamity of losing one's head that is associated with this star it can instead give the 'power of the sword over others', as it evidentially did here. Return Venus is close to natal Moon and conjunct IC of pre birth lunation. A nice return 5th house cusp falls conjunct his very dignified Moon restating the 10th house testimony of previous lunar return, his career aspirations are being expressed through his 5th house compositions and playing. The return Jupiter, dispositor of natal arc Fortuna, is conjunct natal Venus, and the dispositor of natal arc Part of Vocation is Mars, close to natal Sun conjunct Regulus inside the 2nd from 5th thus highlighting the profit from his playing. The return MC is conjunct the antiscion of the natal North Node again suggesting increase and gain in his career and reputation.

New Beginnings in His Career

Debussy's progressed MC passed over fixed star Aldebaran around 1891–92. Aldebaran is suggestive of new cycles and from the new beginnings indicated by the initial progression into Gemini and the winning of the Prix de Rome this is now marked as a major new period in his career. In January 1892 he began, *Prélude interlude et paraphrase finale pour l'après-midi d'un faune.*

In 1892–93 Debussy's progressed Moon conjuncts his natal Sun conjunct Regulus showing he had reached a milestone in his life. August 93–94 Progressed Fortuna followed suit and conjuncts natal Sun on Regulus. In May 1893 Debussy saw Maeterlinck's *Pelléas et Mélisande* and began to set it to music. This really was a new beginning and with the performance of *Preludes après midi d'un faune* in Dec '94 he became known to a wider audience.

Prélude à l'après-midi d'un faune

Debussy's *Prélude à l'après-midi d'un faune* (prelude to the afternoon of a faun) brought him a lot of attention. Later choreographed by Nijinsky for the Ballet Russes, the Debussy score was inspired by the poem *L'après midi d'un faune* by Mallarmé. Again we see Debussy's constant drive towards the

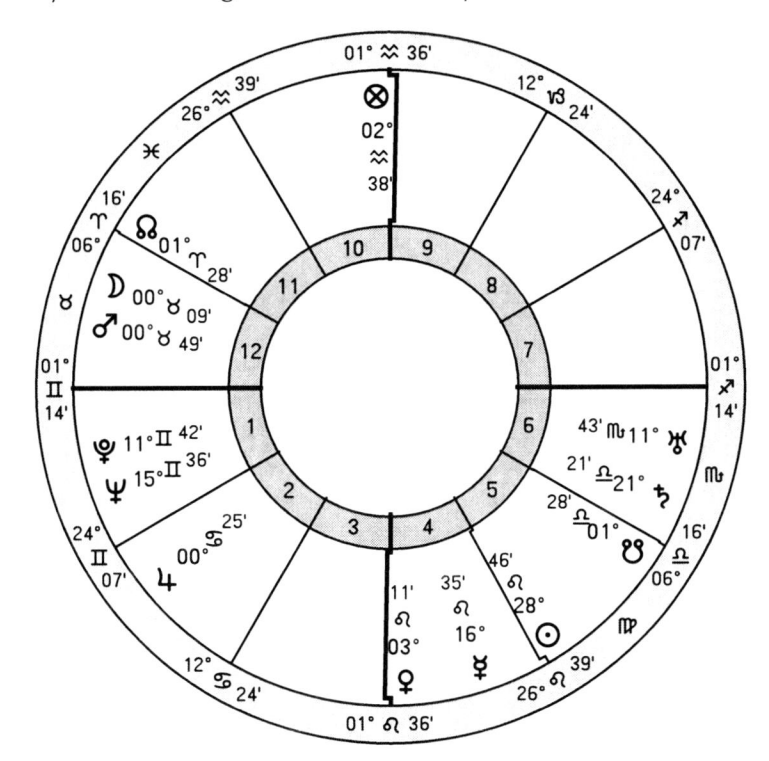

(Fig 37) Solar Return 1894

watery symbolism of his Fortuna. The faune is living in the woods near a river surrounded by marshes. He daydreams about nymphs, and his desires and daydreams weave together and pass back into the unconscious. This fits Debussy's Moon ruled Fortuna perfectly – Moon being natural ruler of images, dreams and water, and Fortuna pointing towards ones deep desires.

Debussy became far better known through this piece of music. It brought him to greater prominence and won him a much wider audience. This is seen in the Solar Return of that year, (Fig 37), where the solar return Sun, itself natal Lord Ascendant, is inside the return 5th. An exalted return Moon is conjunct Mars in the seclusion of the 12th. And Jupiter, natal Lord 5, his creations, has just recently entered its exaltation; Jupiter is also ruler of natal arc Part of Vocation, signifying his career, and natal arc Fortuna is also conjunct the pre birth eclipse MC.

In December 1897 he began a final version of *Nocturnes* and that year Fortuna progressed onto benefic fixed star Spica, (Fig 38). The solar return shows Venus in Cancer placed between natal Fortuna and the Moon. The progressed Fortuna plugs Debussy into the power source of his pre birth eclipse, and brings the power of the eclipse into manifestation as the pre birth eclipse IC is also conjunct benefic Spica thus helping to bring this potential into manifestation.

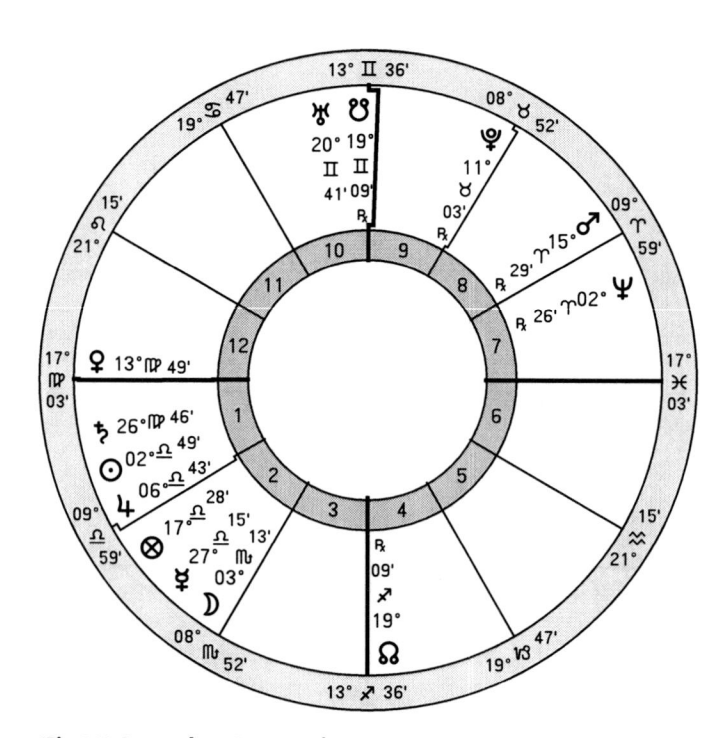

(Fig 38) Secondary Progressions 1897

Fate, Freewill, Fortuna and the Soul

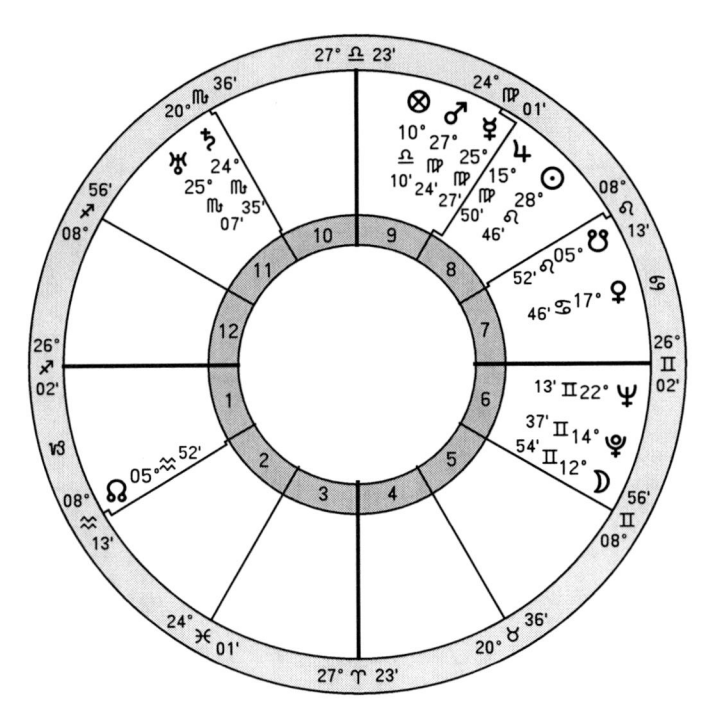

(Fig 39) Solar Return 1897

Prosecuted for Debts

As Fortuna's wheel can rise, so can it fall, and in June 1898 Debussy was prosecuted for debts. In the solar return, (Fig 39), natal Lord 2 Mercury, his finances, is very dignified. But it is heading to conjunct Mars suggesting strife and disagreements. This all happens between natal Jupiter, suggestive of overspending and indulgence, and natal Saturn natural ruler of restriction and debts. Progressed Fortuna opposes natal Mars and then squares natal Moon, showing the waste and loss of his finances with wrangling and contentions over such things. His 2nd house has also been progressing over fixed star Vindemiatrix, which is traditionally suggestive of presumption, overstretching and even wanton folly. The solar return Fortuna is in the vicinity of Vindemiatrix too. Maybe he had been overstretching himself financially, or maybe he was simply being daft with his money due to his love of fine things. As his friend the singer Mary Garden said, 'He also loved the secret and sumptuous and luxurious things. In his craving for things he had the most extravagant brain I have ever known. But he could never do what he wanted because he hadn't the money. He had a deep longing for costly things which he could never satisfy ...'

He Marries Lily

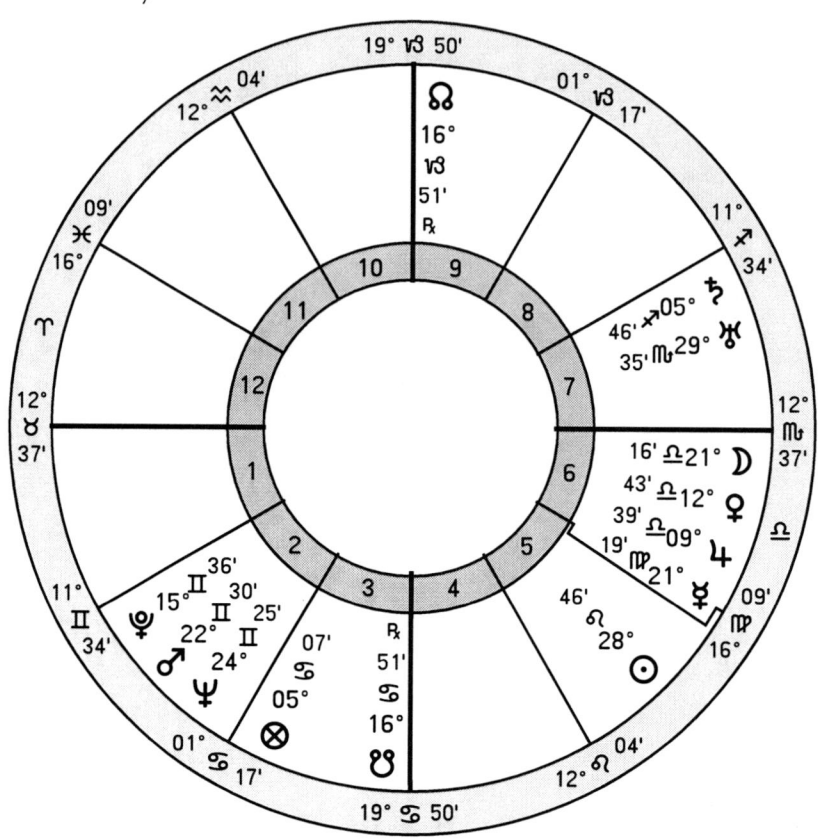

(Fig 40) Solar Return 1898

In the solar return for August 1898 the return Moon trines return Lord 7 Mars. The return Moon and Lord 7 also trines the natal 7th cusp and the return 7th cusp falls on the natal IC. This is suggestive of Debussy thinking about setting up a home with someone significant. In October 1899 Debussy married Lily Texier. Lily was frequently described as pale and beautiful, dear sweet and simple. As Mary Garden said, 'She took care of him like a child. They had worries debts and disappointments but nobody ever got into that little apartment on rue Cardinet to interrupt Debussy at his music, Lily kept the world away so her beloved Claude could work …' This clearly brings to mind Debussy's dignified maternal Moon on the cusp of the 12th house desiring the seclusion of the 12th house while exalting the ruler of his 5th house – his creations, the things he makes. In later years Debussy was unhappy with regret and in a letter to Messager, Mary Garden recalled him saying, 'Oh how I wish I could recapture the happiness of Pelléas et Mélisande! But it is hopeless that joy has vanished forever.'

Fate, Freewill, Fortuna and the Soul

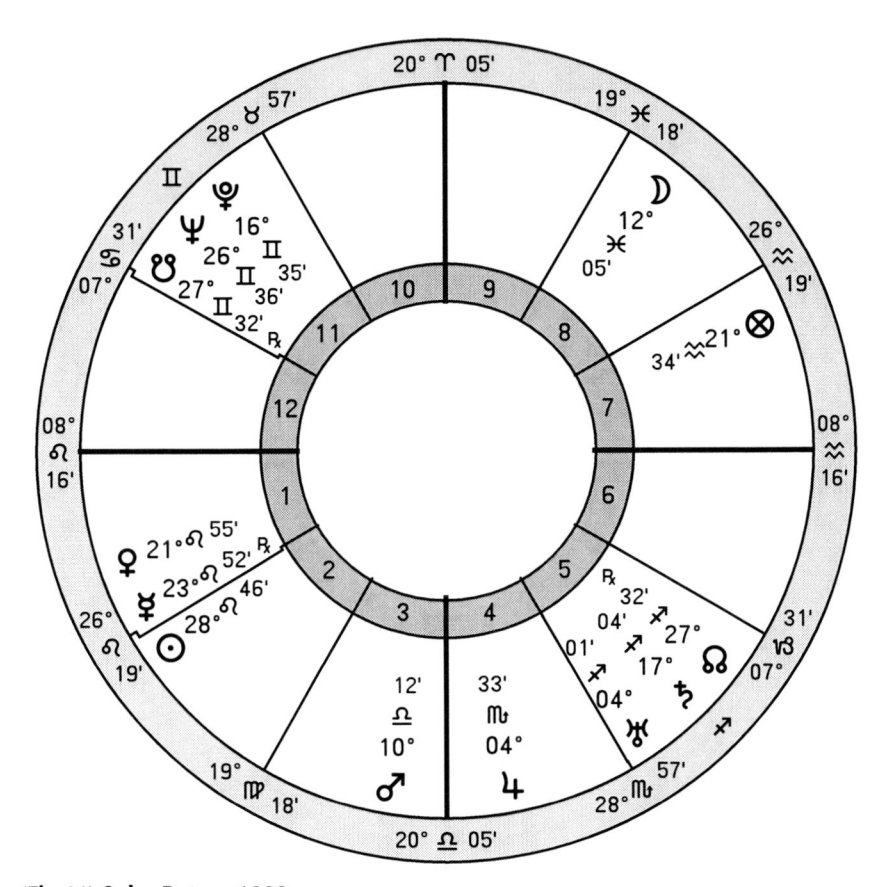

(Fig 41) Solar Return 1899

In the 1899 solar return, the Ascendant/Descendant angles match the pre birth eclipse Ascendant/Descendant. Return Moon is square Saturn, natal Lord 7 and return Lord 7. The return Fortuna is conjunct natal 7th house and return and natal Lord 7, Saturn, is conjunct the natal 5th cusp; he was looking for love, someone to settle down and have children with. And as return Venus Mercury conjunction falls on the natal Ascendant; as well as being in love, he was busy composing his *Nocturnes*.

Appointed Chevalier of the Legion of Honour

In February 1903 Debussy was appointed Chevalier of the Legion of Honour. In the August 1902–03 progressions, (Fig 42), the progressed Sun trines natal Sun conjunct Regulus and thus leads him to the throne. The progressed North Node is conjunct the 5th house cusp suggesting gain via his creations. Progressed Moon quickly opposes Fortuna, squares Mars and opposes natal Moon suggestive of tension within his art. Progressed MC will sextile

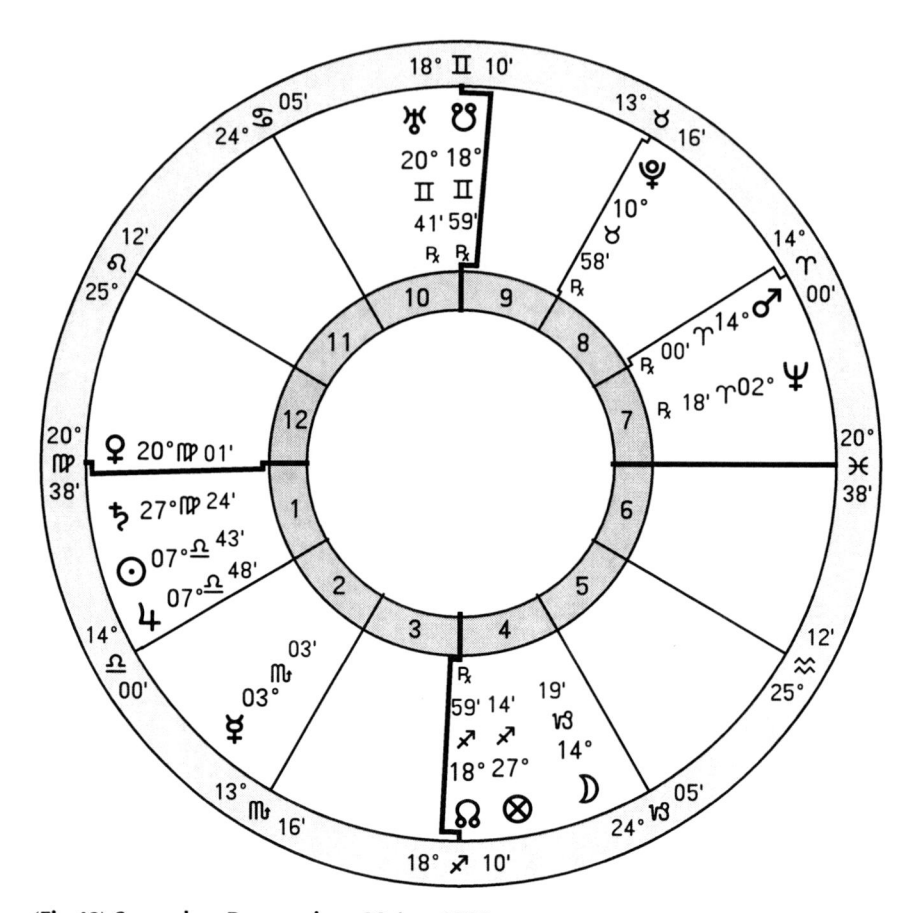

(Fig 42) Secondary Progressions 22 Aug 1902

very dignified natal Mars, natal Lord 9 his art, thus connecting his artistry and his status. His progressed Ascendant falls on the pre-birth eclipse Jupiter, dispositer of eclipse, plugging him into the potentials of the power source that is the eclipse before birth.

Echoing the progressions, in Debussy's solar return August 1902–03, (Fig 43), the Ascendant Descendant axis falls on the pre birth eclipse Midheaven/IC – the 'status potential' of the eclipse is connected and manifested through him, through the physical bodily quality of the Ascendant. Return 9th house cusp is conjunct natal 5th cusp bringing together his artistry and its expression through his 5th house compositions. Natal arc Part of Vocation is conjunct the 5th house cusp of the pre-birth eclipse, showing his desire to plug into the creative potential of the zeitgeist to capture the spirit of the times he was born into. And the fruition of this expression of his 5th house of creativity is shown by the cusp of the return 2nd house from 5th, falling upon his natal Sun on Regulus; very suggestive of the honour he would receive.

Fate, Freewill, Fortuna and the Soul

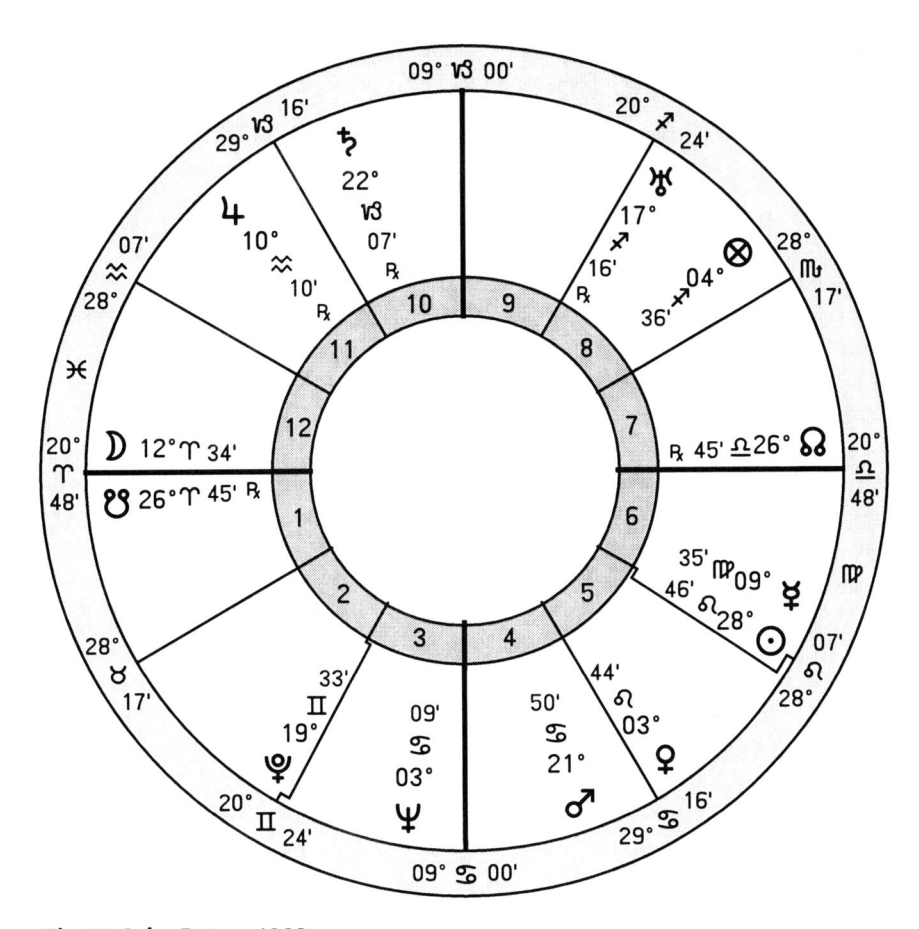

(Fig 43) Solar Return 1902

The lunar returns all echo the progressions and solar return.

In the derived[16] lunar return 6 Jan 1903, (Fig 44), the Ascendant is conjunct Debussy's dignified natal Moon. The 2nd house, is in context that which supports him, his reputation and also his money. Its cusp is conjunct the pre birth eclipse Fortuna and Ascendant. The derived lunar return IC is conjunct natal Lord 5 Jupiter, his creations. Fortuna is close to IC of pre birth eclipse. Derived lunar return Venus and Mercury, twin tools of the creative, are conjunct derived lunar return Saturn, other people, in the return 7th in earth sign Capricorn, thus cementing his reputation in the eyes of the people. Also the derived lunar return Jupiter is the derived lunar return Lord 10. It is conjunct natal arc Part of

---

[16] A derived lunar return is a lunar return set from the solar return of that year. Hence it is derived from the solar return rather than the natal chart. It can often highlight and clarify things that are shown in the solar and regular lunar returns. However it is not in any way a stand-alone chart and it must always be read in light of the natal chart, progressions and returns.

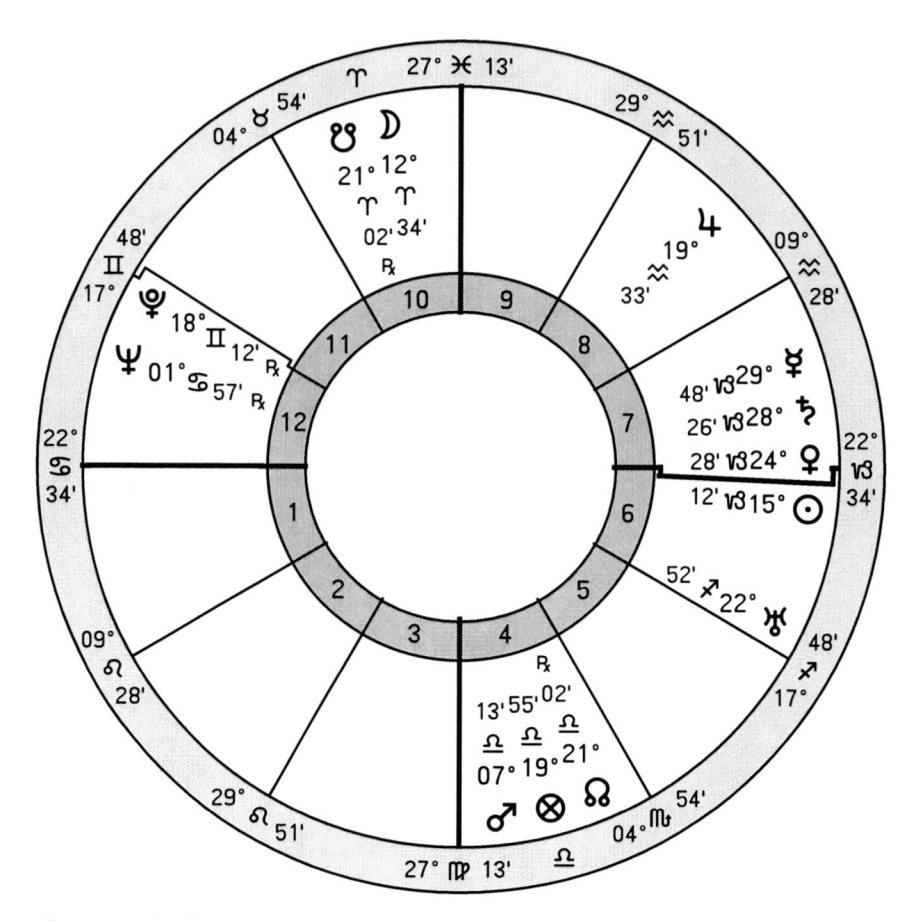

(Fig 44) Derived Lunar Return 6 Jan 1903

Vocation and near natal 7th house cusp, thus showing the expansion of the reputation of his career in the world – natal 7 being, other people.

The 9th of February lunar return, (Fig 45), echoes the previous testimonies. It has Fortuna conjunct natal Part of Vocation and natal arc Part of Vocation is conjunct lunar return 9th cusp. Natal arc Fortuna is conjunct natal Saturn and lunar return Sun is conjunct natal 7th cusp and there is a very nice exalted Venus near the cusp of the 5th house of the return.

Sometimes when looking at events it is worthwhile to look at earlier returns. And we see an example of this here with the earlier lunar return of 13 Jan 1903, (Fig 46). In it a dignified return Lord 10 is about to enter fixed Saturn sign, again this symbolizes the solidifying of Debussy's status. Fixed star Caput Algol is near the Ascendant, again giving him power of the sword over others, as befitting a 'Chevalier', a knight. This is confirmed by the

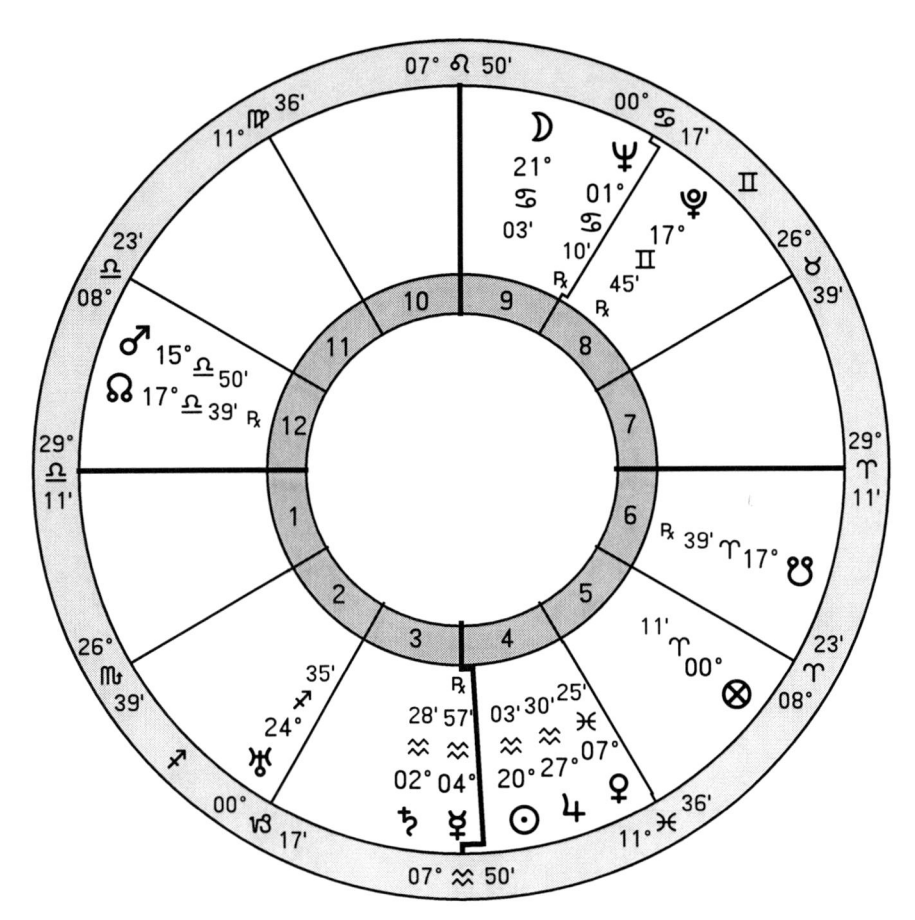

(Fig 45) Lunar Return 9 Feb 1903

Ascendant also being conjunct the dignified pre-birth eclipse Venus. Natal arc Fortuna is conjunct natal Mars, showing his fortune and his art coming together again. The Return 5th cusp is conjunct natal Ascendant, return Jupiter is conjunct natal Descendant. Return Fortuna is conjunct return 7th cusp. Return Sun, natural significator of honour is trine natal Jupiter, his creations, opposing return/natal Moon. And Return 2nd cusp from 7th, is conjunct natal 5th cusp. The esteem of others is connected with his creations and his career. Also natal arc Part of Vocation is conjunct natal 5th cusp and the North Node.

La Mér – *The Sea, Lily, Emma and Chou Chou*

The progressed Ascendant 03–04, (Fig 47), is conjunct progressed Venus sextile natal Moon and progressed Sun is conjunct malefic fixed star

The Pattern of Time

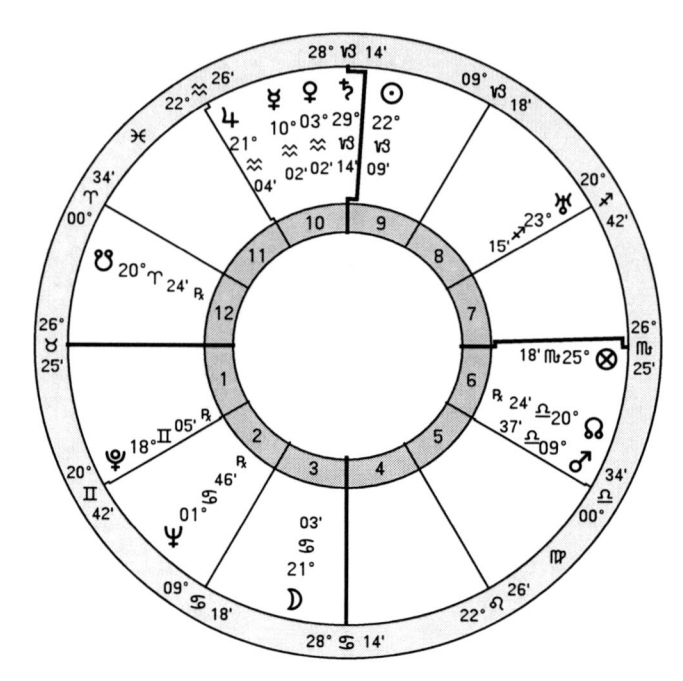

(Fig 46) Lunar Return 13 Jan 1903

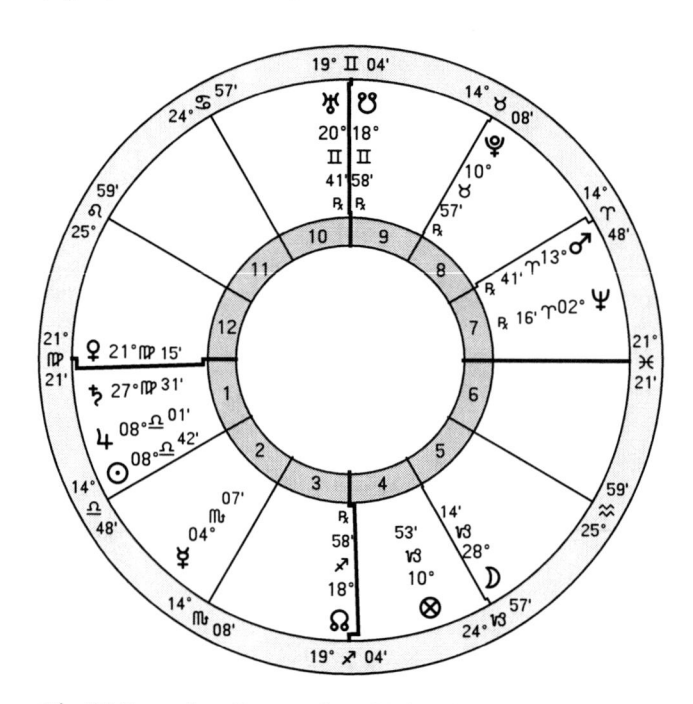

(Fig 47) Secondary Progressions 22 Aug 1903

Vindemiatrix. Vindemiatrix is also traditionally known as the widow maker, and it can be connected with divorce. Progressed Fortuna opposes natal Fortuna, squares natal Mars and opposes natal Moon, natural ruler of his wife. Debussy and Lily did not have any children – he loved Lily but he wanted children as Louis Laloy recalled, 'Later he spoke of her to me with affection only complaining that they had no children. I remember my reply – "you mustn't give up hope …" But sadly, in June 1904, Debussy abandoned Lily for Emma Bardac. The singer and friend Mary Garden, who had played the part of Mélisande, recalled,

> 'he went for his walk one morning and never came back. It was a very cruel thing …'

Lily was utterly devastated. But Debussy was unwavering: natal Lord Ascendant Sun is stubbornly fixed and in the detriment of Lord 7 suggesting he would not listen to her desperate pleas.

The progressions for 05 show progressed Moon opposing natal Sun, again signs of the difficulties they are having and sadly the potential for his divorce.[17] He was divorced from Lily in August 1905.

Debussy desperately wanted children; his natal Moon, dispositor of Fortuna, is exalting Jupiter natal Lord 5, the things he creates, which of course includes his potential children. In October 1905, his only child, daughter, Chou-Chou was born and we see the progressed Ascendant conjunct natal Jupiter, significator of fertility and natal Lord 5: his potential children. The letters and evidence clearly show Debussy loved his wife Lily and, in a different way, he loved his second wife Emma too, though Mary Garden later thought that his daughter Chou Chou may have been the only person that Debussy truly loved. And so we are reminded once again of his powerful Moon, ruler of Fortuna, exalting Lord 5, his daughter.

In 1905 Debussy also composed, *Images, Reflets dans l'eau* – reflecting in the water – again driven by his desire for watery symbolism. And in 1905 *La Mér*, the Sea, which he had begun in 1903, the year he was elected as Chevalier of the Legion of Honour, was first performed. Progressed Fortuna is sextile natal dignified Lord 9.

In the solar return for 22 Aug 1905, (Fig 48), the Ascendant falls on fixed star Antares and the Descendant fall on Aldebaran. This signifies that this period was the end of one phase and the beginning of another. *La Mér* was performed and a baby born this is all very much 5th house, creative stuff. Exalted dignified return Moon is conjunct the cusp of the return 2nd house from 5th; indicative of the fruits of the fifth. The return fifth house ruler, Venus, is between natal Fortuna and natal Moon. The return 9th cusp is

---

[17] This does not mean, *in any way*, that this testimony, or any other, will always indicate divorce in someone's life. If it has not been made clear by now I will repeat clearly: we all have free will. Whether we use this or not is another question, nevertheless, there isn't any testimony in any chart that will mean anything in isolation.

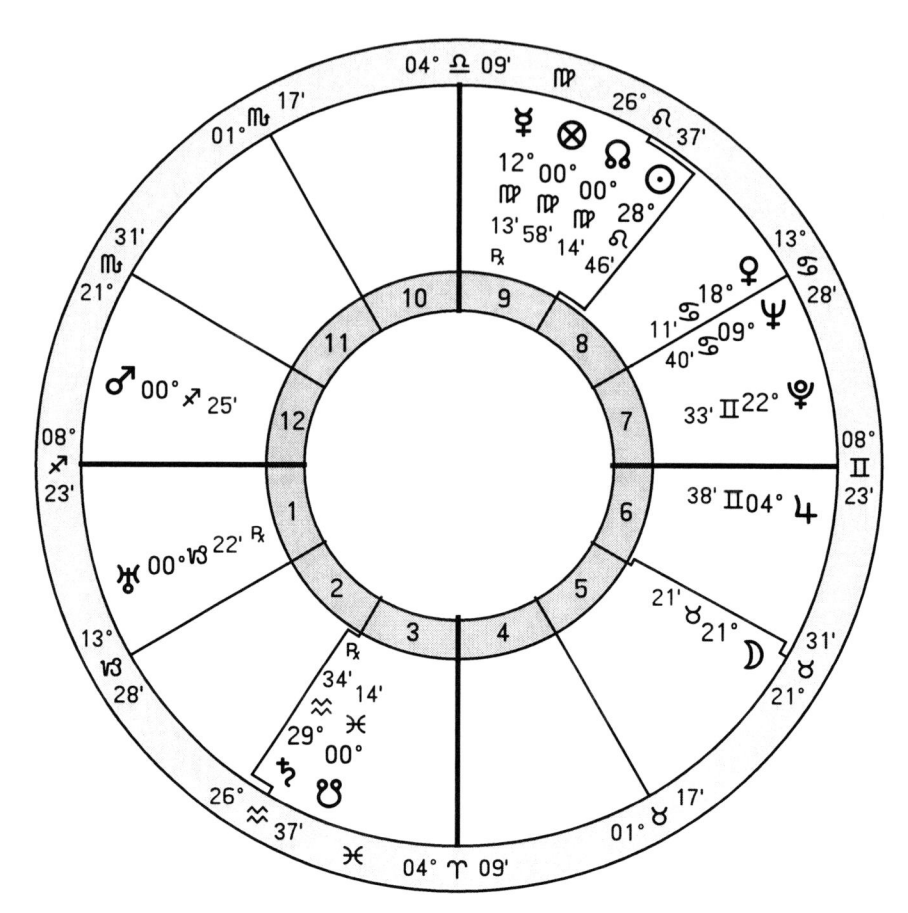

(Fig 48) Solar Return 1905

conjunct Regulus showing honour for his artistry and return Fortuna is conjunct return North Node conjunct natal Mercury. Appropriately, Debussy had completed *La Mér* while staying in Eastbourne, an English seaside town in Kent. It appears the lure of the sea was ever-present. The Premiere of *La Mér* was on 15th October 1905 in Paris. And as Debussy had always wanted, the picture of Hokusai's wave was used on the cover of the 1905 edition of the music.

At the time of the Premiere we see his career, his status and his creations, all connected in a powerful manner in the lunar return of 23 Sept, (Fig 49). Mars natal Lord 9, is conjunct the return 10th house cusp near return Lord 9. Return MC is conjunct natal 5th cusp. Return Venus is conjunct natal Ascendant Sun, and return North Node is also conjunct natal Sun. A watery Cancerian return 5th house cusp is close to his natal Fortuna and his pre birth eclipse. The return 9th house cusp is conjunct the pre birth eclipse 5th

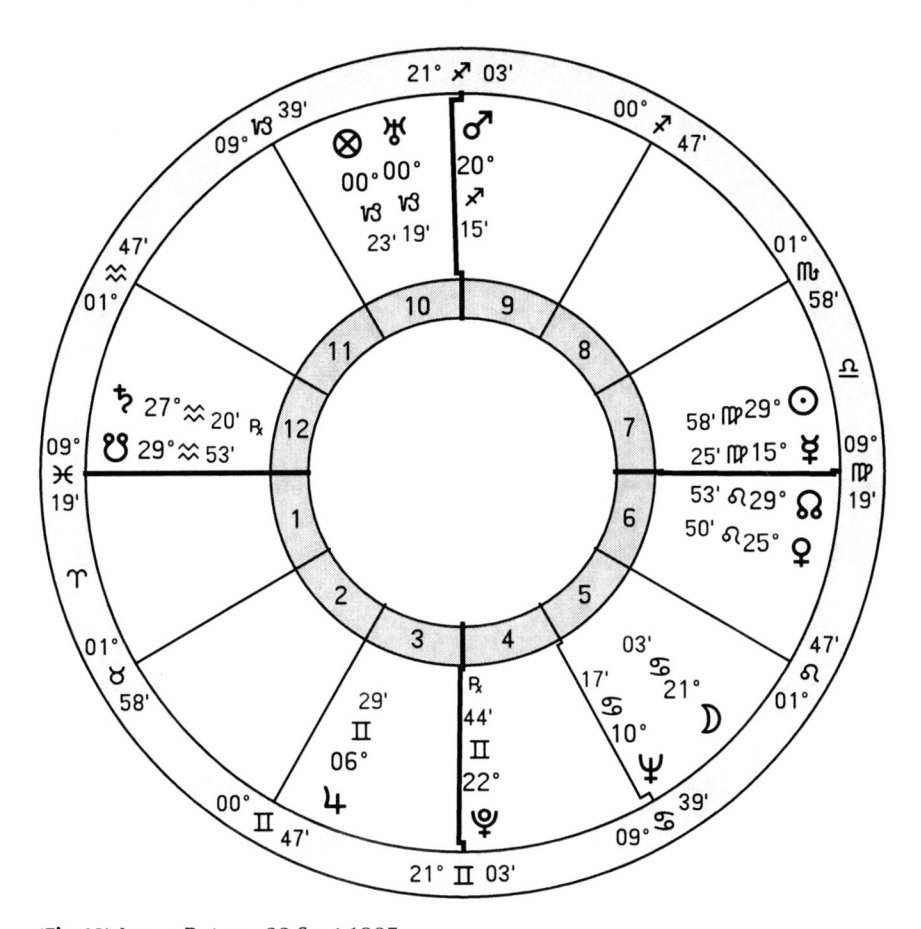

(Fig 49) Lunar Return, 23 Sept 1905

house cusp. This again shows his 9th house artistry plugging into the potential for creative expression that is promised in the eclipse.

On the 21st October there was a lunar return that came just after the Premiere, (Fig 50). The return Ascendant is conjunct natal Lord Ascendant. The expansive fertile overflowing North Node is on the Ascendant: Debussy's baby daughter, Chou-Chou was also born during this lunar return period, on 30th October '05. This is also suggested by the return 5th cusp conjunct fertile natal North Node.

The dignified return Saturn is opposed to natal Sun – initially *La Mér* was not well received as Paris was outraged over Debussy leaving Lily for Emma Bardac. But this attitude would change; in the return we see Venus about to leave its fall and gain major dignity. Venus is the dispositer of return Fortuna inside the return 10th. It is also the ruler of natal 10th – his career is soon to gain major dignity.

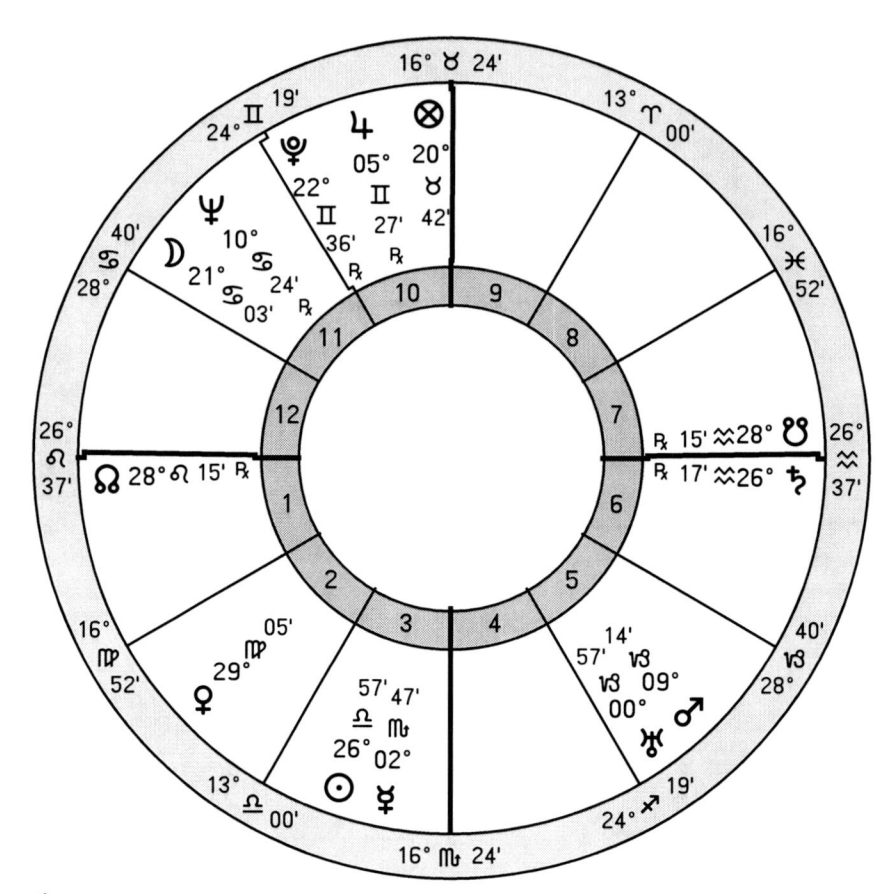

(Fig 50) Lunar Return 21 Oct 1905

As these Debussy charts have shown, in astrology as elsewhere, Fortuna is clearly connected with the 'external goods', exactly as Aristotle and Aquinas had said. But also in astrology, Fortuna seems to have a connection with something else much more mysterious, namely, the soul.

IV. FORTUNA AND THE SOUL

As we saw earlier in the quote from Bonatus, there seems to be a link between Fortuna and the soul. This seems odd. How can something like Fortuna, something so connected with the material in life, also be connected with something utterly immaterial such as the soul?

To answer that question we need to look deeper.

In traditional astrology texts, we sometimes come across details of how to discover the governors or significators of the native's soul. These significators are usually listed as Mercury, the Moon and their respective rulers. As we have seen, Fortuna is essentially a Lunar Ascendant – as Ibn Ezra says, it is the 'part of the Moon' – and this partly explains Fortuna's connection with the soul, the Moon being one of the main 'significators of the soul'. But before going any further, this idea of significators of soul needs some careful thinking and serious qualification.

We could start with what is a soul? Maybe better to start with what is a human being?

A Composite of Spirit and Matter

In Aristotelian and mediaeval scholastic tradition a human being was seen as a hylomorphic being – a composite of spirit and matter. Hylomorphism means a combination of Matter and Form. A human being is not a machine with a soul inhabiting and driving it. A soul is not a ghostly, Hollywood style, ethereal substance at the helm of a fleshy machine. A soul is not even a ghostly substance at all.

Dualism, at its best suggests the soul is the real self, like a sailor in a ship, or at its worst, the soul is the real 'me' imprisoned in a body. On the other hand, materialism suggests that man can be reduced to and completely explained by matter. Between these two extremes there is a middle way: Man as a composite being, a union of spirit and matter.

This is a union that makes a complete substance. After all it is a human *person*, one complete substance that falls in love or flies a kite or enjoys a meal. It is not a soul using a body; we don't fall in love with souls or sophisticated machines. We fall in love with a person.

The Soul

The term soul in Latin is anima – that which animates – it is the principle of life – that which animates the material body. Anything that is alive has a soul with vegetative powers – it is the vital principle of a living body.

When talking about the soul, traditionally it is distinguished into three powers.

– Vegetative: this is the power of the soul that all living things have.
– Sensitive: animals have the vegetative power of the soul and the power of the senses.
– Rational: only human beings have a rational soul. This has the previous powers of vegetative and sensitive and it also has reason, intellect and will.

These are not three types of 'souls' they are three powers of the soul. In Aristotelian and medieval scholastic tradition the soul is the substantial form of a living body. In Book II chapter I of *De Anima*, Aristotle describes the soul via a helpful analogy;

> 'For if the eye were an animal, sight would be its soul. For this is the substance, in the sense of the definable form, of the eye. The eye is the matter of sight, and apart from this it is an eye no longer save equivocally, as with a painted or stone eye.'

So following Aristotle's analogy, as the matter of the eye and sight together would make an eye, therefore the matter of body and soul together are what make a living thing. An animal that was an eye would be defined by the composite between the matter of the eye and its soul which would be sight, hence it would only have one activity and that would be to see.

Each living thing has a soul. Plants are organisms and so they too also have souls which give them the vegetative powers of nourishment, growth and ability to reproduce. Animals have souls that give them a different power to plants, the power of sensing, of appetite and desire and the power to move from one place to another. A human being has all of these powers but the human soul also has the distinctive power that plants and animals do not, the intellect, and thus the power of conceptual thought, judging and reasoning and of making free choices: freewill.

Spirit is the antithesis of matter. It is something that exists or can exist apart from matter. In a human person it is identical with rational soul. The rational soul is a 'subsistent being'. This means it can exist on its own apart from the body. It is the soul's act of existence that activates the whole human being throughout their life. Intellect and will are powers and acts of the rational soul and via intellect and will the soul can act on its own within the complete substance that is a human being. Although the human rational soul is not a complete substance it can still exist in a separated state from the body.

Freedom of the Will

The distinction of that which is material from that which is immaterial is where the route to understanding freewill is hidden.

The intellect and will are not affected by the stars as the intellect and will are immaterial spiritual powers of the immaterial soul. The planets are material bodily substances and the intellect is neither a body nor a bodily power therefore it is impossible for the planets to directly make an impression on it. Vitally, the effects we see in or 'caused by' the movements of the planets are subject to time. And so events that abstract from time entirely are not, and cannot be subject to planetary motion. The intellect in its operation abstracts from time and place and so the operation of the intellect cannot be subject to the movement of the planets.

The fatalistic Stoic philosophers said that man's intellectual knowledge is caused by images of reflection impressed on our minds as a reflection in a mirror or as a page receives letters imprinted on it without doing anything. As Boethius reports in Book V verse 4 of his *Consolation*, '... according to their view it follows that intellective notions are impressed on us by the planets hence Stoics asserted that man's life is directed by a fatal necessity.'

And so too most astrologers would probably agree.

But, this is false, as Boethius goes on to say, 'for understanding combines and separates, compares the highest with the lowest and knows universals and simple forms not found in bodies'. Universals are those things that can be said of many i.e. round is a universal feature of rings, polo mints, tyres etc; Humanness is a universal shared by Europeans, Africans, Americans etc; rectangular is a universal shared by boxes, windows, wardrobes etc.

From the intellect's awareness and comprehension of universals Boethius concludes,

> 'So it is obvious that understanding is not simply receptive of bodily images but has a power higher than bodies since external sensation which is only receptive of bodily images does not encompass the actions mentioned above'.

So though the planets can't be the direct cause of our understanding they can still influence us indirectly. Understanding is not a bodily power, but the operation of understanding cannot happen without the operation of bodily powers – imagination, memory and the cogitative power, which is the sense that enables any animal to determine what may be good or harmful for it.

St John Damascene in *De Fide Orthodox* II 7 says, 'different planets establish in us diverse temperaments, habits and dispositions – so they work indirectly on the good condition of understanding and thus the planets do not cause our will or our choices. As they cannot make a direct impression on our intellect neither can they make a direct impression on our will.'

Though not popular in the modern world, virtues and vices are the traditional principles for acts of choice. Virtues and vices are simply good and bad habits. These good and bad habits are not in us 'by nature' but are things that we learn and acquire and so make of them what used to be called 'a second nature'. Therefore they are not caused by the planets.

In the Canto XVI of, *The Purgatorio*, Dante meets Marco Lombardo, a man who when he was alive, '… had knowledge of the world, and loved that worth at which now everyone hath unbent his bow'. Dante is very troubled; he desperately wants to know why there is so little virtue in the world and so much vice. He feels Marco might know the answer and so Dante speaks to him, 'But I pray that thou point the cause out to me, so that I may see it, and that I may show it to others; for one places it in the heavens and another here below'

Marco Lombardo answers, 'Brother the world is blind, and verily thou comest from it.'

He continues:

> 'Ye who are living refer every cause up to the heavens alone, even if they swept all with them of necessity. Were it thus, Freewill in you would be destroyed, and it were not just to have joy for good and mourning for evil.
>
> The heavens set your impulses in motion; I say not all, but suppose I said it, a light is given to you to know good and evil, and Freewill, which, if it endure the

strain in its first battlings with the heavens, at length gains the whole victory, if it be well nurtured.

Ye lie subject, in your freedom, to a greater power and to a better nature; and that creates in you mind which the heavens have not in their charge.

Therefore, if the world today goeth astray, in you is the cause, in you be it sought, and I now will be a true scout to thee therein.'

Fortuna Unveiled

When William Lilly in *Christian Astrology* tells us the Moon 'governs the vegetative and strength of the brain more near the senses', he is referring to the vegetative and sensitive powers of the soul. When he talks about the reason and intellect he is not referring to the immaterial intellect I described earlier, but the bodily conditions in the particular native with and through which the immaterial intellect operates. Lilly might label Mercury as governing the 'rational soul' but he also says, 'and animal spirits in the brain'. Again, he is referring to the rational souls operation in the body. So this is not the rational intellect itself, which is immaterial and so impossible to delineate in an image, but rather the bodily tools and dispositions the immaterial intellect uses in order to work with the material body.

When Ptolemy in the *Tetrabiblos* speaks of the soul or the 'governors of the soul', he too is referring to the vegetative and sensitive powers of the soul. As we often see Fortuna pointing towards our desires we can now understand the sense of seeing natal Fortuna as the heart's desire. The heart's desires are those things, which command our passions and senses; it is that which we are driven toward. Fortuna in a chart can clearly show such things.

It is important to remember that desire, per se, is not necessarily bad in itself. Freedom from our desires, contrary to opinion, is not a state that we should seek. This in itself would be a contradiction in terms and presuppose desire even if that desire is to be free of desire. Elimination of desire is an outright denial of what we are as human beings. We desire, from our heart as Fortuna shows us, because as hylomorphic beings we are only partially in actuality and partially in potential and therefore we are incomplete. And being incomplete, we desire our completeness and this completeness is what our desires drive us towards. Desire is part of who we are as, via hylomorphism; it is built in to our very being. Therefore it shows that the natural movement towards completeness is also built into our very being. It is not the ceasing of desire that will complete us but the correct ordering of desire. Fortuna, just like Saturn, Mars or indeed Venus won't go away – we can't pretend they are not there – no matter how much havoc they might seem to 'cause' in our lives.

So, unless we make a stand, as Marco Lombardo suggests to Dante, by using our intellect and will to correctly order our desires and passions, it can appear to us that one thing simply follows another in a chain of causes. But, as we have seen, it does not have to be that way.

Boethius, while trying to comprehend what looks to him like all things proceeding by necessity, ponders how freewill can possibly fit into things. He speaks to Philosophia:

> 'I understand, and agree it is as you say. But is there room in this chain of close knit causes for any freedom to the will? Or does the chain of fate bind even the impulses of the human mind?'

Philosophia answers him,

> 'There is freedom' she said, 'for it would be impossible for any rational nature to exist without it. Whatever by nature has the use of reason has the power of judgement to decide each matter. It can distinguish by itself between what to avoid and what to desire, but man pursues what he judges to be desirable and avoids that which he thinks undesirable. So that those creatures who have an innate power of reason also have freedom to will or not to will, though I do not claim that this freedom is equal in all. Celestial and divine beings possess clear – sighted judgement, uncorrupted will, and the power to effect their desires. Human souls are of necessity more free when they continue in the contemplation of the mind of God and less free when they descend to bodies, and less still when they are imprisoned[18] in earthly flesh and blood. They reach an extremity of enslavement when they give themselves up to wickedness and lose possession of their proper reason. Once they have turned their eyes away from the light of truth above to things on a lower and dimmer level, they are soon darkened by the mists of ignorance. Destructive passions torment them and by yielding and giving in to them, they only aid the slavery they brought upon themselves and become in a manner prisoners of their own freedom ...'

---

[18] 'Imprisoned' means enslaved, not literally stuck inside!

7

The Forge of Vulcan

'This god was the first, so it is thought, to see the shameful behaviour of Venus and Mars: for he sees everything before anyone else.'[1]

Apollo the sun god stands in the doorway of the darkened forge. Head lit by a halo and crowned with a green laurel wreath he shines with otherworldly beauty. Apollo calls the blacksmith Vulcan from his work; he has urgent news to deliver to him.

* * *

The masterful Spanish painter Diego de Velázquez was born in 1599. He was called the 'phlegmatic painter' by his contemporaries, the title phlegmatic, being used as a euphemism for lazy. This nickname was given to Velázquez in response to his outrageous, stripped down approach to painting. Instead of creating his paintings gradually, piece by piece, Velázquez wanted to paint rapidly, in a direct manner, with sweeping translucent colour. In order to achieve this he developed his own innovative method of painting. As well as possessing inventiveness and powerful technical abilities Velázquez was an erudite and learned man. He owned a large library of books and by using his knowledge of tradition, coupled with his profound artistic ability Velázquez was able to create powerful religious and mythological paintings filled with symbolism. If we look at these paintings with an attentive eye we can gain new insights into the astrological nature of the planets.

* * *

'Vulcan's senses reeled, and the iron he was forging fell from his hand. At once he began to fashion slender bronze chains, nets and snares which the eye could not see. The thinnest threads spun on the loom, or cobwebs hanging from the rafters are no finer than was that workmanship'

* * *

[1] *The Metamorphoses* Book IV Ovid – All other quotes in this chapter are also from *The Metamorphoses* unless stated otherwise

The Forge of Vulcan

In 1630 when Velasquez was staying in Rome he painted the *Forge of Vulcan*. In his book *Velasquez*, R. A. M Stevenson, the highly respected Edwardian writer on art, described the Forge of Vulcan as painted with '… an almost monochromatic tissue of tone which accompanies and unites the colour of the picture.' From an astrological perspective this, 'monochromatic tissue of tone' that 'unites the picture', alerts us to the binding, structural quality of Saturn as does the gloomy underground cave-like feel of the painting.

Stevenson then elaborates, he tells us that, 'Few strong local tints are embedded in the brown tone of the "Vulcan"; you have nothing in the subject more chromatic than the flesh tints of the dark blacksmiths, and the light ones of Apollo, a yellow drapery, and, on the anvil, one spot of glowing iron.' Again, if we look at this astrologically, we see the overriding presence of Saturn and the illumination of the Sun via the light tones of Apollo. The Blacksmiths and the 'one spot of glowing iron' lead us directly to Mars.

Velázquez painted the Forge of Vulcan to illustrate a scene from Ovid's Metamorphoses. He chose the scene where Ovid describes the adultery of Venus. The traditional way for an artist to portray this scene was to paint images of Venus and Mars caught in mid-embrace, or with Venus in bed while Mars is hiding somewhere in the bedroom. But Velázquez approached this subject in a different manner. There is no image of Venus in the Forge of Vulcan and though there's a hint of Mars with the 'glowing iron' there's no actual image of Mars either. We shall have to look closer to try to understand what this dark and mysterious painting is all about. If we do this we will learn more about the relationship between Venus and Mars and this will, by extension, shed more light on the underlying nature of romantic relationships in general. It is this underlying nature that Ovid with his words and Velázquez with his paint are alluding to.

* * *

'Moreover, he made them to yield to the slightest touch, and to the smallest movement. These he set skilfully around his bed.'

* * *

On the left hand side of the picture, where our eyes naturally fall, Velázquez shows us the sun god Apollo standing in the doorway of Vulcan's forge. Apollo has come to deliver the news that Vulcan's wife Venus has been unfaithful. It is appropriate that this news is delivered via the sun god as the sun is the traditional symbol for Truth. Though truth should be what we always seek it is not what we always want to hear. It is no accident that Velázquez placed Apollo where our eyes will first fall. From this primary position in the painting, it is truth, in the guise of Apollo the all seeing sun god, which illuminates the darkness of the forge. It is through this illumination from outside that Vulcan learns his wife is having an affair. Velasquez depicts Vulcan in such a manner that Vulcan, despite being a god, has the appearance of human-like shock. Stunned at the deliverance of the tragic news of his wife's infidelity he could even be seen as simply a man suffering a very human drama. To add to the humanity of the painting, Vulcan's assistants, normally depicted as Cyclops, are painted by Velázquez as ordinary workers. In another masterful touch, there is a piece of armour in the corner of the workshop that Vulcan and his assistants have been working on. This is a suit of armour that has been requested by Vulcan's wife Venus. Unknowingly for Vulcan, this suit is a present from his wife that is destined for his rival Mars.

Devastated by the news, Vulcan plots revenge. He decides to craft a net with which to catch his adulterous wife and her lover. Using his skill and ingenuity, Vulcan makes the net so fine that it could not be seen and he places it over the bed where the lovers will meet. When Venus and Mars make love in the bed, the trap will be sprung.

*   *   *

'When his wife and her lover lay down together upon that couch, they were caught by the chains, ingeniously fastened there by her husband's skill, and were held fast in the very act of embracing.'

*   *   *

This trapping of the lovers by the restrictive net is symbolic of the bonds that relationships always place on lovers. It is worth noting that in the days before people could get married in swimming pools or floating in hot air balloons, weddings were traditionally celebrated on a Saturday – the day of the week ruled by Saturn. It was a Saturnian restriction and fixing, mirrored in the marriage vows, of the Venusian romance. This is not a forcing on the happy couple of Saturn's restriction but a willingness to announce to the world that this is a restriction they freely choose. Ovid's tale of Mars and Venus, depicted by Velázquez in an ordinary human setting, shows us that despite the desire of lovers for it to be different; the love story will always come with restriction. It could not happen otherwise. Whether the lovers can see this or not, as in the transparency of Vulcan's fine mesh net, is neither here nor there as the ties of love will bind just as strong. But, there is a major difference between Saturn restricting for the benefit of a strong and stable foundation in a relationship and Saturn manifesting as the gossamer thin restrictive mesh that Venus and Mars are trapped and thrashing about in.

Vulcan invites the other gods to come and make fun of the lovers who are trapped in the finely woven net.

The Forge of Vulcan

* * *

'Immediately, the Lemnian Vulcan flung open the ivory doors, and admitted the gods. There lay Mars and Venus; close bound together, a shameful sight. The gods were highly amused; one of them prayed that he too might be so shamed. They laughed aloud, and for long this was the best known story in the whole of heaven.'

* * *

Discovered and mocked by the gods at the end of the tale, we should remember that at the very beginning, Venus and Mars had been seen by another god. Initially they had been seen by Apollo as Ovid said at the beginning of his tale, 'for he sees everything before anyone else'. The sun illuminates all; it is the symbol of truth. It was the announcement of truth that Velázquez had chosen to paint as it was truth, delivered in the guise of Apollo that led to the discovery of Venus and Mars. The lovers had believed they could outwit Vulcan, but illumination would enter the picture and lead to them being uncovered. Truth often appears in this guise, like a shining light 'from outside'. It can appear in a flash and clearly show things to be what they really are. This is similar to when a precious item that we've held onto is brought into the light of day. It can appear to be something quite different than what we thought. When we see by the light of truth we often see that it is tarnished and the lustre, that in the half light was so alluring to us, is now gone.

Saturn, by its nature restricts, yet it is only by seeing things via the illumination of truth that we can see which restrictions we might willingly choose. And to see them clearly is very important, because no matter what, there will always be restrictions. This is exactly what Venus found out. In her embrace with Mars she broke her Saturnian marital bonds and yet simultaneously she found herself trapped, bound together with her lover in a net that neither of them could see. Entwined upon the couch, 'caught in the very act of embracing', they were unable to escape the truth of the situation. The ivory doors had been flung open and there they lay, uncovered, 'a shameful sight' in full view of the gods.

Instead of escaping the restrictions of Saturn the lovers were trapped; bound together within the net of the severely limited possibilities of their relationship.

8

Act and Potency – The Nature of Change

Born c. 515 BC, the pre-Socratic philosopher Parmenides denied that anything in our world changes. To us this might seem bizarre, but Parmenides clearly did not think so. You may believe that this morning you got out of bed, cleaned your teeth and made some tea; you may even think that you were once a teenager and now you are not, but Parmenides would say, your senses deceive you.

Why? Because, Parmenides argued, everything that exists is a 'being'. Something that does not exist is 'non-being', or simply nothing. The only thing that can cause change is that 'being', somehow mixes with or is acted upon, by something else. But Parmenides tells us there isn't anything else that exists, there is only 'being', and so there cannot be anything such as change. Everything is in fact 'one' and therefore everything stays the same. You may ask why anyone would believe such a bizarre thing. A follower of Parmenides called Zeno invented arguments, called paradoxes, to persuade people that Parmenides was correct and despite what we might think, nothing in this world changes. One of Zeno's paradoxes, 'Achilles and the Tortoise', nicely illustrates why someone might believe change is an illusion.

Achilles and the Tortoise

The Greek hero Achilles is on the starting line of a race track, limbering up, preparing to have a race with a tortoise. The tortoise is given a head start, as after all, he is a tortoise and Achilles is a Greek hero. Despite the tortoise having a head start, the winner of the race seems a foregone conclusion. But not according to Zeno. He thought that Achilles, despite being a hero and very fast, could never really catch up and pass the tortoise because even though the tortoise was very slow he was still moving. No matter if it appears to our senses that Achilles nigh on immediately passes the tortoise; he simply couldn't have. Because in order for Achilles to pass the tortoise first he would have to cross the distance between him and the tortoise and by the time he reaches where the tortoise is the tortoise will have moved. We can extrapolate from this and say that Achilles doesn't move at all. First he has to cross half the distance but before he reaches that point he has to cross half

Act and Potency – The Nature of Change

of that distance and before he does that he has to cover half of that. If we follow the argument through, we can see, contrary to our senses that Achilles doesn't even leave the starting line! It is logically impossible for him to move and therefore impossible for him to change position and we only believed that it was possible because our senses deceived us. Therefore there cannot be anything called change that exists in the world.

Heraclitus

Slightly earlier than Parmenides, another pre-Socratic philosopher, Heraclitus, born c. 535 BC, had the opposite view. He denied there was anything that ever stayed the same. Heraclitus believed that, 'you could never step into the same river twice', and so contrary to your senses, nothing is ever the same in life. The only thing that there truly is, is change. You were once a teenager and now you are not – is there anything that remains of the teenager you once were? Heraclitus believed not. Another example that illustrates this type of thinking is the burning candle: A candle burns and we stare at the flame. The flame seems constant but Heraclitus would say that this is an illusion. Though it appears to be constant the candle is in fact being consumed by the flame. The wax is melting and the entire candle is continually disappearing into smoke. Therefore the only thing there is in the world is change.

But, the truth of change and permanence lies in the middle of these two extremes. Things in our world do indeed change as Heraclitus argued, but there is an underlying subject that has permanence and it is in this that the change happens.

Plato

Plato was the first to begin to resolve this dilemma by postulating a world of forms, of which, our world is but a shadow, an imperfect projection of the true world of forms. The 'form' is that which gives each particular thing its identity, almost like its own particular unique shape and this 'form' is in-filled with matter. Each original form exists in the mind of God and the things we see around us are simply projections of these. And so yes, in reality there is permanence, in the fact that the world of forms does not change and yet there is also change as can be seen by the things around us constantly changing, constantly coming to be and passing away.

In *The Republic*, Plato told his myth of the cave.

There are people living within a cave. Chained and unable to turn their heads they face the wall at the end. Behind them, towards the mouth of the cave, is a fire upon a walkway. As the people in the cave are chained, they cannot escape, but can only watch and listen to what is before them. They hear sounds in the cave and see images in front of them and believe these sounds and images are reality. But they are merely shadows cast by people passing in front of the fire on the walkway behind them. These people are sometimes chatting to each other, and they carry little objects such as statues of humans and animals and it is these things that are projected onto the cave wall. If the prisoners can somehow tear themselves away and escape from the cave they will see the truth of all this. Emerging from the cave they will see the true light, what Plato called the Good, which the fire in the cave is but an echo of. Outside the cave they'll see the true unchangeable forms and thus see reality as it truly is and no longer be deceived by the shadows and projections they saw before them.

Aristotle

Plato's student Aristotle later developed this idea by his realisation that there was no world of forms out there, somewhere beyond our world, but there was still such a thing as a form. The form of say a table, exists both in the mind of the person looking at the table and in the table. So a form exists in the mind and also in the thing itself. And each thing is a better or worse example of its form – which is almost like its blueprint – the perfect example of what it should be.

Aristotle also divided everything into what he called Act and Potency; this is where he solved the problem and how he explained change. Aristotle thought that both Parmenides who said nothing changed was partly right and Heraclitus who said that there was only change was also partly right. Something does indeed change and yet that something which changes also somehow remains the same. Yes you were a teenager once and now you are not – you have clearly changed and yet you clearly remain the same.

You may ask, what does any of this have to do with astrology?

The answer is it has everything to do with astrology.

The Nature of Change in Astrology

The nature of change in astrology is no different to change anywhere else in the world – the problem is that it is often treated as if it is different. In astrology, change is often seen as something that you can somehow arrange, as if astrology is like a Fairy Godmother who, if we plead with her enough, will grant us three astro wishes. This is an illusion.

When we look at change in the world, change is always change into something. When something in the world changes there is always an underlying subject in which the change takes place, and something which is either gained or lost. Change always ends in a new state of being for the subject that has undergone the change. We work and we are tired – we, the subject, remain the same subject and yet we change by attaining the state of tiredness.

Act and Potency – The Nature of Change

Aristotle, in book I chapter 7 of the *Physics*, says, '... we say not only "this becomes so- and so," but also "from being this, it comes to be so-and so," as "from being not-musical comes to be musical".'

Aristotle is explaining that change is not random; it is rooted in what the thing is in itself.

Act and Potency

Whatever a thing is, it is made up of act and potency. The word act, tells us what a thing is or has; for example, a human being has such things as life, rationality and substantiality it also has senses; seeing, hearing, tasting, all these things are acts. Potency on the other hand is the power, the potential, the capacity or aptitude for something. This potency is something that a being also has but in a different way to how it has actuality. For example the un-musical man has the potential to be musical and the baby has the potential for speech. The colour blue has the act of blue and the colour yellow has the act of yellow and both have the potency of green. And green has the actuality of green but is potentially blue and yellow. And so the full reality of anything is what it actually is, together with its potentials. A potential painting is not the same thing as a real painting but nonetheless it is not no-thing because a potential painting is still the potential of the paint, brushes and canvas that sits in the painter's studio. And though that particular painter may be drinking tea and not painting at that particular time, he is still capable and has the potential to be painting, which is more than the man who does not have the knowledge or the ability to paint. And so potency or potential is indeed a real thing, and, most important to remember, it is rooted within the being itself. Pure potential does not exist – a possibility or potential must always be a possibility or potential of something – it only has reality and meaning in relation to a real actuality.

Aristotle defined change as 'the act of a being in potency in so far as it is in potency'. St Thomas Aquinas said that a thing may be in any one of three situations: in act only, in potency only or somewhere between act and potency. An entirely potential thing is not in a state of change; neither is a thing finished and in perfect act in a state of change. Change therefore is the state of being in between.

This may seem far removed from astrology yet it underpins everything. Consider some examples of horary:

> 'Is this the man or woman for me?' Is this Mr or Mrs Right?

In such a query we are looking at the potential of this particular person actually becoming, or being, Mr Right.

> 'Is there any profit in this investment?'

Here we are looking at the real potential of profit of a particular investment.

The Pattern of Time

'Do I have what it takes to be a successful pianist?'

We are looking at the potential the querent has as a professional pianist.

In order for these potentials or any others to be real they have to be grounded in the actuality of the situation and the people involved and not in thin air or fantasy.

In natal work we are also looking at potentials. As with horary, the common trap is to regard potential as something that we can dream up if we close our eyes and try hard enough. This, of course, is the astro Fairy Godmother again! Potential is always potential for something and this is always the potential that resides within the thing itself. There is a certain set of possibilities that belong to whatever it is we are looking at. So the full reality of say the finest cut of European Spruce tree will include the potential to be the top for a steel string guitar whereas a thick off-cut of pine will not have that potential. It may have the potential to be a pine table top maybe, but not a fine steel string guitar.

This is why in natal astrology we have to build upon the temperament – the cloth from which we are cut – and why all further detail will only ever be embroidered upon this. The temperament is the foundational layer in the natal figure that will allow certain possibilities in and rule certain possibilities out. This is similar to when we look at a patch of land; it will have the inherent potential for us to grow some things and yet other things will wither and fall. In the modern world, for some reason, it is now believed that potential is somehow democratic and that we all have it in equal measure. There is some truth in this – we do all have potential in somewhat equal measure – the difference is what that potential is for.

The particular circumstances must also be taken into consideration. This is clearly seen when we look at situations of profit and loss. For instance, in a potential property sale a querent can easily imagine it is simply a matter of realising the profit inherent within the deal. But this presupposes there is always profit in the deal. This is not always true. We can see this in situations when the querent wants to buy property as an investment to later sell on at a profit. Sometimes, even when the buying price for the property is low, there is still not always potential profit in the situation. This can be difficult for the querent to understand especially if they have seen others profit from similar deals. The idea that if the chap over the road has profited then I will too, is of course, not true. We also see this when the potential to profit from a sale does not exist, simply because the querent's partner does not really want to sell. Even if they receive a good offer for their house, they will not let it go.

In any situation we have the potentials of the situation itself and the potentials of the parties involved. Very often the hopes, desires and wishes of the querent are projected onto the situation and are seen as potentials when they are but merely wishful thinking. Though we must be very careful here as this does not imply the accountant who tells his friend the musician to, 'be realistic' and 'get a real job' is necessarily making a valid objective judgement of his friend's musical abilities and potential for success. This type of thing usually has more to do with the accountant projecting his own musical inability and lack of understanding onto his friend's situation. Some plants may take a long time to grow and bear fruit. This is not a defect, it is simply their nature: some things take a long time for their potentiality to become actuality. The thing to remember is that however long that potential may take it is still potential that is rooted and grows from within the thing itself. When we look at a natal chart we often see that despite difficulties many still do manage to actualise their potentials. And it is in a natal chart where we can clearly see how potential is rooted and contained within an individual's being and nature. Many people can look at situations and think, 'I could do that' – 'I'm no different'. But they are different. Yes they could probably could 'do that', whatever 'that' is, but the results would be different due to their different potentials and the particular possibilities inherent within them and the situation.

The Cycle of the Elements

In order for things to change, to go from potency to actuality, they have to pass through the elemental cycle, what the medieval philosophers sometimes referred to as the cycle of Empedocles.[1] This often means agitation and difficulty. In astrology this points towards squares and oppositions. As much as people don't like it, all those squares and oppositions are necessary; they show the strife and friction that is needed so something can actually happen. This can be seen clearly if we observe the elemental make up of aspects. It is largely their elemental make up that describes what an aspect is and why it works in the way it does.

Medieval astrologer Abraham Ibn Ezra, in his book *The Beginning of Wisdom* tells us that, 'an aspecting planet is like a person looking for a thing he desires.' This 'thing he desires' refers to the Aristotelian concept of teleology. Teleology tells us that all natural things are inherently pointed towards something and this 'pointed towards' is simply part of its nature – it is built into it. This is similar to when we hear of something loving or hating something else. The words, loving and hating, suggest that one thing 'wants' to be near or apart from another thing. It is important to remember that we are speaking analogously here and this idea of wanting or desiring does not mean that, for instance, in the earlier example of a slice of European Spruce

---

[1] Empedocles was a pre Socratic philosopher and a follower of Pythagoras. When discussing the elemental cycle medieval philosophers often referred to Empedocles, his theory of the elements and the two powers of Love and Strife. Hence the pattern of change illustrated by the movement of matter through the elements was often called 'the cycle of Empedocles'.

the wood itself wants in some kind of autonomous way to be a top of a guitar rather than a chair. No, it simply means that it is inherent in its nature. It is by the virtue of what it is to be directed to its potentiality to be a top for a guitar. The analogous quality is that this wanting or desiring is similar, but not the same as, wanting or desiring in us. It is this similarity with our wanting and desiring that enables us to see and understand this quality in nature.

The 'person looking for' part in Ibn Ezra's statement refers to the geometric relationship of the planets or what we would call an aspect. The word aspect is from the Latin aspectus meaning, 'a seeing', a 'looking at' or a 'view'. The traditional aspects are opposition, square, trine and sextile.

The Opposition

The opposition of a planet in Aries and a planet in Libra can be understood by looking at exactly what qualities they are opposed to. Aries is hot and dry, Libra is hot and moist. They are opposed by the qualities of dryness and moisture. They come together easily, due to the affinity of their temperature but they fall apart due to the contrary qualities of dryness and moisture. The opposition traditionally shows things coming together and falling apart or coming together and regretting it. Like two lovers coming together, the planets recognize similarities in each other, almost a kindred quality in their outlook and yet end up, sometimes very quickly, rueing the day they ever met. But it is only in coming together that they realise how essentially opposed and far apart they are in reality. This is emphasised by the essential dignities.[2] Speaking somewhat loosely, a planet in Aries loves Mars and the Sun and it hates Saturn and Venus. A planet in Libra loves Venus and Saturn and hates the Sun and Mars. Yes they may come together for a moment drawn by that shared quality of temperature but pretty quickly they realize they hate each other and so they fall apart – as Ibn Ezra's tells us, the opposition is 'like two people fiercely fighting each other'.[3]

The Square

The Square of a planet in Aries and a planet in Scorpio brings together the qualities of Hot and Dry and Cold and Moist. There is no middle ground here. There is no affinity. As Ibn Ezra tells us, a square is 'like two people each one seeking authority for himself.' There are two mixtures of temperature and quality that are in strife each trying to overcome the other and to gain the upper hand exactly as Ibn Ezra describes. Yet, as with the opposition, without this strife and agitation nothing would change.

---

[2] See Appendix and the *Table of Essential Dignities*, which is used to determine the dignities that each planet falls in.
[3] Ibn Ezra, *The Beginning of Wisdom*

Act and Potency – The Nature of Change

The Trine

The trine of a planet in Aries and a planet in Leo brings together the qualities of hot and dry and hot and dry. This is the coming together of two things in signs with a total similarity of elemental structure. It is traditionally seen, as Ibn Ezra says, as the aspect of friendship. Like two people coming together with a shared outlook and mutual background. There may not be the spark for lovers, for that spark you need agitation, like flint striking flint, but there is the shared outlook of friends. Illustrating exactly this point, Ibn Ezra tells us a trine is like, 'two people of the same nature'.

The Sextile

The sextile of a planet in Aries and a planet in Gemini brings together two signs with similarity of temperature but a difference of moisture. This is the same elemental mix of an opposition but without the 180 degree hatred of what the other loves. The shared outlook of temperature is also reminiscent of a trine but without the similarity of element. In the example of a trine we had fire and fire, in this sextile we have fire and air. Fire and air are both hot, but the difference between fire and air together with the difference in moisture shows the lack of glue or spark of dynamism. Yes they get along, they are the same temperature, as in a trine, but it is no big deal – though there is a sense that it might possibly develop into something. This can be seen in practice, as a sextile often performs like a weak trine, just as a lukewarm friendship is a weak friendship. This sense of, it might develop into something, is illustrated by Ibn Ezra telling us that a sextile is like 'two people seeking each other's friendship'.

The Conjunction

The conjunction is not technically an aspect. As I said earlier an aspect is from the Latin aspectus meaning, 'a seeing', a 'looking at' a 'view', and a conjunction brings two planets together in totality, therefore as they occupy the same space, they cannot see each other. This is two lovers coming together; two becoming one as in the traditional view of marriage. The difference with friends and lovers is among other things an elemental balance. With the friendship of a trine we have Aries, hot, dry and cardinal and Leo, hot, dry and fixed; there is great similarity here but they are not the same thing. Whereas two planets conjunct in Aries share the same heat, the same dryness and the same place, as Ibn Ezra says, 'Conjoining planets are like two people joining each other'. Conjunction was often used as an equivalent term for sexual intercourse.

It is in these combinations of the elemental cycle that we see things changing from potency to actuality, or in traditional terminology, being reduced from potency to act. It is always important to remember, as I mentioned earlier, that it is not some random potential that things change into; potential is always an as yet unrealised part of the nature of the thing itself.

As Aristotle says in his *Physics* Book I chapter 5 188a 19–27,

> '… in nature nothing acts on, or is acted on by, any other thing at random, nor may anything come from anything else, unless we mean that it does so in virtue of a concomitant attribute. For how could "white" come from "musical", unless "musical" happened to be an attribute of the not-white or of the black? No, "white comes from "not white" – and not from any "not- white", but from black or some intermediate colour. Similarly, "musical" comes to be from "not-musical," but not from anything other than musical, but from "unmusical" or any intermediate state there may be.'

This is clearly seen by us learning to play a musical instrument. We start out having musical ability in potential but not in actuality. And via our practicing upon our instrument and working upon our musical potential we go through a process of intermediate states whereby we pass from un-musical to musical in actuality. Again this is not random or pure chance, as Aristotle continues to tell us,

> 'Nor again do things pass into the first chance thing; "white "does not pass into "musical", '… but into "non white" – and not into any chance thing which is not white, but into black or an intermediate colour; "musical" passes into "not musical" – and not into any chance thing other than musical, but into "unmusical" or any intermediate state there may be.'

In Aristotle's *Physics* we are also told that, '… everything that comes to be or passes away comes from, or passes into, its contrary or an intermediate state. But the intermediates are derived from the contraries – colour for instance, from black and white. Everything, therefore, that comes to be by a natural process is either a contrary or a product of contraries.'[4]

Hence, in a very obvious example, it takes a man and a woman to make a child.

It is the contrary that causes the strife, the friction for something to happen as St Thomas Aquinas tells us, when discussing what the ancients thought in his commentary on Book 1, chapter 5 of Aristotle's *Physics*, 'Others, however, held that the cause of generation and corruption[5] is strife and friendship that is, the cycles of Empedocles, which are also better known to reason …'

---

[4] Aristotle *Physics* Chapter 5 188a27

[5] The term generation and corruption means coming to be and passing away – it means change. Three excellent books I recommend to deepen understanding of the underlying philosophy are, *An Introduction to Philosophy – Perennial Principles of the Classical Realist Tradition* by Daniel J. Sullivan, *Aristotle for Everybody – Difficult Thought Made Easy* by Mortimer J. Adler, and *Aquinas* by F. C. Copleston.

Act and Potency – The Nature of Change

Strife and friendship and all in-between are illustrated by the relationships we call aspects: the opposition, square, sextile, trine and conjunction and the qualities that come from the elemental nature of the signs. It is through these relationships that things pass in order to bring their potentials into manifestation. And it is by bringing these potentials into manifestation, by going from potency to act, that things in our world move from one state to another.

It is how things change.

9

Impressionism, Saturn and Ivory Black

If we peer within the deep caves of Western France we can still see the horses of our ancestors galloping past. Upon the cave walls of Lascaux they charge in vivid swirls and striking compositions, in red earths and deep greens, yellow ochre and black. Mighty bulls, bison and athletic deer are also there. Outlined in haunting black pigment, they remain visual echoes of the past crafted upon the simple cave surface.

The colour black is ruled by Saturn. And reflecting the steadfastness of Saturn, it has been uninterruptedly used in painting since the Lascaux caves of prehistoric France. Uninterrupted that is until we reach the 19th Century, when the Impressionists, a group of painters in modern France, decided they would abandon black. Since then it has never regained its former reputation and it remains a somewhat forgotten colour that only the traditionally minded painter uses.

There were several ways the traditional artist could make their black pigments. Ivory black was made by burning ivory. A good black pigment could also be made by burning the leg of a chicken, traditionally a capon, which is a sterilized male chicken, Saturn being the ruler of sterility as well as the ruler of black. The pigment made from the leg of a capon was known as bone black. Black could even be made from the stone of a peach; this was called peach black. Saturn rules stones as well as bones, but ivory black was, and still is,[1] the very best black.

Ivory Black

Ivory black was an essential colour on the palette of the traditional artist. It was used to great effect by the powerful Renaissance and Baroque painters known as the Old Masters. In a finished painting it is difficult to distinguish one black from another, but if black's the colour that's flowing from your brush, then ivory black is unsurpassed in fineness and versatility. As opaque as ivory is, when it is burned to make a pigment it produces a black that is very dark yet also transparent. This quality of darkness and transparency makes it a very useful tool for the painter; excellent for describing the contours of light

---

[1] Ivory black is no longer made from Ivory. Instead it is usually a high-grade bone black made to reproduce the handling and visual qualities of the traditional colour.

and shade. We clearly see the Saturnian quality of boundaries here, the boundary between light and shade and the Saturn-like qualities of solidity and weight. These are all qualities the paintings of the Old Masters had.

However, the 19th Century Impressionists complained that though black did indeed do these things, it also deadened the canvas, 'dead' being another apt description of a Saturnian quality. So in order to fulfil the Impressionist drive to capture the freshness and freedom of the ephemeral, these French artists tried to leave black off their palette. But as the qualities of Saturn are required in order to preserve the things of this world, they could not banish black completely. He would only ever be waiting in the wings. And one Impressionist painter, Pierre-Auguste Renoir, after abandoning black early in his career eventually decided to return black to his palette. He did this after many years of careful experimentation and soul searching. And he did it as a clear statement to distance himself from Impressionism and re-align himself with the Old Masters. If we can trace the path he took astrologically, we may gain insight into the complex relationship between freedom and structure and the endless struggle between modernity and tradition.

Pierre-Auguste Renoir, Ivory Black and the Old Masters

As a child Pierre-Auguste Renoir was natural at art but his main talent seemed to be singing. He was a pupil of Charles Gounod, the choir master of the church of St Roch. Gounod wanted his pupil to follow a musical career and he tried to persuade Renoir's parents of the considerable talent and ability of their son. But due to financial difficulties Renoir had to leave school at 13 and he had to stop his music lessons.

Because of Renoir's artistic ability he was then sent to become an apprentice to a porcelain painter. During any time off from porcelain painting, the young Renoir wandered the galleries of Louvre where he carefully studied the paintings of the Old Masters that hung upon the walls. The master painter of the porcelain factory recognized the talent of his apprentice and he told Renoir's parents that their son was too good for porcelain painting. He suggested their son should train as an artist.

While continuing to work at the porcelain factory, Renoir took lessons to prepare for entry into the École des Beau-Arts, the premier art establishment of the day. In 1858 the porcelain factory went mechanised and Renoir turned to painting fans, window blinds and other household goods to pay for his art lessons. He continued to spend many hours copying the Old Master paintings in the Louvre. By 1862 he'd saved enough money to study art full time. He enrolled at the École des Beau-Arts and at the same time Renoir entered Charles Gleyre's studio. Here he met fellow artists, Claude Monet, Alfred Sisley and Frederic Bazille.

The Pattern of Time

In Claude Monet's documents there is a passage[2] where Monet recalls this time:

> 'In Gleyre's studio I found Renoir, Sisley, and Bazille ... While we sketched from a model, Gleyre criticized my work:
>
>> "It is not bad," he said, "but the breast is heavy, the shoulder too powerful and the foot too big."
>
> 'I can only draw what I see,' I replied timidly.
>
>> "Praxiteles[3] borrowed the better elements of a hundred imperfect models in order to create a masterpiece," retorted Gleyre dryly. "When one does something, one must go back to the ancients."
>
> 'The same evening I took Sisley, Renoir, and Bazille aside: Let us leave, I told them. This place is unwholesome: there is no sincerity here. We left after two weeks of lessons of that kind ... and we did the right thing.'

In this defiant action lay the beginnings of the Impressionist movement in art.

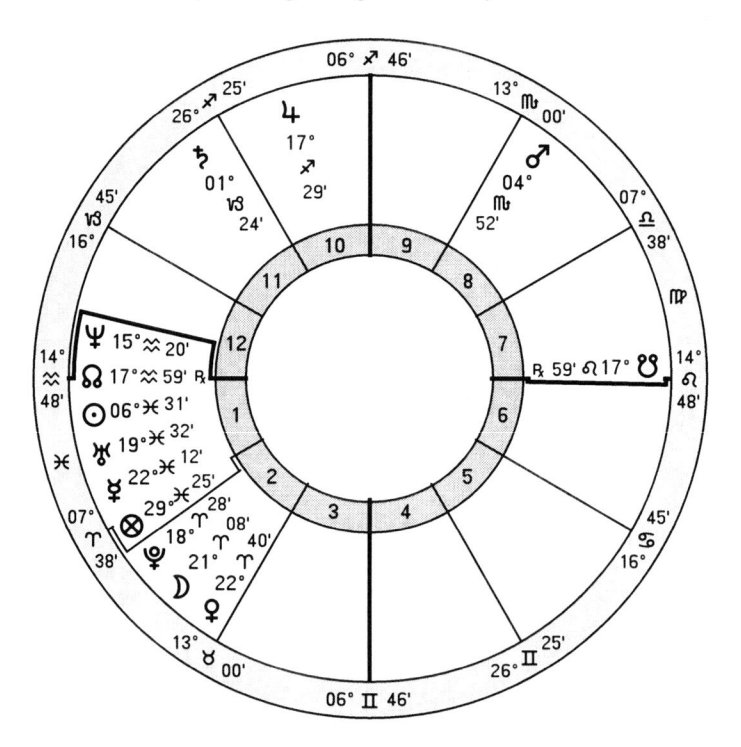

(Fig. 51) Pierre-Auguste Renoir, 25 Feb 1841, 6.00 am LMT, Limoges, France

[2] Included in *Painters on Painting*
[3] Praxiteles was the renowned Greek sculptor (4th Century BC). He was famous for his beautiful sculptures of nudes, especially his *Aphrodite*.

Impressionism, Saturn and Ivory Black

The Impressionists

The French Impressionists stood against academic tradition and the view that art should improve upon nature and nature was to be subsumed to drive the 'big idea'. Their academic predecessors had drawn their subjects from the grand themes of mythology and religion but the Impressionists felt the transient qualities of day to day life were subjects equally worthy of depiction. But these subjects, from the perspective of academic art, were considered too mundane. And the Impressionist use of colour in trying to capture the transient was considered a garish horror. One of the many statements the Impressionists made against academic painting was to eliminate black from their palette. This was done in order to lighten the palette; as they saw no black in nature therefore they thought it had no place on their palette. And instead of painting solely in their studios they also painted outdoors, 'a plein air', to better capture the fleeting quality and subtleties of nature.

The Forest of Fontainebleau

Near Paris was the Forest of Fontainebleau and in the spring and summer of 1862 Claude Monet organized painting trips there. Setting easels up amongst the trees, squeezing paint upon their palettes, Monet, Sisley, Bazille and Renoir filled canvas after canvas trying to capture the dappling light and changing colours that Fontainebleau poured out. Previous generations of artists had travelled to the forest to study nature and gather material for the backgrounds of their paintings, but Monet and his friends went there to create paintings in their own right. With each brush stroke they put pure colour upon the canvas, each artist attentively watching the movement of the vibrant greens and yellows of the trees, the whites and purples of the wild flowers. Intent on keeping sensitive to the changing light they'd paint all day and watch the sun pass overhead and the atmosphere turn a sultry orange as it neared sunset. This attentive approach paid off but there was a major problem with Renoir's materials. He used a lot of black bitumen in his paintings. Though he was striving to capture colour and light, a lot of Renoir's work from this period was dark due to the bitumen on his palette.

Bitumen is a sticky, brown-black substance used by 19th century painters to create deep shadows and form in their paintings. Astrologically this again suggests the influence of Saturn, as Saturn is also the natural ruler of tar-like substances like bitumen. In Renoir's solar return for that year, (Fig 52), Saturn, natural ruler of black and bitumen is close to debilitated Jupiter. This placement suggests excess, that there is 'too much' of something. In this return Saturn and Jupiter are conjunct the 5th house cusp of Renoir's pre birth eclipse. This pre birth eclipse 5th house is, in context, symbolic of the potential paintings of the age that he was born into. Saturn and Jupiter are also opposing his own natal Lord 5, showing that this excess of black and bitumen was clearly afflicting his ability to produce paintings that would reflect his contemporary life and times. Saturn is also retrograde in the return; this nicely suggests that as well as the potential for excess black at the time, Renoir also had the potential for it to retreat from his palette. And this is exactly what happened.

It was in the summer of 1862, in the Forest of Fontainebleau, that Renoir first decided to lighten his palette. In the forest he met the Barbizon landscape painter Narcisse Virgile Diaz de la Peña. Diaz de la Peña encouraged Renoir. He bought him materials that Renoir was too poor to buy and he kindly opened a line of credit for him at his colour merchants. And crucially, he told Renoir to remove black, and bitumen, from his palette.

Renoir's temperament, as befitting such a fluid painter, is very moist, a combination of sanguine and phlegmatic. His Moon is conjunct Venus in the movable cardinal sign of Aries: this suits impressionism, as the Moon, receiver of impressions, is in a cardinal sign exalting the light of the Sun.

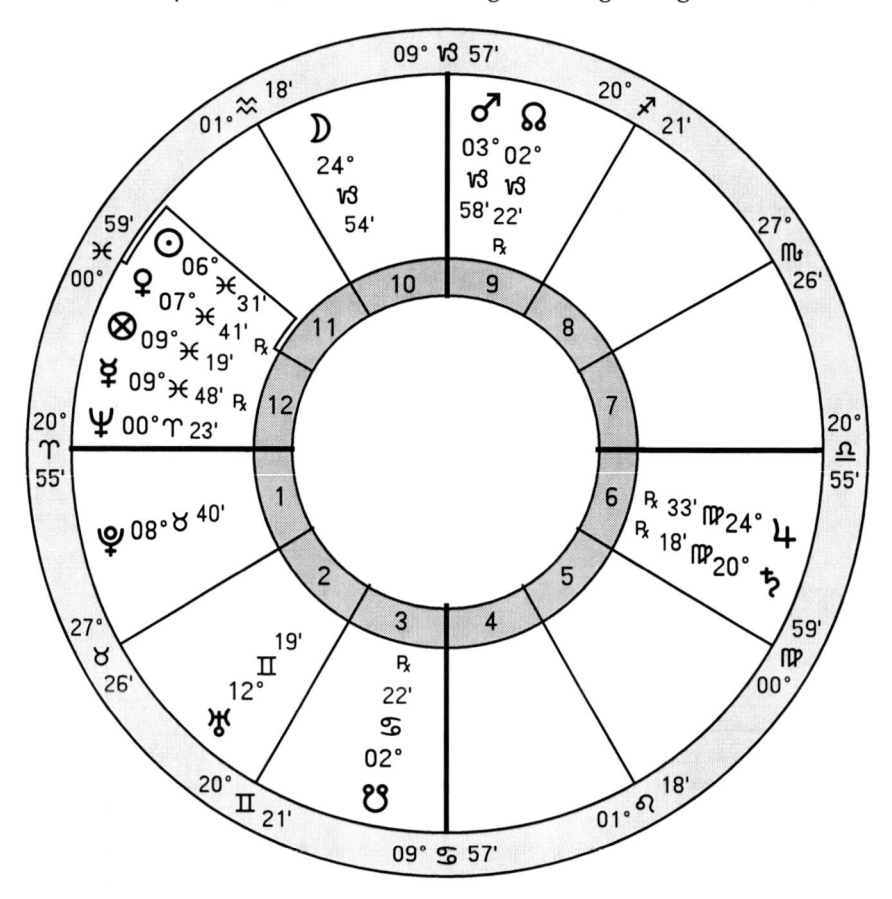

(Fig 52) Solar Return 1862

Impressionism, Saturn and Ivory Black

Yet astrologically there are also signs of tension here in his approach to things. His natal Lord Ascendant is Saturn strong in its own sign and in the 11th house. It is in a cold dry sign and in the detriment of the Moon which is conjunct Venus. Saturn also exalts Mars Lord 9 which as an artist is indicative of his artistry. As he exalts this, it suggests that he expects a lot of himself, his ideas and his art – sometimes he expects more than he can realistically give. And Lord 9, his artistry itself, is in the detriment and fall of impressionistic Venus and the Moon. In an astrological sense it is no surprise that at some time he would have to face a dilemma with his creative expression – the choice between Impressionism and tradition.

His paintings are shown by Lord 5, Mercury in Pisces exalting Venus, ruler of his 3rd house. The 3rd house is indicative of Renoir's method, his mode of communicating the artistry of his 9th. And, the public loved his way of painting, his method, as we see illustrated astrologically by the Sun, natal Lord 7, indicative of other people, exalting Venus Lord 3.

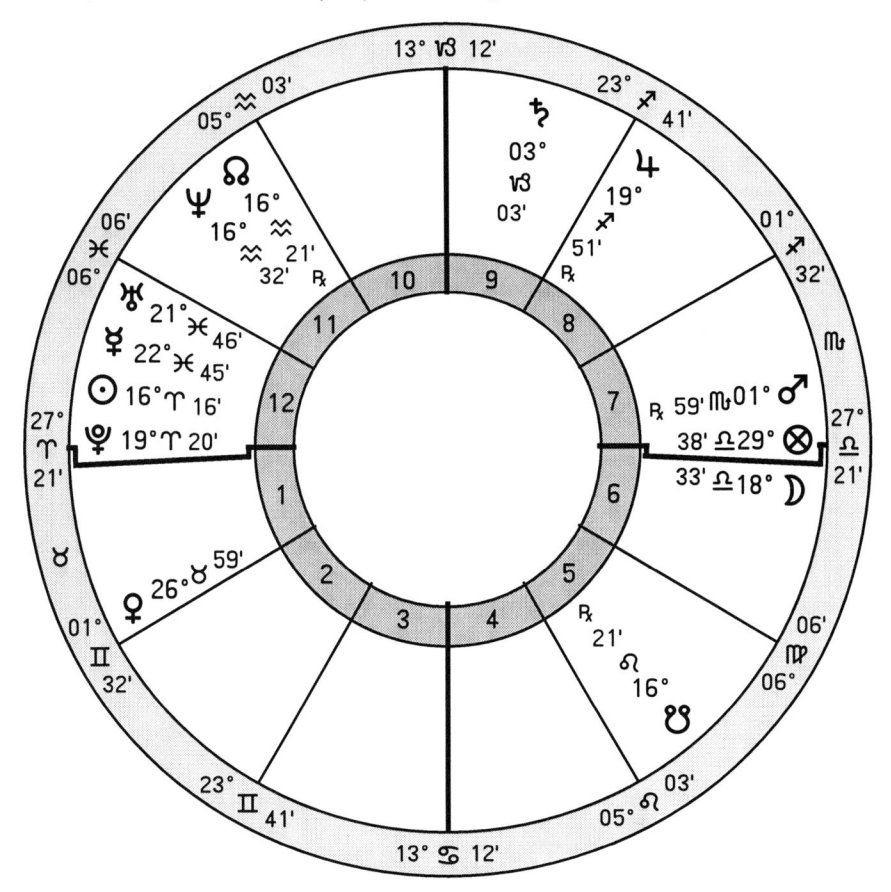

(Fig 53) Secondary Progressions 25 Feb 1881

His First Doubts ... and the Trip to Italy to See the Old Masters

In 1880 Renoir began to have his first doubts about his art. In 1881 he took a trip to Italy to see the paintings of the Old Masters first hand. He'd seen the work of the Old Masters in the Louvre since he was an apprentice porcelain painter but now he wanted to see the Italians in their own environment.

The progressed Ascendant on his birthday that year, (Fig 53), had recently entered Saturn terms, appropriate for the Old Masters. Progressed Sun too is in a trine with Jupiter, dispositor of his natal Fortuna, though it will perfect the following year, almost as a realization of what he will have seen in Italy. This impending trine suggests the, 'solidity of judgement in achieving his affairs and designs ...' that William Lilly mentions for this progression[4]. As Jupiter is ruler of Fortuna we see that he was searching for a way to realize his deep drives and passions.

Writing from Naples in 1881 Renoir said,[5]

> 'I'm still afflicted with the malady of research I don't like what I do and I paint it out and I paint it out again. I hope this mania will come to an end ...'

The progressed Moon opposes natal Mercury and Fortuna. This shows that as inspiring as this trip to Italy might be it could lead to dissatisfaction and frustration at his own ability to realize his desires. This drive is also echoed in the return for that year with the return Ascendant falling close to natal lord 9, Mars, and his natal 9th house cusp of long journeys and study.

In the same letter from Naples Renoir also went on to say, 'I'm like a child at school. The white page must always be evenly written and slap! Bang! I'm still blotting and I'm forty years old. I've been to see the Raphael's in Rome. They are very fine and I should have gone to seen them sooner. They are full of knowledge and wisdom. Unlike me he didn't go in search of impossible things ...'

In the solar return, (Fig 54), return Venus is conjunct natal Venus. This is a Venus return, if this appears in a solar return chart set for an artist, and it follows on from the progressions, then it can show a significant time. In this return, Venus is also close to return Jupiter and return Saturn, Saturn being both Lord Ascendant and ruler of Part of Vocation, and of course, natural ruler of the Old Masters – thus spelling out in astrological language Renoir's search for the wisdom of the Old Masters. Natal Lord 5 is Mercury and in the return Mercury is close to natal Mercury falling in the return 5th house of creativity and paintings.

---

[4] I am speaking somewhat loosely here. Lilly did not use progressions—he used primary directions for moving a natal chart through time. However, a planet is a planet, a cusp is a cusp and an aspect is an aspect whether it is in a primary direction or a progression, or in any other method that symbolically moves a chart through time. Therefore a testimony will not, in essence change, whatever method one uses to move the chart.

[5] *Letter to Paul Durand-Ruel*

Impressionism, Saturn and Ivory Black

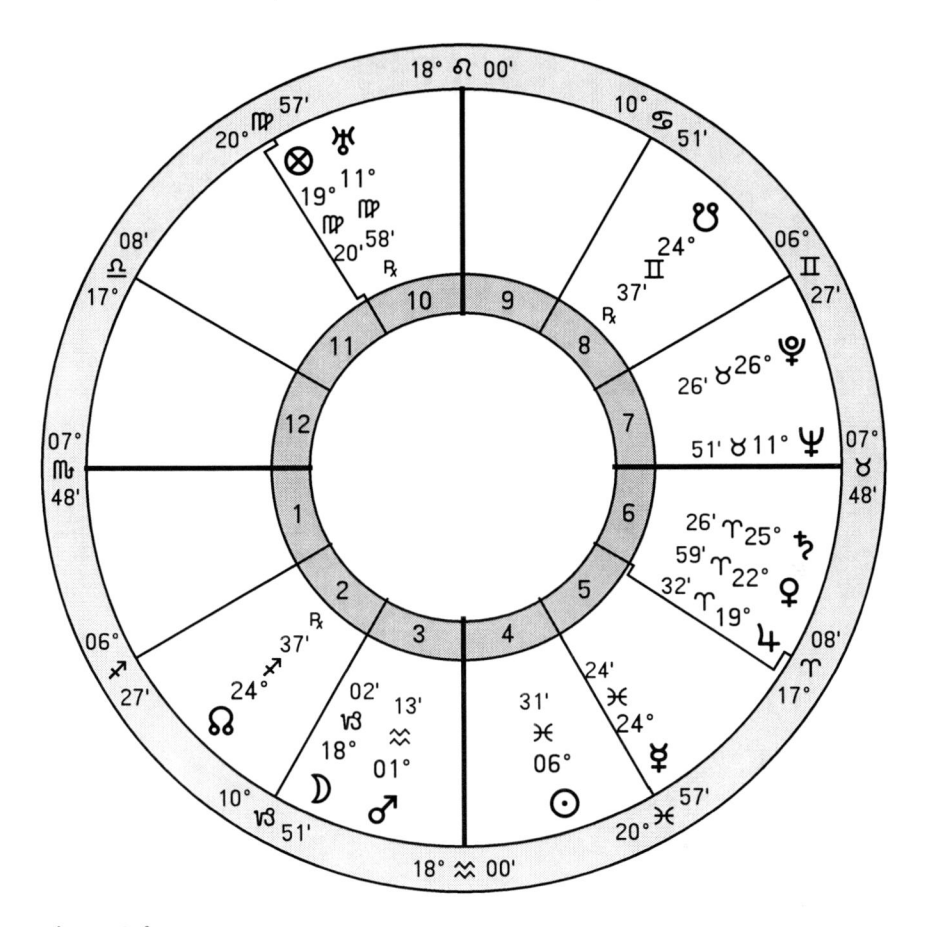

(Fig 54) Solar Return 1881

The solar return Midheaven – his career at that time – is conjunct natal South Node and close to natal 7th house cusp. In context showing him trying to develop his career by looking at others and suggesting that no matter how beneficial this approach might be, it would still give him strife and worry. This is an echo of the difficulty in his natal chart regarding the receptions between Saturn and Mars, the impressionistic Moon Venus combination, and the receptions between Jupiter and Lord 5 Mercury. And it of course suggests the inherent difficulties in his attempts to resolve these conflicts. But return Moon, hidden away in the natal 12th is soon to conjunct natal Part of Vocation – despite the difficulties and seeming impossibility he does eventually find what he is looking for. Natal arc Fortuna falls close to return North Node and natal Jupiter, echoing the quality of his quest: one side you win, via the North Node, and the other side you lose, via the South Node. This affects his whole concept of how his work fits into the bigger picture of the world as shown by return Fortuna being conjunct the 5th house cusp of creativity in the pre birth eclipse. That he had been struggling since his doubts in 1880, is shown by progressed Venus having been passing over malefic star Caput Algol forcing him to see things as they really are and not how he would want them to be. And upon realising how they really are, forcing him to make a clear decision and choice about things.

The Dry Period

Renoir had an artistic crisis after his trip to Italy, he said,

> 'About 1883 something like a break occurred in my work. I had reached the end of "Impressionism", and I had come to realize that I did not know how to paint or draw. In short I found myself in a deadlock'.[6]

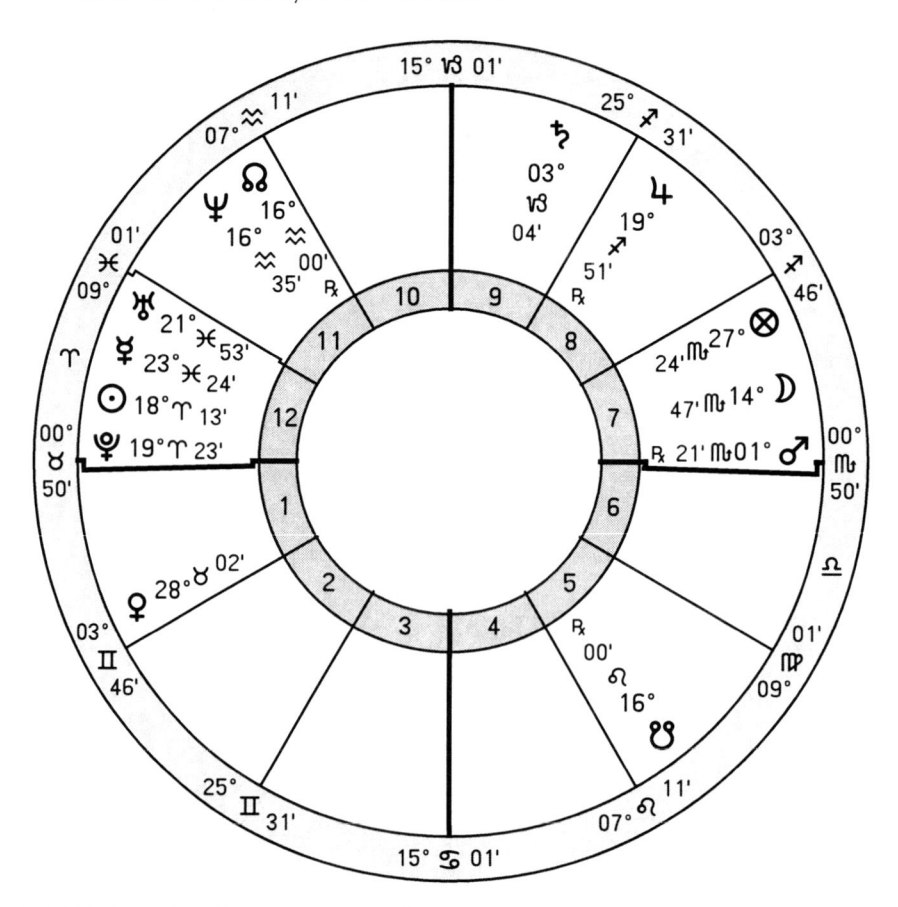

(Fig 55) Secondary Progressions 25 Feb 1883

[6] *Renoir* Ambroise Vollard

Impressionism, Saturn and Ivory Black

1883 marked the beginning of what is known as Renoirs 'dry period'. The dry period was a turning point. We see the progressed Ascendant has just entered a new sign, (Fig 55). Appropriately this is a Venus sign, Venus being ruler of art and aesthetics and natal 3rd house ruler: his technical approach. It was his dissatisfaction with his abilities after returning from Italy that drove this dry period and the progressed Ascendant is now applying to a trine with cold dry Saturn in cold dry Capricorn. For someone so moist this dryness must have been awful for him; apparently he destroyed many of his paintings from the 'dry period'.

Progressed Venus is applying to fixed star Alcyone. Alcyone is the brightest star of the Pleiades, the weeping sisters, the daughters of Atlas. It is often indicative of emotional turmoil. Maybe the tears of the daughters of Atlas can provide Renoir with some much needed moisture? But no, alas their tears are bitter in light of the restrictions that have been placed upon their father whose task it was to bear the weight of the sky upon his shoulders. And so too with Renoir who struggled under the draining emotional weight of it all.

The progressed Sun is now separating from natal Jupiter – he has realised that he needs to change something to do with his work. With realisation and revelation comes responsibility. Now he must come to terms and deal with this realisation, hence the impending trine of progressed Ascendant to natal Saturn. For this direction, Lilly suggests it will show such things as, 'to have familiarity with men of good years viz ancient grave men, and that his commerce or society with them shall be more for his reputation than profit ...'[7] We can imagine Renoir standing in front of his easel conversing in his head with the ghosts of the long gone Old Masters: Renoir, brush and palette in hand, quizzing the ghosts of Michelangelo and Raphael, Titian and Tintoretto, desperately seeking from them the means to solve his technical problems. Renoir was preoccupied with balancing drawing with painting, or contour suggested by Saturn, and colour suggested by the natal Venus and Moon conjunction exalting the Sun.

The solar return, (Fig 56), shows Venus conjunct Fortuna in the 9th house. This again suggests the journey, the long journey, of looking to those who have gone before for their artistry and inspiration. As this is all conjunct natal Part of Vocation this will affect his deep drives and desires towards action. Again, more signs that all this caused him grief are seen by the pressure of the angular return Mars, natal Lord 9 being both on the Midheaven of the solar return and conjunct the natal Ascendant and natal North Node.

Return Jupiter in its detriment, is close on natal 5th in the detriment of his paintings, it dislikes his paintings, and thereby shows Renoir's dissatisfaction with the work he was creating. It is also on the pre birth eclipse Ascendant thus showing that this dissatisfaction runs deep. And so as well as technical

---

[7] *Christian Astrology* William Lilly

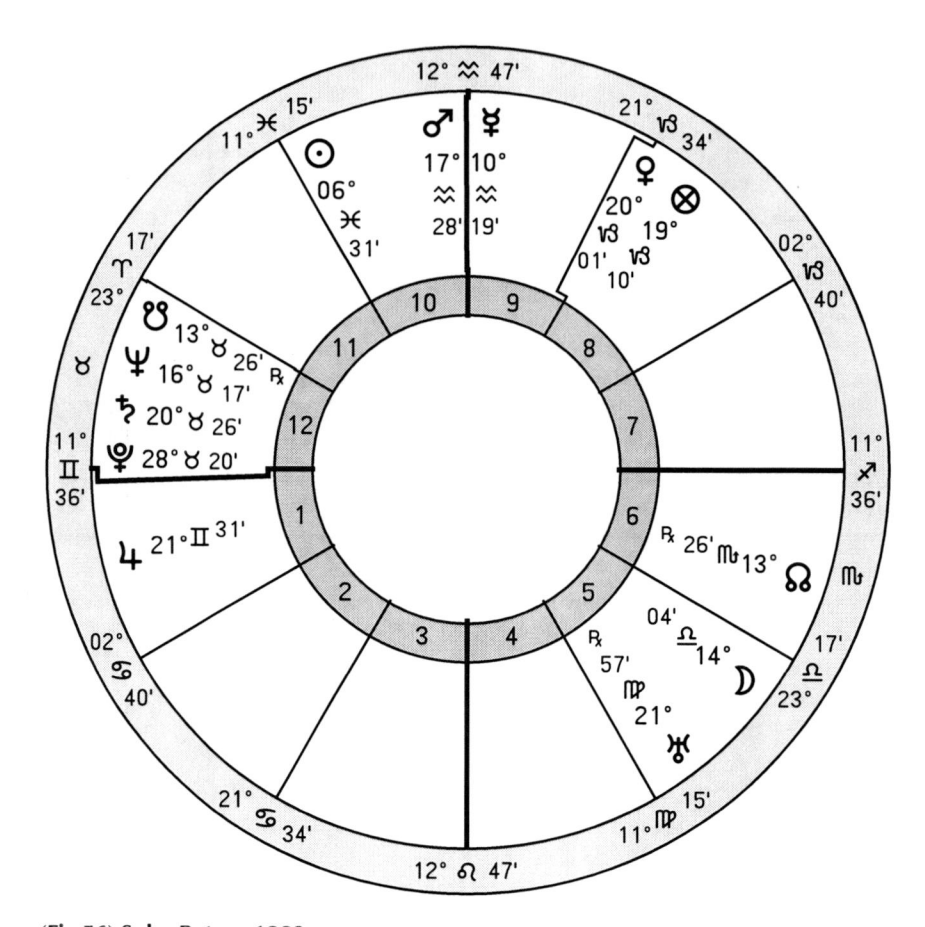

(Fig 56) Solar Return 1883

struggles there was an inner tension shown by natal arc Fortuna opposing natal arc Part of Vocation. This suggests a contrast between what he wants in life and his desire for action, which seem to cancel each other out and frustrate each other.

Renoir's struggles continued through the years of the dry period and are illustrated in an 1885 letter to Paul Bérard where Renoir says,

> 'I'm involved in lots of things and not one of them is finished. I wipe out, I start over. I think the year will go by without one canvas, and that's why I turn down visits from painters, no matter who ... I stopped Durand-Ruel from coming to see me ... I WANT TO FIND WHAT I AM LOOKING FOR BEFORE GIVING UP. Let me look ... I have gone too deeply into the series of experiments to give up without regret ... Success may be at the end.'[8]

[8] *A letter to Paul Bérard 1885*

The Dry Period is Over

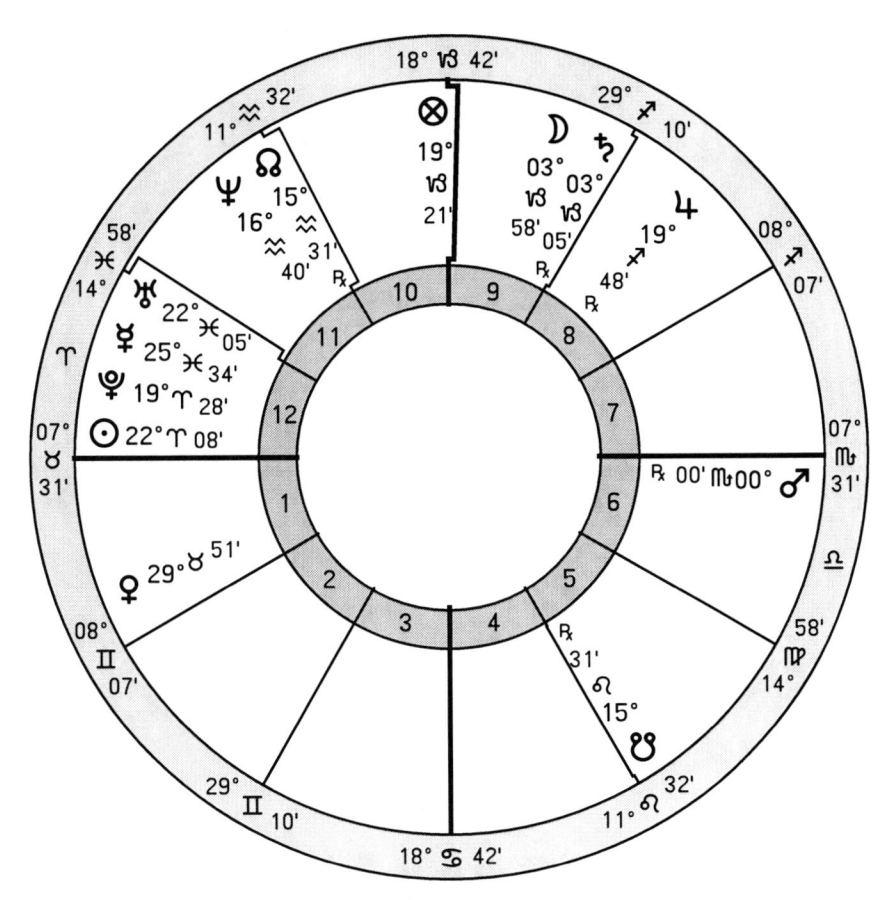

(Fig 57) Secondary Progressions 25 Feb 1887

In 1887–88 his dry period was considered to be over and the difficulties somewhat resolved. We see this shown astrologically as progressed Lord 9 Mars, his artistry, and progressed Venus, natural ruler of art and his technical approach both change sign. That his troubles in this area were not over is clearly shown by the fact that though they both change sign, they change out of their essential dignities. Still, be that as it may, the dry period passed and Renoir moved on.

This is echoed in the solar return of 1887, (Fig 58). Return Lord Ascendant Mercury, is conjunct natal Mercury, natal Lord 5. Solar return Jupiter, dispositor of natal arc Part of Vocation is conjunct natal Mars, showing there is tension with his ability to act in his work. Solar return Mars is conjunct natal arc Part of Vocation. This suggests, in context, that though he now realised what he needed to do with his approach to his paintings, doing it was another

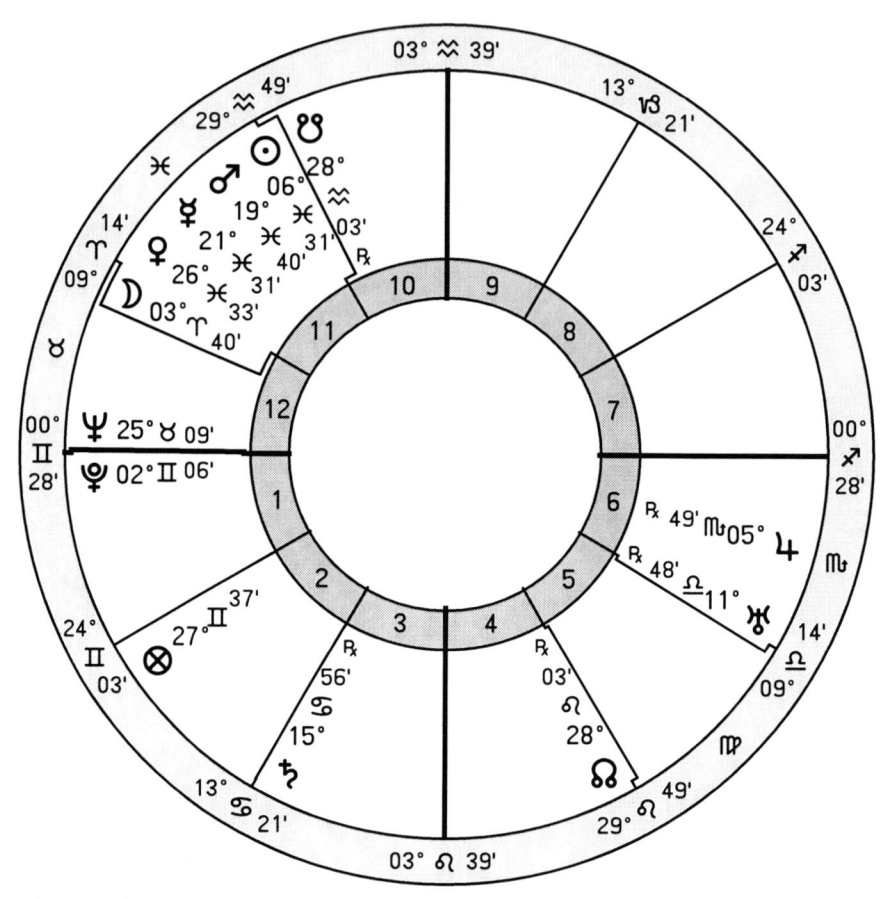

(Fig 58) Solar Return 1887

matter.

Natal arc Part of Vocation is conjunct solar return watery Saturn, suggestive of painting, on the cusp of 2 from 5, the fruit of his creative efforts. Renoir was preoccupied with and dearly wanted these fruits of his creativity. But accompanying this desire was the fact that he was still so dissatisfied with what he was doing. This is shown by watery Saturn being in its detriment. Saturn is natal ruler of Part of Vocation and also his natal Lord Ascendant – it is not happy in this position.

And neither was Renoir.

But three years or so later in late 1891 or early 1892 Renoir was asked by the French minister of fine arts Henri Roujon, to paint a substantial painting to be purchased by the Musée du Luxembourg, the museum devoted to paintings by the top living artists. Renoir painted, *Jennes filles au piano* – (young girls at a piano).

Impressionism, Saturn and Ivory Black

Alexandre, writing in 1920, recalled the process Renoir went through,

'I remember the infinite pains he took in executing the official composition which a well meaning friend had take the trouble to gain for him ...' 'Renoir began this painting five or six times, each time almost identically. The idea of a commission was enough to paralyze him and to undermine his self-confidence'. Tired of the struggle he finally delivered the painting to the Beaux-Arts the picture that today is at the museum, which immediately afterwards he adjudged the least good of the five or six'.[9]

Though there are only minor compositional differences in the variations there is a big colour change if you have eyes to see and you know what you are looking for. In the Luxembourg version the painting is warm and golden – the others are a lot cooler. Crucially, in the last version, Renoir had decided to eliminate the colour blue from the shadows. The Impressionists were known and ridiculed for their use of blue in the shadows of their paintings. We saw earlier that traditionally the shadows would have been modelled with black; as Aristotle had said in *On Colour*, '... all things appear black of the kind from which a very small amount of light is reflected this is why shadows appear to be black'. The Impressionists had thrown black away a long time ago and now Renoir was getting rid of blue. Not from his palette, but from his shadows, but with no black and no blue this would pose him another technical problem. And it would increase the difficulties of creating form in his paintings. Despite this, he still left it out. And, as John House points out, 'Renoir rarely used blue as an important means of modelling form in his pictures after this date'.[10]

It was shortly after this, sometime in the mid 1890's, Renoir took an unprecedented step in an attempt to resolve his artistic difficulties. Having learnt from his studies of the past he decided to distance himself from Impressionism and clearly re-align himself with the tradition of the Old Masters. In a bold move, 'He proudly declared that he had restored black as an essential colour on his palette – banished since the mid 1870s from all his paintings except a few commissioned portraits.'[11]

In 1894 progressed Mercury Lord 5 is square natal Saturn, ruler of black, and progressed Moon also squares Saturn, (Fig 59). In the solar return, (Fig 60), again we see Saturn, ruler of both black and natal Part of Vocation, retrograde, returning, coming back. It is in its exaltation and high in the chart: this is not just any old return but a triumphant return. Saturn, in its exaltation and high in the chart and trine return Venus conjunct pre birth eclipse and solar return Mars, natal Lord 9 is also in its exaltation. Solar return Jupiter is near Algol. Solar return Moon is near natal 9th cusp and return 5th cusp, his paintings, is conjunct natal 3rd house cusp: the expression and manifestation of the artistry of the 9th house. As Jupiter, dispositor of natal arc Part of

---

[9] A. Alexandre, *Renoir sans phrases*
[10] John House, *Renoir*
[11] John House, *Renoir*

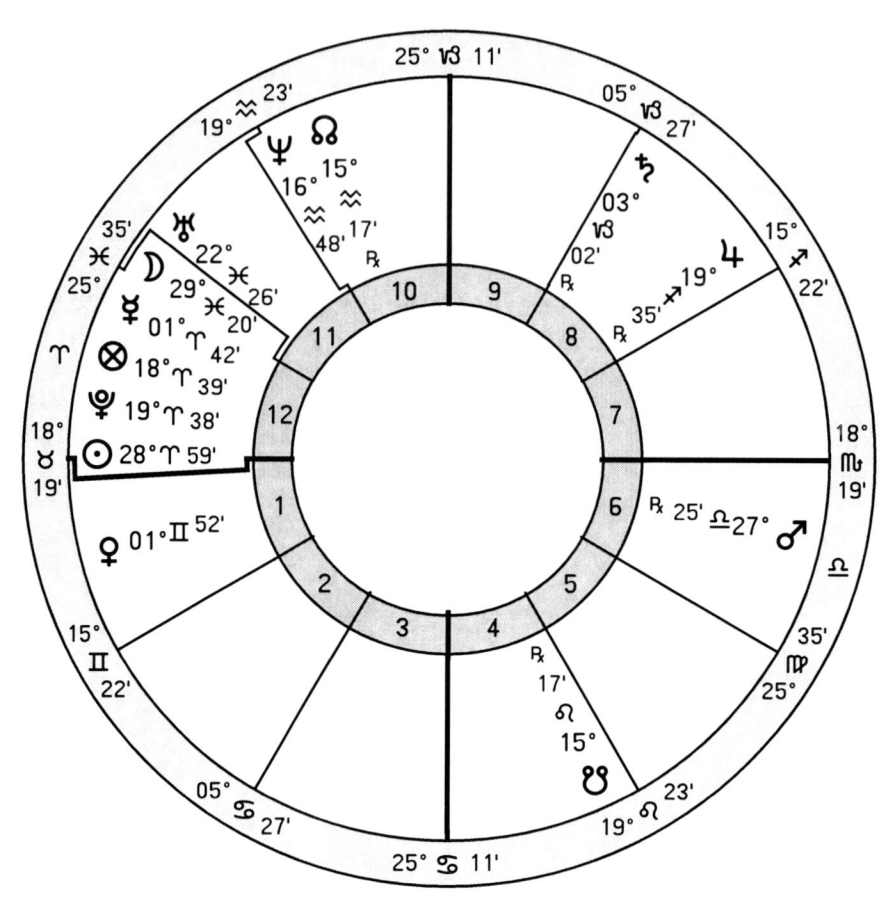

(Fig 59) Secondary Progressions 25 Feb 1894

Vocation is on Algol this clearly suggests a choice had to be made. And a choice was made. Renoir proudly reinstated black to his palette.

A Return to Tradition

This decision to develop a more traditional approach influenced his handling of form and by 1897, 'Renoir had largely abandoned the coloured modelling of the Impressionist reintroducing black to his palette as a declaration of his return to traditional methods.'[12] Soon after he completed the painting *Yvonne and Christens Lerolle at the piano*, in 1897, Renoir told Julie Manet that, 'in painting there is nothing but black and white'.[13]

[12] *Renoir* John House
[13] *Journal* J Manet Paris 1979

Impressionism, Saturn and Ivory Black

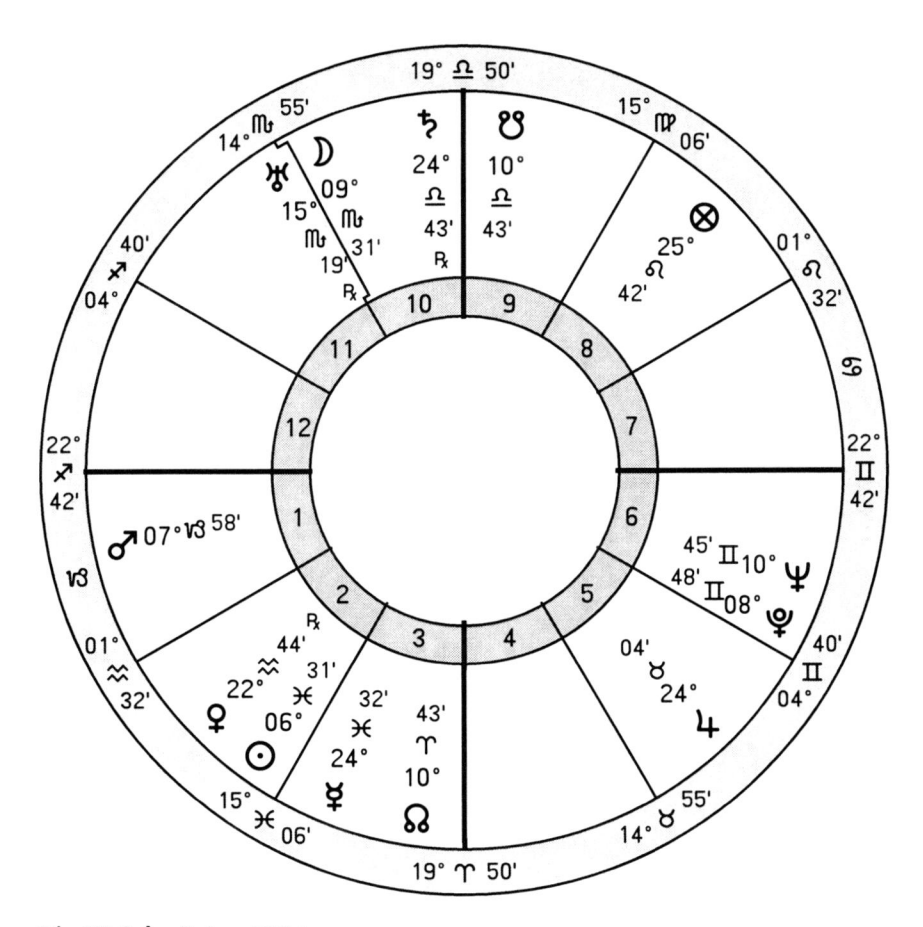

(Fig 60) Solar Return 1894

After his artistic and technical struggles Renoir finally saw form and colour in painting as generated from two colours: Black and White, dark and light, almost as if they were the fundamental principles or building blocks of colour. This may seem very odd to us in the early 21st century, dazzled by colour everywhere we look. But, let us not forget, this was Renoir, the Impressionist and master of colour, who had said this. And that was only after deep and torturous exploration. In doing so, he was echoing Aristotle who in his *Physics* had said, '... the intermediates are derived from the contraries – colour for instance, from black and white.'[14]

And in *On Colour*, Aristotle elaborates and links the colours with the elements, he says,

'Those colours are simple which belong to the elements, fire, air, water and earth.

---

[14] Aristotle, *Physics* Book I Chapter 5 188a 27

For air and water are naturally white in themselves, while fire and the Sun are golden. The earth is also naturally white but seems coloured because it is dyed. This becomes clear when we consider ashes; for they become white when the moisture which caused their dyeing is burnt out of them, but not completely so, for they are also dyed by smoke, which is black. In the same way sand becomes golden, because the fiery red and black tints the water. The colour black belongs to the elements of things while they are undergoing a transformation of their nature but the other colours are evidently due to mixture when they are blended with each other for darkness follows when light fails. The rest of the colours come from a mixture of these simple colours white red and black.'[15]

On a value scale, which is something that is used to illustrate the darkness or lightness of a colour, red will fall somewhat midway between white and black. To illustrate this further, think about how reds look in a black and white photograph where three dimensional coloured objects are seen without colour. Though values in a photograph are compressed and do not truly represent how we see things, this idea of a black and white representation of something is a good example of the modelling of a subject. This modelling of form was understood to its greatest degree by the Old Masters; those artists who had silently accompanied Renoir through his creative journey ever since he was a young porcelain painter wandering the galleries of the Louvre.

In *On Colour* Aristotle had mentioned that, black belongs to things while 'they are undergoing a transformation of their nature'. It was through Renoir's struggles with black that his understanding of colour and his art of painting were transformed. Renoir found that without black, form and then colour fell away. But it is understandable, in the effort to break new ground that he would try to do without black. After all black was the colour of Saturn, the natural ruler of boundaries and restriction. In trying to pioneer a new approach, these Saturnian qualities can be seen simply as obstacles to be overcome, as walls waiting to be breeched.

This happens to us in all areas of life. It is similar to being frustrated, fed up and held back, constrained by the difficulties of Saturn. Struggling under such things we may attempt to rid ourselves of our fetters. Yet exactly as the Old Masters knew, it is Saturn that brings structural ability, the gift to preserve, capture and hold something in place. Patience, solidity and resilience, are all Saturnian qualities, which, if given to us by Grace, can help us persevere when we may feel like giving up. As all these qualities are restrictive we may still try to do without them, to throw them off in the name of freedom of expression. But in casting these things aside, we may well find that by losing our restrictions we will also lose both our freedom and our expression.

Still, just like Renoir, we do have another option. We can always choose to return Saturn back to our palette.

---

[15] Aristotle, *On Colour*

10

Epiphany

One always hopes that a book can end with an epiphany, most don't of course, such is the nature of things, and yet this one will.

There is probably more nonsense talked about the star that lead the Three Wise Men to the stable in Bethlehem than almost anything else in the whole history of astrology. And yet, as this is an Epiphany we are talking about, it is worth remembering amid all the mad cap astro-talk of conjunctions at Christ's birth, Super Duper Comets etc that whatever the validity of any of these theories might be – this star – this particular star, the one that led the Magi to the stable, could not have been in the firmament.

Some traditional reasons:

- They may have seen the star in the East but the Magi are said to have most likely come from Persia. This was also somewhat to the North. This star then led them to the West and to the South to where the stable was. That is an odd star.
- Stars move with a regularity that we can predict they do not randomly interrupt their movement. The movement of this star was interrupted – it stopped, it rested, it started up again etc.
- It gave light to the Magi during the day. And before someone mentions that at certain times Venus is visible by daylight let us remember that if you literally followed Venus you'll simply end up standing in the garden morning and evening craning your neck up to the sky. You won't go anywhere and ditto for a 'super conjunction' of anything: You certainly won't saddle up some camels and trek across the desert.
- In order for the Magi to find the exact place they were looking for the star would have to be reasonably close to the ground; after all, it came to rest exactly over the place where the child lay.

They followed a star from Persia to Bethlehem – they did not sit in front of astrological software and punch some keys.

During their journey the Magi went to Herod's palace. Upon entering the city they suddenly found that they could no longer see the star they had followed for so long. It was only later that they would understand: it was not above the palace that the star shone but above the stable. When they were in the city they had in effect turned aside from their divine celestial guidance in order to seek the aid of Herod's scribes and prophets. It was of course then, that they could no longer see the star. The moment they sought the guidance of those who served the kings of this world was the moment that they lost the true light.

But as we know, this was not the end of the story, for when the star rose and shone before them again they 'rejoiced with exceeding great joy'. As Pseudo–Chrysostom explains in his Gloss on St Matthew's Gospel, '... By the mystery of this star they understood that the dignity of the King then born exceeded the measure of all worldly kings.' And so when they left King Herod and all his scribes and prophets behind, the Magi's hope was renewed in their hearts, as Pseudo-Chrysostom explains, 'They rejoiced, because their hopes were not falsified but confirmed, and because the toil of so great travel had not been undertaken in vain.'

When the Magi finally arrive at the end of their journey, Pseudo-Chrysostom tells us the Epiphany is complete,

> 'Mary His mother, not crowned with a diadem or laying on a golden couch; but with barely one garment, not for ornament but for covering, and that such as the wife of a carpenter when abroad might have. Had they therefore come to seek an earthly king, they would have been more confounded than rejoiced, deeming their pains thrown away. But now they looked for a heavenly King; so that though they saw nought of regal state, that star's witness sufficed them, and their eyes rejoiced to behold a despised Boy, the Spirit shewing Him to their hearts in all His wonderful power, they fell down and worshipped, seeing the man, they acknowledged the God.'

Appendix

The Table of Essential Dignities

Sign	Ruler	Exalt-ation	Triplicity		Term					Face			Detri-ment	Fall
			Day	Night										
♈	♂	☉ 19	☉	♃	♃ 6	♀ 14	☿ 21	♂ 26	♄ 30	♂ 10	☉ 20	♀ 30	♀	♄
♉	♀	☽ 3	♀	☽	♀ 8	☿ 15	♃ 22	♄ 26	♂ 30	☿ 10	☽ 20	♄ 30	♂	
♊	☿		♄	☿	☿ 7	♃ 14	♀ 21	♄ 25	♂ 30	♃ 10	♂ 20	☉ 30	♃	
♋	☽	♃ 15	♂	♂	♂ 6	♃ 13	☿ 20	♀ 27	♄ 30	♀ 10	☿ 20	☽ 30	♄	♂
♌	☉		☉	♃	♄ 6	☿ 13	♀ 19	♃ 25	♂ 30	♄ 10	♃ 20	♂ 30	♄	
♍	☿	☿ 15	♀	☽	☿ 7	♀ 13	♃ 18	♄ 24	♂ 30	☉ 10	♀ 20	☿ 30	♃	♀
♎	♀	♄ 21	♄	☿	♄ 6	♀ 11	♃ 19	☿ 24	♂ 30	☽ 10	♄ 20	♃ 30	♂	☉
♏	♂		♂	♂	♂ 6	♃ 14	♀ 21	☿ 27	♄ 30	♂ 10	☉ 20	♀ 30	♀	☽
♐	♃		☉	♃	♃ 8	♀ 14	☿ 19	♄ 25	♂ 30	☿ 10	☽ 20	♄ 30	☿	
♑	♄	♂ 28	♀	☽	♀ 6	☿ 12	♃ 19	♂ 25	♄ 30	♃ 10	♂ 20	☉ 30	☽	♃
♒	♄		♄	☿	♄ 6	☿ 12	♀ 20	♃ 25	♂ 30	♀ 10	☿ 20	☽ 30	☉	
♓	♃	♀ 27	♂	♂	♀ 8	♃ 14	☿ 20	♂ 26	♄ 30	♄ 10	♃ 20	♂ 30	☿	☿

(Fig 61) The table of essential dignities

This table shows the essential dignities that each planet is in wherever the planet is placed in the zodiac. The numbers in the table are ordinal numbers. This means that a planet in the early part of Aries is in Jupiter terms until 5 degrees 59 minutes. When it reaches 6 degrees of Aries it is in Venus terms.

Bibliography

Adler, Mortimer J., *Aristotle for Everybody – Difficult Thought Made Easy* (New York: Simon Schuster1978)
Alexandre, A., *Renoir sans phrases* (Paris Les Arts 1920)
Aristotle., *De Anima*
Aristotle., *Eudemian Ethics*
Aristotle., *Metaphysics*
Aristotle., *Nicomachean Ethics*
Aristotle., *On Colour*
Aristotle., *Physics*
Aristotle., *Rhetoric*
Boethius., *Consolation of Philosophy*
Bonatus., *Liber Astronomiae,* trans. Robert Zoller
Buonarroti., Michelangelo, *Poems and Letters,* trans. Anthony Mortimer (Penguin Classics 2007)
Bucklow, Spike., *The Alchemy of Colour: Art, Science and Secrets from the Middle Ages* (London: Marion Boyars 2009)
Cennini, Cennino d'Andrea., *The Craftsman's Handbook 'Il Libro dell' Arte'* (New York: Yale University Press 1933)
Condivi, Ascanio., *Life of Michelangelo* (1553) (C B Holroyd translation)
Copleston, F. C., *Aquinas* (Penguin 1955)
Dante Alighieri., *Inferno*
Dante Alighieri., *Purgatorio*
Dante Alighieri., *Paradiso*
Ibn Ezra, Abraham., *The Beginning of Wisdom* (12th Century), trans. Meira B. Epstein (Arhat Publications 1988)
Ibn Ezra, Abraham., *The Book of Reasons* trans. Meira B. Epstein (1991)
Frawley, John., *The Horary Textbook* (London: Apprentice Books 2005)
House, John., *Renoir* (London: Arts Council of Great Britain 1985)
John Damascene, St., *De Fide Orthodox*
Le Begue, Jehan., *Experimenta de Coloribus* (Manuscript 1431)
Lilly, William., *Christian Astrology* (1647)
Lull, Ramon., *Treatise on Astronomy,* trans. Kris Shaper (Berkley Springs: Golden Hind Press 1994)
Macrobius., *Saturnalia*
Manet, Julie., *Journal, 1893–1899* (Paris 1979)
Merrifield, Mrs Mary P., *On the Arts of Painting* (1849)
Nichols, Roger., *Debussy Remembered,* (London: Faber and Faber 1992)
Oxford Companion to Classical Literature
Ovid., *Metamorphoses*
Plato., *The Republic*
Ptolemy., *Tetrabiblos,* trans. F. E. Robbins (Loeb 1940)

Robson, Vivian., *The Fixed Stars and Constellations in Astrology* (1923)
Stevenson, R. A. M., *Velázquez,* (London: George Bell and Sons 1902)
Sullivan, Daniel J., *An Introduction to Philosophy – Perennial Principles of the Classical Realist Tradition* (Bruce Publishing 1957)
Thomas Aquinas, St., *Commentary on Aristotle's Peri Hermeneias*
Thomas Aquinas, St., *Commentary on Aristotle's Physics*
Thomas Aquinas, St., *Commentary on the Sentences (of Peter Lombard)*
Thomas Aquinas, St., *Compendium Theologiae*
Thomas Aquinas, St., *Summa Contra Gentiles*
Thomas Aquinas, St., *Summa Theologica*
Thompson Daniel V., *The Materials and Techniques of Medieval Painting* (New York: Dover Publications, 1956)
Various, Edited by Protter, Eric., *Painters on Painting* (New York: Grosset and Dunlap 1971)
Vasari Giorgio., *Lives of the Most Excellent Sculptors, Painters and Architects* (1568) trans. George Bull
Worsdale, John., *A Collection of Remarkable Nativities* (1799)
Worsdale, John., *Celestial Philosophy or Genethliacal Astronomy*

Index

accidental dignities (description of) 3
act and potency 117–19; *see also* change
Adler, Mortimer J 122 n
Aegina 64
Alighieri, Dante, *see* Dante
Angels 70–1
anima 105; *see also* Soul
Andromeda 8–9
Apollo 110–1, 113
Aquinas, *see* Thomas Aquinas, St
Arabic Parts:
    Part of Fortune 9, 16–19, 41, 50–1, 59–61, 73–6, 78, 81–2, 84, 86, 88–9, 90–3, 95, 98–9, 101–2, 104, 108, 130–4; *see also* Fortuna
    Part of Fame 12–13, 18, 21
    Part of Marriage 53
    Part of Vocation 9, 10, 15–16, 20, 81–2, 89–90, 92, 96, 98–9, 130, 134–8
Argo, The 80
Aristotle 59, 62, 72, 105–6, 116, 137, 139–40
    De Anima 105
    Eudemian Ethics 64–5
    Metaphysics 64
    Nicomachean Ethics 63
    on chance and fortune 62–5
    On Colour 137, 139, 140
    on fortunate people 64
    on the external goods 63
    on the hidden causes 62
    Peri Hermeneias 67
    Physics 62, 117, 122, 139
    Rhetoric 63
antiscia, antiscion (description of) 4
Athena 80
Bardac, Emma 101, 103
Bazille, Fredric 125–6
Beginning of Wisdom, The 21, 75, 115

Berard, Paul 134
Bethlehem 141
bitumen 127–8
body, bodily 68–9
Bonatus, 104
Bramante 12–13, 15
Bucklow, Spike 34 n
Byzantium 34, 59
Cassiopeia 8
Cause (general) 61–2, 66–8
Cause (specific)
    accidental, per accidens cause 63; *see also* chance
    chain of causes 109
    contingent cause 64, 66–7
    higher cause 66
    indeterminate cause 61–2, 64
    incidental cause 63
    primary and secondary causes 66–7
    secondary causes 72
    universal cause 66
Celestial Philosophy 46
Cennino d'Andrea Cennini 32–5
Cesena, Biagio 19
chance 60–3, 65–6, 70, 72–3
change 68, 114, 117, 123
    the nature of 114
    Parmenides 114
    Achilles and the tortoise 114
    Heraclitus 115
    Plato 115–16
    Aristotle 116
    nature of change in astrology 116–17
    act and potency 117–19
    from potency to act 121–23
    cycle of the elements 119–20
Christian Astrology 4, 33, 39, 74, 108
Christmas Day 17–19, 21
Choleric 38, 77
Chou Chou 99, 103

Collection of Remarkable Nativities 46
Colours:
  of the Watchers of the Heavens 32
  of Saturn 33
  of Jupiter 33–4
  of Mars 34
  of Sun 34
  of Venus 34–5
  of Mercury 35–6
  of Moon 35
Condivi, Ascanio 1–4, 7, 11, 13–15, 18
Conjunction (description) 121
Copleston F.C. 122 n
Consolation of Philosophy 59–60
Cornucopia 61
corporeal, *see* bodily
cusps 3 n, 23 n
Damascene, *see* John Damascene, St
Dante 68, 107
Debussy 75–78, 81–86
Debussy:
  natal chart 76
  temperament 77
  Fortuna 78
  Canopus and Fortuna 78–80
  and Orpheus 80–1
  beginnings of Debussy's career 82–87
  Paris Conservatoire, 82–83
  enters Guiraud's composition class 86
  Prix de Rome 86–87
  wins first prize at Prix de Rome 87–90
  appointed Chevalier of Honour 95–9, 101
  marries Lily 94
  prosecuted for debts 93
  La Mér, Lily, Emma and Chou Chou 99–103
  Première of *La Mér* 102–03
  Claire de lune 81, 86
  En Sourdine 86
  Images, Reflets dan l'eau 101
  La Mér 80–1, 99, 101–3
  L'après midi d'un faune 91–2
  L'enfant prodige 87
  Mandoline 86

Nocturnes 81, 92, 95
Pelléas et Mélisande 81, 91, 94
derived lunar returns, 97, 97 n
De Romilly, Madame Gerard 81
desire(s) 108
Determinism 67, 70
Dignities :
  essential, (description of) 3
  accidental, (description of) 3
  table of 143
Diana 56
Diaz de la Peña, Narcisse Virgile 128
Divine Grace 9, 21
Durand, Jacques 80–1
Eastbourne 102
Empedocles 122
eloquence, eloquent 6, 80
Epiphany 141–2
essential dignities 3
Experimenta de Coloribus 31
external goods 63
fate 59, 61, 65, 67, 71–2; *see also*
  Thomas Aquinas, St
fixed stars:
  Acrux 13, 18
  Acubens 48
  Aculeus 44
  Agena 53
  Alcyone 56, 87, 89, 133
  Aldebaran 16, 32, 56, 89, 91
  Alphecca 81
  Alhena 7
  Alphard 53
  Antares 32, 54
  Bootes 7
  Bungula 9
  Canopus 78, 80
  Caphir 53
  Caput Algol 23, 90, 98, 132, 138
  Castor 44
  Cetus 8
  Copula 43
  Deneb Adige 4, 6
  Difda 8
  Facies 7, 8
  Fomalhaut 17, 32
  Markeb 44
  Pelagus 4, 9, 53

Index

Pleiades (constellation) 56, 87
Pollux 44, 78, 81
Princeps 7
Procyon 51
Rasalhague 42
Regulus 18, 32, 43, 53, 77, 87–8, 90–1, 96, 102
Scheat 42
Seven Sisters 56
Sharatar 51
Southern Cross (constellation) 13, 18
Spica 20, 92
Vertex 43
Vindemiatrix 93, 101
Wega 126
Feast of All Saints 11, 15
Fixed Stars and Constellations, The 4, 32, 48
Flood, The 13, 87
forest of Fontainebleau 127
Forge of Vulcan, The 110–113
   tonal make–up of *Forge of Vulcan* 111
   composition and description of painting 111–12
   the bonds of relationships 112–13
Fortuna
   in astrology 60–1
   classical meaning of fortune 61–2
   calculation of Fortuna 73
   as part of the Moon 74
   traditional astrological meaning 74–5
   in a horary and natal chart 75–6
   natal Fortuna 76–104
   Fortuna through time 81–104
   relation to the Soul 104–109
Fortune 61–4, 73, 76–7
Frawley, John 24
freedom of the will 107–9
Garden, Mary 93, 94, 101
Gauguin, Paul 43–4
Ge 8
Genethliacal Astronomy 46
Gold 3, 34
goods of fortune 75
Gounod, Charles 125
governors of the soul 108

Guardian Angels 70–1
Heraclitus 115–16
Herod 141–2
Hidden Causes 62
Hippocrene 9
Hokusai 80, 102
Horary 23 n, 24, 30, 75
   'Is my job safe?' 26–28
   'Take job?' 25–26
   timing with horary 24
   'Will this job come through? Will it happen? When?' 28–30
   'When will either I or my wife get some work?' 22–25
Horary Textbook 24
Humane 6
Hylomorphism 105, 108
Ibn Ezra 74, 119, 121
Impressionism 124–9, 132
Iron 31, 34
Ivory Black 124
John Damascene, St 69, 107
Laloy, Louis 101
Lapis Lazuli 32–3
Lascaux 124
Lavignac, Albert 82
Liber Astronomiae 75
Light of Time 4, 6, 43
Lilly, William 4, 10, 14, 33–6, 39, 74, 108, 130
Linsey Woolsey 35
Lombardo, Marco 107
Long, Marguerite 78
Lord of the Geniture 4, 38, 40–1
Lorenzo the Magnificent 10
Lull, Ramon 42
Macrobius 60
Manet, Julie 138
Marmontel, Antoine 82–3
Maeterlinck, Maurice 81, 91
Magi, The 141–2
Mallarmé 91
Masha'allah 74
von Meck, Mme Nadezhda 83–4, 86
Medusa 8
Melancholic 3–4, 38
Michelangelo :
   dispute over birth data 1–2

Michelangelo *cont.*
  natal chart 2
  temperament, manner and quality of mind 3–10
  pre birth eclipse and lunation 5–7
  progressions and returns 11–21
  Medici Gardens 10–11, 21
  Sistine Chapel ceiling 7, 11–16
  Dying Slave, The 4
  Last Judgement, The 16–17
  Rebellious Captive, The 4
  'sonnet 5'
  'sonnet 285'
  'sonnet 289'
  'sonnet 292'
Monet 126
Mount Olympus 44
Murex purple 34
Muses, The 9, 60, 80
Naples 130
Nativity of a Lady 46
  natal chart 47
  temperament 47–8
  quality of mind 48–9
  family, background and inheritance, 49
  friends in high places 50–51
  passions and loves of a lady 51–54
  in a carriage from the opera house 54
  honour and preferment 54–56
  charts for progressions and returns 57–8
necessity 60, 62, 65, 67, 72, 109
Nereids 8
Nijinsky and the Ballet Russes 91
Oxford Companion to Classical Literature 61
Old Masters 124–5, 130, 137, 140
Opposition (description) 120
Orpheus 80
Ovid 110–12
Parmenides 114, 116
Paschal Calendar 2
Pegasus 9
Perseus 8–9
Persia 141
per accidens cause 63

Phlegmatic 38–9, 47–8, 51, 128
Plato 59, 115
Praxiteles 126
primary and secondary causes 66
poetry 6, 9
Pope Julius 12
potentials 36, 117–18
Philosophia 72, 109
providence 65–6, 71–2
Pseudo-Chrysostom 142
Ptolemy 69, 74, 108
Purgatorio 107
Raphael 12–13, 15, 130, 133
Renoir 125–9
  singing 125
  as a porcelain painter 125
  École des Beaux-arts 125
  Gleyre's studio 125–6
  natal chart 126
  forest of Fontainebleau 127
  first doubts about his work and the trip to Italy 130–32
  Dry Period 132–5
  commission for Musée du Luxembourg 136–7
  unprecedented step 137–38
  return to tradition 138
  Jennes filles au piano 136–7
  Yvonne and Christens Lerolle at the Piano 138
Regiomontanus 23 n
Republic, The 115
Robson, Vivian 4, 32–3, 43–4, 48, 51, 53
saffron 34
Sangallo (Pope's architect) 13
sanguine 38, 40, 128
Saturnalia 60
Savonarola, Girolamo 4
self-employed 24
sextile (description) 121
Sisley, Alfred 125–6
Sistine Chapel 7, 11, 16, 18, 21
Soul 59, 104–6
square (description) 120
Stevenson R. A. M. 111
Stoic philosophers 106
Strozzi, Roberto 4

Index

Sullivan, Daniel J. 122 n
Tchaikovsky 83
Thomas Aquinas, St 62, 65–72
    on providence 65–6
    on primary and secondary causes 66–7
    on choices 67–70
    on Guardian Angels 70–1
    on fate 71–2
    Commentary on Aristotle's Physics 122
    Commentary on Aristotle's Peri Hermeneias 67–8, 72
    Commentary on the Sentences 71
    Compendium Theologiae 66
    Summa Contra Gentiles 65, 69, 71
    Summa Theologica 65–6, 70, 72
Truth 42–3, 111, 113
temperament 4, 38, 47, 118; *see also* Choleric, Melancholic, Phlegmatic, Sanguine.
Thompson, Daniel V. 34
Tyche 60, 61
Tetrabiblos 78, 108
Texier, Lily 94, 101
teleology 119
Theodoric, King 59
ultramarine 332–4
universals 107

van Gogh, Vincent
    natal chart 37
    temperament 38, (39–40)
    manner 38–9
    quality of mind 39–41
    fixed stars 41–45
van Gogh, Theo 45
Varchi, Benedetto 1, 18
Vasari, Giorgio 1, 10, 18–19, 21
Velásquez 110–13
Verdigris 34
Vermillion 36
vices 107
Virgin Mary, The 20, 142
virtues 107
visions and dreams 6–7, 81
voiced sign 4, 6
void of course Moon 26
Vuillermoz, Emile 80
Vulcan 110–12
watchers of the heavens 32
Wealth 60
Weeping Sisters, the Daughters of Atlas 56, 87, 133
Wise Men 141–2
will 68–9
Worsdale 46–78, 49–56
Yellow House, The 43–4
Zeno 114
Zeus 44